NOBEL PRIZE WINNERS

NOBEL
PRIZE WINNERS

Edited by

L. J. LUDOVICI

ILLUSTRATED

ASSOCIATED BOOKSELLERS

WESTPORT, CONN.

First Edition, 1957

Library of Congress Catalog Card Number: 57-10102

Printed in U.S.A.

CONTENTS

	PAGE
EDITOR'S NOTE	ix

LITERATURE

Thomas Stearns Eliot, O.M., by Arthur Mizener	1
Sir Winston Spencer Churchill, K.G., by D. C. Somervell	23
William Faulkner, by W. S. Merwin	43
André Gide, by Martin Turnell	61
Ernest Hemingway, by M. J. C. Hodgart	85
Rudyard Kipling, by Charles Carrington	101
Thomas Mann, by Edmond Vermeil	116
François Mauriac, by Martin Turnell	128

SCIENCE

Albert Einstein, by J. Bronowski	151
Sir Alexander Fleming, by L. J. Ludovici	165
Thomas Hunt Morgan, by S. C. Harland, F.R.S.	178
Hermann Joseph Muller, by S. C. Harland, F.R.S.	185
Lord Rutherford, by Norman Feather, F.R.S.	189
Sir Charles Sherrington, by Macdonald Critchley, M.D., F.R.C.P.	216

LIST OF ILLUSTRATIONS

FACING PAGE

T. S. Eliot	I
Sir W. S. Churchill	38
William Faulkner	39
André Gide	39
Ernest Hemingway	98
Rudyard Kipling	98
Thomas Mann	99
François Mauriac	99
Albert Einstein	151
Sir Alexander Fleming	174
T. H. Morgan	175
H. J. Muller	175
Lord Rutherford	212
Sir Charles Sherrington	213

EDITOR'S NOTE

A Word about Nobel Awards

CERTAIN members of the Nobel family made their names and fortunes as pioneers in the extraction and refinement of naphtha products from the South Russian oilfields, but Alfred Nobel, as is well known, made his name and fortune through his researches into explosives. When he died on December 10th, 1896, he left about 33¾ million kronor for the foundation of Nobel Prizes.

Nobel Prizes are international, and Alfred Nobel, Swedish by birth, clearly stipulated in his will that no attention should be paid to any question of nationality, only to the question of who deserved them. They were to be awarded to men and women who had made the most material contribution to the benefit of humanity in the preceding year.

Nobel drafted his will without the assistance of a lawyer. As a result it contained flaws, and it was not until 1899 that difficulties of interpretation were overcome. In the spring of that year articles for the Nobel Foundation were drafted and the moneys left by Nobel handed over to it for use. The Foundation is administered by a board consisting of a chairman and a vice-chairman, together with four members and two deputies, selected by a committee of trustees appointed by the prize-awarding institutions.

These prize-awarding institutions are the Swedish Academy of Science, which selects the winners in physics and chemistry; the Caroline Medico-Surgical Institute, which selects the winners in physiology and medicine; the Swedish Academy, which selects the winner in literature, and the Nobel Committee of the Norwegian Storting, which selects the winner of the Peace Prize. The presentation of the prizes takes place on December 10th, the anniversary of Alfred Nobel's death, the scientific and literary awards being given at Stockholm and the Peace Prize at Oslo.

Nobel deliberately omitted to leave detailed instructions in his will as to how the Nobel Laureates should be chosen, in order to leave those entrusted with its execution the greatest possible latitude. It is, for example, often impossible to ascertain exactly when an invention which has required lengthy preparatory work has been completed.

There are also objections to making an award for a discovery which has not fully been proved and tested. Nobel's chief desire was to help those who needed assistance with their work. He felt himself under a debt to pioneer researchers in pure science whose discoveries he had turned to practical use. He wanted those who had devoted themselves to research without a thought of personal gain to benefit from his scheme. He wanted those engaged in promising enterprises to have enough money to render them completely independent for the future, so that they could work without financial embarrassment.

A few months before his death he said: 'I would not leave anything to a man of action. Such a man would thus be tempted to give up work. On the other hand I would like to help dreamers, who find it difficult to get on in life. Dreamers such as possess the gift of poetry, but are unknown to the many, or are misunderstood by them, meditative young research workers who are on the very threshold of a great discovery in physics, chemistry or medicine, but lack the means to achieve it.'

Those responsible for awarding the Nobel Prizes have endeavoured to conform as closely as possible to Alfred Nobel's innermost intentions—in so far as they have been able to ascertain these.

For those who may be interested, Alfred Nobel's will, omitting certain clauses relating to personal legacies, reads as follows:

I the undersigned Alfred Bernhard Nobel hereby declare after mature consideration that my last will with regard to the property which I may leave on my death is as follows:

With the residue of my convertible estate I hereby direct my

Executors to proceed as follows: They shall convert my said residue of property into money, which they shall then invest in safe securities; the capital thus secured shall constitute a fund, the interest accruing from which shall be annually awarded in prizes to those persons who shall have contributed most materially to the benefit of mankind during the year immediately preceding. The said interest shall be divided into five equal amounts, to be apportioned as follows: One share to the person who shall have made the most important discovery or invention in the domain of Physics; one share to the person who shall have made the most important Chemical discovery or improvement; one share to the person who shall have made the most important discovery in the domain of Physiology or Medicine; one share to the person who shall have produced in the field of Literature the most distinguished work of an idealistic tendency; and, finally, one share to the person who shall have done most to promote the Fraternity of Nations and the Abolition or Diminution of Standing Armies and the Formation and Increase of Peace Congresses. The prizes for Physics and Chemistry shall be awarded by the Swedish Academy of Science (Svenska Vetenskapsakademien) in Stockholm; that for Physiology or Medicine by the Caroline Medico-Surgical Institute (Karolinska Institutet) in Stockholm; the prize for Literature by the Academy in Stockholm (i.e. Svenska Akademien) and that for Peace by a Committee of five persons to be elected by the Norwegian Storting. I declare it to be my express desire that, in awarding of prizes, no consideration whatever be paid to the nationality of the candidates, that is to say, that the most deserving be awarded the prize, whether of Scandinavian origin or not.

This is my only valid Will and cancels any previous testamentary dispositions that may come to light after my death.

It is moreover my express will and injunction that my veins shall be opened after my death, and that when this has been done, and competent doctors have noted definite signs of death, my body shall be burned in a crematorium.

Paris, the 27th November, 1895. Alfred Bernhard Nobel.

PART ONE

Literature

T. S. Eliot

Thomas Stearns Eliot, O.M.

by ARTHUR MIZENER

Arthur Mizener, an American, was educated at the Hill School, then took his degrees at Princeton and Harvard. He did his thesis for a doctorate at Princeton and is a Ph.D. of that university.

He began his career in the academic world by teaching at Yale and later at Carleton College, Minnesota. He has been Professor of English at Cornell University since 1951.

When Scott Fitzgerald's daughter made a gift of her father's papers to Princeton, Arthur Mizener had the task of looking through them and getting them in order. His interest in Scott Fitzgerald was roused and the result was a biography of that writer entitled *The Far Side of Paradise*.

I

IT is not easy at this point to define the quality or to estimate the value of Mr. Eliot's work. During what he has called 'twenty years largely wasted, the years of *l'entre deux guerres*,' he produced in English literature a revolution in taste and critical judgment which has involved us all; as one writer put it, 'the poetry got into your head like a song-hit.' There is something to be said—Mr. Eliot himself has often said it—for being moved by poetry in this way, before you understand it. The danger is that you are never sure how much you have been moved—as people have been moved in other times by Shelley's *Cenci* or Tennyson's *In Memoriam* or Swinburne's *Atalanta*—to some temporary, 'period' response, and how much to a sense of what Mr. Eliot has called the horror and the glory beneath the period feelings.

Mr. Eliot himself has been disturbed by the popularity of his early poetry. At least there is an excess of irritation in his remark in 1931 that 'when I wrote a poem called *The Waste Land* some of the more approving critics said that I had expressed the "disillusionment of a generation," which is nonsense. I may have expressed for them their illusion of being disillusioned, but that did not form a part of my intention.' It is understandable that so religious and moral a poet as Mr. Eliot was annoyed to find himself described as disillusioned in the way popular writers of the twenties were and to find himself thought of even by serious critics as without beliefs ('Mr. Richards's statement that a certain writer [i.e. T. S. Eliot] has effected "a complete severance between his poetry and *all* beliefs" is to me incomprehensible'). But if Mr. Eliot's poetry did not, in the twenties, express the disillusionment of a generation, it certainly spoke to something in that generation more potent than either its opinions—almost all of which Mr. Eliot disliked—or its sentimentalities. 'It was you,' as Mr. Auden put it,

> Who, not speechless with shock, but finding the right
> Language for thirst and fear, did most to
> Prevent a panic.

For whatever Mr. Eliot's opinions and convictions, whatever the occasional extravagances of his powerful personality, whatever, even, the limits of his sensibility, his work has given us the basic perception of our time, and done so in a language so fine that—when they were first published—the New York *Herald-Tribune* thought *The Waste Land* a hoax and the *New Republic* thought *Four Quartets* prose.

Poetry of this order is the product of sharp insight and deep feeling under the discipline of a powerful intelligence; as Clive Bell once put it in his slightly acid way, 'if T. S. Eliot were not a famous poet, he would be known as a remarkably clever man.' This unremitting control of feeling by intelligence characterises Mr. Eliot's poetry and is the main subject for discussion in his criticism; it requires an unusual degree of self-awareness, a lifelong cultivation of what he once called 'the two forms of self-consciousness ['which must go together'], knowing what we are and what we ought to be'; and, despite Mr. Eliot's expressed preference for a regional culture ('a small and mostly self-contained group attached to the soil'— no doubt somewhere in Chelsea), it is difficult not to feel that his constant movement from one culture to another has given special intensity to an awareness originally established by his admirable puritanical habit of testing every feeling against the whole culture of the West. This is a guess; for a famous man,

Mr. Eliot has applied his 'theory of impersonality' with remarkable success to his personal life; and the indulgences of vanity in his career have been few and obscure.

2

He is a descendant of Andrew Eliot, who emigrated from East Coker, Somerset, to Beverly, Massachusetts, in the late seventeenth century, a fact which provides the personal sense for 'East Coker's' 'In my beginning is my end.' For several generations the family consisted of merchants and clergymen (one of them at least a strong Congregationalist and a professed enemy of Episcopalianism). In 1834, Mr. Eliot's grandfather moved to St. Louis, Missouri, where he founded the city's first Unitarian church. There he also helped to build Washington University and served as its chancellor. Mr. Eliot's father was a St. Louis business man; in 1868 he married Charlotte Stearns of Boston, who was descended from one of the original settlers of the Bay Colony. Mr. Eliot, the seventh and youngest child of this marriage, was born in St. Louis, September 26th, 1888, and lived there for the first seventeen years of his life. From this experience his poetry has drawn a few of those sharp visual images to which his feelings characteristically attach themselves; they help to explain why he has referred to the influence of the Big River on his poetry:

> His rhythm was present in the nursery bedroom,
> In the rank ailanthus of the April dooryard,
> In the smell of grapes on the autumn table,
> And the evening circle in the winter gaslight.

As a young man, too, he spent summers at Cape Ann ('where the hermit thrush sings in the pine trees').

He spent his last year of college preparation at Milton Academy and went on to Harvard, where in 1909 he completed the work for his degree in three years. There are a few glimpses of him during these years, 'of a singularly attractive, tall, and rather dapper young man, with a somewhat Lamian smile, who reeled out of the door of the Lampoon on a spring evening, and, catching sight of [Conrad Aiken], threw his arms about me. . . . "And that," observed my astonished companion, "if Tom remembers it tomorrow, will cause him to suffer agonies of shyness." And no doubt it did: for he *was* shy.' After a year of graduate work at Harvard, Mr. Eliot spent two years at the Sorbonne and then returned to Harvard for further study and a year of teaching. Again it is Conrad Aiken who remembers him going to dances as a discipline for shyness and, for the same reason, learning to box and—in his own phrase—'to swarm with passion up a rope.' He spent the summer before the outbreak of the war at Marburg and the following winter at Oxford ('Come, let us desert our wives, and fly to a land where there are no Medici prints, nothing but concubinage and conversation. Oxford is very pretty, but I don't like to be dead').

Despite this extravagant but not altogether frivolous fooling, he settled in England. In 1915 he married Vivienne Haigh (Mrs. Eliot died in 1947), and after a year of teaching at Highgate School went to work in a London bank. He was now a young poet about London, smiling what Wyndham Lewis called his 'Giaconda smile' in Pound's small sitting-room while Pound applied his tireless and tactless publicity to 'Prufrock,' or enduring with disciplined silence what must have been further agonies of shyness while Pound unceremoniously removed the brown-paper wrappings from a pair of second-hand shoes he had carried to Paris for Joyce. When he became editor of *The Criterion* in 1923, joined Faber & Gwyer, and, in 1927, became a British subject, he emerged as a public figure on the London literary scene.

There are certain things worth emphasising in these glimpses of Mr. Eliot's life before he completed his public *persona*. There is the energetic and discriminating sensibility; there are the intelligence and the appetite for knowledge. There are the temperamental extravagance and shyness and the vigorous, reforming self-awareness with which they are disciplined. And there is the deliberately repeated resort to a larger culture together with the effort to make the sensibility grow up to and into it—'mixing,' as one of Mr. Eliot's memorable phrases puts it, 'memory and desire.' Speaking of another great American poet, Emily Dickinson, Mr. Allen Tate once observed that the moments of great awareness are those where two cultures cross. We know that Mr. Eliot's family was unusually conscious of its cultural inheritance; when his mother's dramatic poem, *Savonarola*, was published in 1926, Mr. Eliot remarked in the introduction that 'this Savonarola is a disciple of Schleiermacher, Emerson, Channing, and Herbert Spencer.' Good American that he is, Mr. Eliot has never forgotten the sense of infinite promise this world gave him ('But where is the penny world I bought / To eat with Pipit behind the screen?'). But even Harvard must have shown him its inadequacy, offered him a more complex conception of his tradition's memory to adapt desire to. It was a process he was to repeat again and again.

As a consequence his poetry has always been constructed around the contrasts of different ways of life which he possesses. The young man who submitted himself to the discipline of Boston parties knew the Boston world of 'Cousin Nancy' Ellicott, who 'smoked / And danced all the modern dances'; he also knew the exiled Boston culture of his inheritance which did not forget 'Matthew and Waldo, guardians of the faith, / The army of unalterable law.' Like so many of Mr. Eliot's later poems, 'Cousin Nancy' is a judgment of both worlds. Perhaps the provincial talent in America can realise itself only by adaptation to another culture. Such an adaptation produces a sensibility different from that of the original or the adopted culture. Mr. Eliot is a complex American finally made over into an Englishman and an Anglo-Catholic. If the most important thing about him is his talent, the precise shape of his talent has been determined by that process of making over. All his perceptions of the world around him have the precision and intensity of a foreigner speaking a language nearly perfectly:

Now the light falls
Across the open field, leaving the deep lane
Shuttered with branches, dark in the afternoon. . . .
In a warm haze the sultry light
Is absorbed, not refracted, by grey stone.

The peculiar sharpness of this perception—and it is characteristic—is that of a man for whom what he sees still has, for all
its familiarity, some element of the surprising about it.

3

From the time Mr. Eliot began to publish verse in the
Harvard *Advocate*, his poetry has shown the consequences of
this commitment to the attitude expressed in the epigraph of
the first essay in his first book of criticism: 'Eriger en lois ses
impressions personnelles, c'est le grand effort d'un homme s'il
est sincère.' In one of his best-known and earliest essays,
'Tradition and the Individual Talent' (1917), he set forth the
use of personal feelings in poetry that this attitude required.
'Poetry,' he said, 'is not a turning loose of emotion, but an
escape from emotion; it is not the expression of a personality,
but an escape from personality.' 'But, of course,' he added,
'only those who have personality and emotions know what it
means to want to escape these things.' The escape from being
'laid waste by the anarchy of feeling,' then, is to find some
form which provides impersonal occasions and motives unrelated to the writer's for the feelings he wishes to express, 'to
commit the feelings,' as John Crowe Ransom once put it, 'to
their determination within the elected figure.' It follows that
the more highly conventionalised the form is, the better (though
not necessarily—as Mr. Eliot sometimes seems to suggest—
that the more 'unrealistic' it is the better). This is not a theory
for writing poetry without involving the personality and the
emotions but a theory for writing poetry which will make the
best possible use of them by giving them the greatest formal and
therefore public order.

Given Mr. Eliot's temperament and the cosmopolitanism of
his sensibility, it inevitably became for him a theory for
committing the feelings, step by step, to the full tradition of
Western culture by 'a continual surrender of himself as he [was]
at the moment to something which [was] more valuable.' This
includes, as Mr. Eliot presently realised in a way perhaps only
the heir of Congregationalists and Unitarians could, the
Catholic Christianity which is the heart of that culture.

'Culture,' as he said, 'after all, is not enough, even though nothing is enough without culture.' This feeling is responsible for Mr. Eliot's lifelong dislike of liberalism in politics and religion and his distrust of 'the possessors of the inner voice [who] ride ten in a compartment to a football match at Swansea, listening to the inner voice, which breathes the eternal message of vanity, fear and lust.'

It may seem odd that this conception of poetry was once thought to be an impersonal one, but Mr. Eliot himself is partly to blame for that. Some combination of slyness and humility makes him almost always approach his subject with an indirectness which is very misleading, as when he throws away with his 'But, of course . . .' the most important statement in this argument. This indirectness can approach absurdity—'Mr. Richards's statement that a certain writer . . .' as if every reader did not know this writer was Mr. Eliot; 'when I wrote a poem called *The Waste Land* . . .' as if it were not, in 1931, the most famous of poems. It has occasionally driven critics like Mr. Edmund Wilson to grumble (in his review of *Ash Wednesday*) that he wished Mr. Eliot would not talk like an old man at forty. It is hard not to suspect that the bad boy in Mr. Eliot takes a certain pleasure in trapping critics into these complaints.

On the rare occasions when his intellectual commitments outrun his feelings, he can give the impression of real arrogance: 'The non-Catholic, certainly the non-Christian philosopher, feeling no obligation to alter himself, and therefore no cogent need to understand himself, is apt to be under the sway of his prejudices . . .'; or, 'I have little hope for America until . . .'; or, 'I am reproaching a world in which blasphemy is impossible.' 'Puritanism,' Mr. Eliot has said, 'became repulsive only when it appeared as the survival of a restraint after the feelings which it restrained had gone'; something like that is also true before the feelings have come.

> How unpleasant to meet Mr. Eliot!
> With his features of clerical cut,
> And his brow so grim
> And his mouth so prim

And his conversation, so nicely
Restricted to What Precisely
And If and Perhaps and But. . . .
How unpleasant to meet Mr. Eliot!
　　(Whether his mouth be open or shut.)

It is only just, however, to remember that Mr. Eliot himself wrote these verses, and to remind ourselves of how effective his Great Cham manner can be, as, for instance, when he said in 1933: 'I would even say that, as [Communism] is the faith of the day, there are only a small number of people living who have achieved the right not to be communists. My only objection to it is the same as my objection to the cult of the Golden Calf.'

Moreover, occasions when his manner is in excess of his perception are rare, for Mr. Eliot is the last man to imagine what he says with some justice Mr. Pound has imagined in the *Cantos*, 'a Hell for the *other people*, the people we read about in the newspapers, not for oneself and one's friends.' The abiding impression of his work is that of an extraordinary integrity. Nothing could have been more mistaken than Paul Elmer More's conviction that his poetry and criticism are not in accord—and nothing, incidentally, more honest than Mr. Eliot's comment: 'At the moment when one writes, one is what one is, and the damage of a lifetime, and of having been born into an unsettled society, cannot be repaired at the moment of composition.' The early realisation and lifelong development of this conception of poetry, so well fitted to Mr. Eliot's temperament, has enabled him to write a kind of poetry which is very rare in any time and perhaps unique in ours, a poetry at once profoundly personal, an expression of Mr. Eliot's deepest private feelings, and completely public, a universally valid judgment of our world.

4

The technical equipment with which Mr. Eliot has conducted these 'raids on the inarticulate' derives from the circumstances of his time and the pervasive influence of Ezra Pound, '*il miglior fabbro*,' as Mr. Eliot called him in the dedication of

The Waste Land. Pound's commitment to imagism is only one manifestation of a theory of perception which was perhaps fundamental to his whole period. Its history has still to be written, but its appearance in such different forms as Joyce's 'epiphanies,' Virginia Woolf's 'moments,' and Hemingway's 'the way it was' indicates how widespread it was. Essential to it is the belief that every pattern of feelings has its pattern of objects and events—whether as cause or only as participating occasion —and that if the poet can set down the pattern of objects and events in exactly the right relations, without irrelevances or distortions, they will evoke in the reader the pattern of feelings. 'An "Image,"' as Pound put it, 'is that which presents an intellectual and emotional complex in an instant of time.'

From the first the structural units of Mr. Eliot's poems were of this kind; they suited his talent, with its remarkable visual and aural perception, perfectly.

> The showers beat
> On broken blinds and chimney-pots,
> And at the corner of the street
> A lonely cab-horse steams and stamps.
> And then the lighting of the lamps.

The last two lines here illustrate particularly well the power of such images. Poetry of this kind depends greatly on the poet's ability to control, by rhythm and diction, the tone of voice, for it is mostly by the tone of voice that an attitude is suggested. Here again Mr. Eliot's talent suited his method; perhaps the quality of his poetry that haunts the memory most vividly is its magnificent voice, with its control of every tone from the precise irony of

> I shall not want Honour in Heaven
>   For I shall meet Sir Philip Sidney
> And have talk with Coriolanus
>   And other heroes of that kidney

to the quiet intensity of

> I do not know much about gods; but I think that the river
> Is a strong brown god

and the full eloquence of

> After the torchlight red on sweaty faces
> After the frosty silence in the gardens
> After the agony in stony places
> The shouting and the crying. . . .

Mr. Eliot's personal modifications of the imagist method are characteristic. His sense of the fantastic encourages him to specify attitudes with extravagant figures ('I am aware of the damp souls of housemaids / Sprouting despondently at area gates'), and his will to an exact judgment leads him to let his speaker be ' moved by fancies that are curled / Around these images, that cling. . . .' The major problem for poetry of this kind is the problem of length. Perhaps a fiction of any length is impossible without narrative and its concomitant, sustained characters, and narrative is impossible without a commitment to temporal sequence. This problem did not arise as long as Mr. Eliot wrote short poems, but it had to be met with *The Waste Land*, *Ash Wednesday* and *Four Quartets*. Mr. Eliot met it in what must certainly be the best way an imagist can, by devising an essentially static pattern of repetitions with varia-tions loosely analogous to the pattern of the sonata. This form is completely exemplified by *Four Quartets*, but less full-developed forms of it are used in the other long poems. It might even be described as making the best of a bad bargain, for Mr. Eliot's experiments in play-writing indicate that, for all his sharp perception of people, he has little sense of—even little patience for—the running pattern of motive and event which is the reality of everyday perception and therefore of verisimilar narrative. His characteristic way of seeing experience is as a tapestry ('Pray for Floret, by the boarhound slain between the yew trees') or as palimpsest ('There I saw one I knew, and stopped him, crying: "Stetson! / You who were with me in the ships at Mylae " ').

5

Mr. Eliot's poetry did not, of course, arrive at this fully developed form immediately. The poems of *Prufrock* (1917) and *Poems* (1920) are mainly dramatic monologues and short poems which exploit his sense of cultural contrast, often in a form of serious *vers de société* like 'Conversation Galante.' As we move through the short poems of this period, we can see the simpler contrasts of Cousin Nancy with Arnold and Emerson or of the narrator's recollection of La Rochefoucauld with Aunt Harriet growing richer. In 'Sweeney Erect,' for example, we are given an anecdote of Sweeney indifferently continuing to shave while the woman in his bed has an epileptic fit. The ladies of the corridor 'deprecate the lack of taste' in the affair; Mrs. Turner, the landlady, draws attention to the unimpeachable reputation of her house; and Doris shows her humanitarian kindness by 'bringing sal volatile / And a glass of brandy neat.' The poem's judgment of these modes of life is implicit in the image itself. But it is characteristically reinforced by a comment:

> (The lengthened shadow of man
> Is history, said Emerson
> Who had not seen the silhouette
> Of Sweeney straddled in the sun.)

It is further reinforced by an extravagant figure, a contrast between Sweeney and Theseus:

> Display me Aeolus above
> Reviewing the insurgent gales
> Which tangle Ariadne's hair
> And swell with haste the perjured sails.

The full sorrow of romantic betrayal realised in the Ariadne story gives us a further measure of Sweeney's complacent conviction that he 'knows the female temperament,' of the mean vanities of the ladies and Mrs. Turner, of Doris's inadequate good-heartedness.

But the Ariadne story is being placed, too. The Elizabethan language, while beautiful, is a little overripe, for a reason which is indicated clearly by the poem's epigraph, a passage from a scene in Beaumont and Fletcher's *Maid's Tragedy* where the deserted heroine finds her maids at work on a tapestry of Ariadne's story. She assures them that their Ariadne is not nearly pathetic enough, makes an eloquent speech which concludes: 'and behind me / Make all a desolation; see, see, wenches,' and strikes a properly pathetic pose. Mr. Eliot's conviction that this scene is a skilful sentimental fraud is indicated by his quoting a variant reading of this passage which, out of context, has a quite different meaning: 'and behind me / Make all a desolation. Look, look, wenches!' The degree of Mr. Eliot's disgust with Sweeney's world is indicated by the brutal biological pun of his title, but the poem is none the less aware that Sweeney's world is real and that the world of Theseus and Ariadne becomes a sentimental dream if we forget it.

By 1920 Mr. Eliot's consciousness of the decayed worlds available to the contemporary imagination had thus become very complex. In 'A Cooking Egg,' after presenting a whole series of them, he asks: 'Where are the eagles and the trumpets?' Not here, certainly; they are history, 'buried beneath some snow-deep Alps.' Here there are only 'weeping, weeping multitudes / Droop[ing] in a hundred A.B.C.'s.'

Of the dramatic monologues of this period, 'Gerontion' is the finest. Its form is a skilful, 'impersonalising' adaptation of the Jacobean dramatic soliloquy (perhaps particularly the one quoted from Tourneur in 'Tradition and the Individual Talent' and echoed near the end of 'Gerontion'). The speaker's weary old age is another impersonalising device. Moreover, both the form, with its free association, and the character, with his long memory and imprisoning Pyrrhonism, are cunningly suited to express Mr. Eliot's passionate sense of contemporary man's failure to possess his tradition and his feeling of despair in the face of apparently insuperable unbelief. The poem's limiting element is its insufficient sense of the speaker's character, which collapses under the weight of all Mr. Eliot requires him to say. None the less the poem has an intensity of image and an eloquence of voice no earlier poem achieves:

> Gull against the wind, in the windy straits
> Of Belle Isle, or running on the Horn,
> White feathers in the snow, the Gulf claims,
> And an old man driven by the Trades
> To a sleepy corner.

Though we see the movement of the ventriloquist's lips here, it is none the less magnificent.

'Gerontion' also illustrates clearly what has been a stumbling-block for many of Mr. Eliot's readers, a habit no doubt encouraged by both his imagism and his acute ear; this is his dependence on verbal echoes of passages in his reading which have precipitated the feelings he wishes to evoke in his poem. 'The Word within a word, unable to speak a word' echoes a sermon of Lancelot Andrewes; 'In depraved May, dogwood and chestnut, flowering judas' echoes the opening of Chapter XVIII of *The Education of Henry Adams*; 'Vacant shuttles / Weave the wind' echoes the first chapter of *Ulysses*; 'I have lost my sight, smell, hearing, taste and touch' echoes a letter of Peter Damian; etc., through A. C. Benson's life of Edward FitzGerald, Middleton's *Changeling*, Jonson's *Alchemist*, The Scriptures, and Mr. Eliot alone knows how many others. When the innocent reader learns that these puzzling lines are echoes, he may think Mr. Eliot has played him false; when he looks them up and finds their contexts unenlightening, he may think Mr. Eliot has played him falser. 'Clear visual images,' says Mr. Eliot of Dante's, 'are given much more intensity by having a meaning—we do not need to know what the meaning is, but in our awareness of the image we must be aware that the meaning is there too.' This is in fact the way Mr. Eliot's echoes work, when they are not—as they sometimes are—too compressed to take visual or aural shape in our minds.

By deliberately collapsing the character of the speaker, *The Waste Land* (1922) extends the dramatic soliloquy to include all the occasions Mr. Eliot is preoccupied with. These occasions are dealt with in the manner of the early lyrics, reminding us of traditional values by images of historical occasions and by literary echoes, so that we may feel it is the decay of these values which has left the contemporary world wandering in a waste land, somnambulised by the death of meaning, as is the typist home at tea-time, or at best tortured by its own sterile lack of purpose, as are the great lady (' "Do / You know nothing? Do you see nothing? Do you remember / Nothing?" ') and Lil. For the coherence of the speaker's character he substitutes the coherence of reiterated images, particularly images which contrast dryness, sterility and deadness with water, fertility and life. These images are grouped around the allusions to the myth of the fisher-king, and they also allow Mr. Eliot to introduce an essentially religious view of the contemporary world. The poem ends with the echo of a prayer, but that prayer is only one of the fragments the protagonist has shored against his ruins. 'Shall I at least set my lands in order?' he asks, but can only answer, 'London Bridge is falling down falling down falling down,' for this 'least' is the last, not the first thing to be done. Thus the protagonist ends in a confusion of mistaken hope, insight, a glimpse of the promise of purgation —'*Poi s'ascose nel foco che gli affina*'—and a prayer. No wonder he reminds himself of Hieronymo, who made a poem out of the tortured fragments of his madness. *The Waste Land* approaches an emotionally logical reduction to absurdity of the 'materialist' conception of experience. 'The Hollow Men' (1925) carries this process to its radical conclusion:

> This is the way the world ends
> Not with a bang but a whimper.

It was five years before Mr. Eliot found the way up from this darkness, the figure of the ten stairs with its echoes of perceptions from Dante and St. John of the Cross to 'The Jolly Corner.' *Ash Wednesday* (1930) is a scrupulously honest realisation of the need for submission to what *The Waste Land* had called the cruellest of all months. If Mr. Eliot was not yet capable of disciplining 'the lost heart' which in everyone

> stiffens and rejoices
> In the lost lilac and the lost sea voices,

even when he does not 'wish to wish these things,' he was able to see that

> The single Rose
> Is now the Garden
> Where all loves end

and to

> pray I may forget
> Those matters that with myself I too much discuss
> Too much explain.

He was thus able to see the Christian faith as the vivifying centre of the tradition of Western culture to which he had committed himself from the beginning, and so to pray:

> Teach us to care and not to care
> Teach us to sit still.

('I have often said that all the troubles of man come from his not knowing how to sit still.' Mr. Eliot's comments on 'a Jansenism of the individual biography' in his essay on Pascal's *Pensées* are revealing.)

Ash Wednesday is stylised—perhaps the word is ritualised— into a moving but skeletal vision of what experience would be like if the whole awareness were to be disciplined to this conception of it. These bones sing as truly as they can, but their singing is only 'chirping / With the burden of the grasshopper' in the waste land, where desire shall fail because memory has. No more than the prophet can the poem say whether these bones shall live; it can only accept.

> Under a juniper-tree the bones sang, scattered and shining
> We are glad to be scattered, we did little good to each other, . . .
> Forgetting themselves and each other, united
> In the quiet of the desert.

6

It took Mr. Eliot more than a decade to bring his whole perception of experience under the control of this vision in a usable way. This was by far the most formidable act of discipline he had attempted, and it must have made this a period of immense imaginative effort. Meantime he experimented in the drama, first with a pageant, *The Rock*, and then with what is still his most successful play, *Murder in the Cathedral*. Its central insight is very like *Ash Wednesday*'s, though it has absorbed more of experience.

> They know and do not know, that acting is suffering
> And suffering is action. Neither does the actor suffer
> Nor the patient act. But both are fixed
> In an eternal action, an eternal patience

To which all must consent that it may be willed
And which all must suffer that they may will it,
That the pattern may subsist, for the pattern is the action
And the suffering, that the wheel may turn and still
Be forever still.

The play on words here has to carry a heavy load of meaning, but it shows Mr. Eliot moving towards the paradoxes which will allow him to control a great deal of experience for this vision in *Four Quartets*.

Murder in the Cathedral is a remarkable application of the dramatic theories Mr. Eliot the critic had been working out from the start of his career. He began with a series of essays on Elizabethan drama which ought to have revolutionised the academic conception of it; to these he added a number of general essays on the drama. Given Mr. Eliot's conception of poetry and his sense of reality, it is no surprise that these essays sought for a contemporary form of drama which would give formal and impersonal expression to the most deeply felt, personal perceptions, and that the Elizabethan essays express his dislike of realism and an insufficient commitment to convention. 'The great vice of English drama from Kyd to Galsworthy has been that its aim of realism was unlimited. In one play, *Everyman*, and perhaps in that one play only, we have a drama within the limitation of art. . . .'

His first experiment, in the early twenties, was the attempt in the unfinished *Sweeney Agonistes* to adapt the popular form of the music hall to a serious purpose; he apparently found that impossible. In *Murder in the Cathedral* he reversed the experiment and adapted a form like *Everyman*'s to the modern theatre. 'Within the limits of art' thus provided, he develops a subject which is clearly relevant to our time with its concern for 'the art of temporal government,' in which there is 'nothing quite conclusive.' Since the actual events of the play occurred eight hundred years ago, they are free from irrelevant contemporary prejudices and at the same time emphasise Mr. Eliot's sense of the permanent existence in time of the play's conflict. The play is also beautifully imagined by Mr. Eliot in a design which seems to accord both with his deepest feelings about our world and with his deepest feelings about himself:

> I know that the pride bred of sudden prosperity
> Was but confirmed by bitter adversity.
> I saw him as Chancellor, flattered by the King,
> Liked or feared by courtiers, in their overbearing fashion, . . .
> His pride always feeding upon his virtues,
> Pride drawing sustenance from impartiality,
> Pride drawing sustenance from generosity,
> Loathing power given by temporal devolution,
> Wishing subjection to God alone.

Murder in the Cathedral was followed by *The Family Reunion*, which reversed the experiment again and tried adapting drawing-room comedy to something like Orestes' tragedy. Drawing-room comedy is almost hopelessly inadequate for such a purpose, and the play's distinction is almost entirely in the lyric poetry of the trance-like speeches of Harry and Agatha, speeches which are very close to certain passages in the *Four Quartets*. Mr. Eliot's failure to measure the limits of the conventionalised realism of drawing-room comedy tells us something about the unperceived limits of his sense of everyday actuality; this, in turn, helps to explain why his later plays, *The Cocktail Party* and *The Confidential Clerk*, are disappointing. In both Mr. Eliot has pushed the serious implications into the background—so far, in *The Confidential Clerk*, that they can hardly be discerned. He then concentrates his visible effort on what is never very real to him, the daily life of ordinary people, whom he has from the beginning been inclined to see as grotesques answering to names like Mrs. Phlaccus and Professor Channing-Cheetah. If these late plays control this extravagance, they hardly find a substitute for it. 'The dramatist,' as he once said quite rightly, 'need not understand people; but he must be exceptionally aware of them.' Mr. Eliot, to use his own revealing language, is acutely aware of 'the reality of moral synthesis . . . behind the motions of his personages,' but he cannot make these 'shadows of the human world' solid for us. If the abstract theory behind these last plays is sounder than the abstract theory behind *Murder in the Cathedral*, as it probably is, Mr. Eliot's persistent attempt to put it into practice despite the limitations of his perceptions is a kind of wrong-headed heroism.

7

In any event, it was in the *Four Quartets* that he found a form perfectly suited to his resources and to his now fully realised vision, with the result that it is his greatest as well as his most perfectly designed poem. In it his protagonist's meditation is formally organised down to the smallest detail and is at the same time free to elaborate as dramatically natural discoveries every aspect of the necessary subjects of his meditation. Each quartet has the same five-part structure, and in each quartet each part goes over again the subject of the same part in the previous quartets, with a greater understanding which yet includes all that has preceded it. The poem's lucidity of perception and brilliance of expression could be conveyed only by a line-by-line commentary.

But perhaps something can be shown by an illustration; this is the opening strophe of the first part of the final quartet, 'Little Gidding.'

> Midwinter spring is its own season
> Sempiternal though sodden towards sundown,
> Suspended in time, between pole and tropic.
> When the short day is brightest, with frost and fire,
> The brief sun flames the ice, on pond and ditches,
> In windless cold that is the heart's heat,
> Reflecting in a watery mirror
> A glare that is blindness in the early afternoon.
> A glow more intense than blaze of branch, or brazier,
> Stirs the dumb spirit: no wind, but pentecostal fire
> In the dark time of the year. Between melting and freezing
> The soul's sap quivers. There is no earth smell
> Or smell of living thing. This is the spring time
> But not in time's covenant. Now the hedgerow
> Is blanched for an hour with transitory blossom
> Of snow, a bloom more sudden

Than that of summer, neither budding nor fading,
Not in the scheme of generation.
Where is the summer, the unimaginable
Zero summer?

This passage is governed by Mr. Eliot's sense of history's pattern of timeless moments, so that it makes us see the full meaning of 'Burnt Norton's' 'Only through time time is conquered' and of 'East Coker's' awareness both of history's knowledge that 'in my beginning is my end,' and of the timeless knowledge that 'in my end is my beginning.' This is the full realisation of that historical sense Mr. Eliot had been striving for from the beginning, 'a sense of the timeless as well as of the temporal and of the timeless and the temporal together.'

This strophe is first of all, therefore, a description of an unseasonal season, what we sometimes call a spring-like day in midwinter. But this language falsifies what seems to Mr. Eliot its complete reality, for it assumes that time is ultimate, that this day is 'really' a midwinter day and only seems spring-like. Mr. Eliot is very anxious not to ignore the limited but genuine reality of time, which is vividly evoked in 'East Coker's' description of the rustic dancers

> Keeping the rhythm in their dancing
> As in their living in the living seasons
> The time of the seasons and the constellations
> The time of milking and the time of harvest
> The time of the coupling of man and woman
> And that of beasts. Feet rising and falling.
> Eating and drinking. Dung and death.

The intimacy between our senses of Nature's life and of man's when we think of them as existing in time is clearly recognised here; and if the modulation at the end of the passage sets the limit of the reality of time, it does not deny that reality.

But if we recognise the limit as well as the reality of time, then we recognise that, except within this limit, this unseasonal season is not merely spring-like; it is, taken quite simply for what it is, 'its own season,' neither an odd 'winter' day nor an

odd 'spring' day but 'midwinter spring.' As such it is 'sempi-
ternal'; only, to be sure, 'sodden towards sundown.' It is
'suspended,' but it is also 'in time.' The next two lines sustain
this double perception of the occasion, holding sharply before
us both our temporal and our intrinsic senses of it ('When the
short day is brightest, . . . / The brief sun . . .'), and fix our
attention on the occasion's special quality. This quality is
hinted at in 'between pole and tropic'; it is made overt in 'with
frost and fire'; it is re-emphasised by 'The brief sun flames the
ice.'

But because *men* are always 'living in the living seasons,' this
unseasonal season is, in both its temporality and its suspense,
a season of the heart as well as a season of Nature. Thus 'the
brief sun flames [it does not merely make a flame-coloured
reflection on] the ice, on pond and ditches, / In windless cold
that is [it is not merely like] the heart's heat.' We should,
parenthetically, ponder Mr. Eliot's horror of that cold wind
that blows frequently in his poems like a draught through an
uninhabited universe, leaving his protagonists feeling like 'a
dull head among windy spaces' where thoughts are only
'tenants of the house.' From this point on the language of the
strophe keeps us aware of all these meanings. 'Reflecting in a
watery mirror / A glare that is blindness in the early afternoon.'
This does complete justice to the natural phenomenon, the
uneven reflecting surfaces of ponds and ditches, the merely
uncomfortable glare of natural sunlight which, we remind
ourselves, need be endured only for 'the early afternoon.'
But it is also charged with an awareness which will become
overt in the next four lines, the awareness that this is also a
season of the heart, that the watery surface of man's nature has
reflected a flash of the blinding glow that has, in the words of
'Burnt Norton,' 'glittered out of the heart of light.'

If the emphasis of these first eight lines has been on the
natural phenomenon, with the human one kept mainly
implicit, the emphasis of the next four lines is on the human
phenomenon, with the natural one, however, kept constantly
before us by phrases which, if they are metaphors for the season
of the heart, are literal references to the season of Nature ('In

the dark time of the year,' 'Between melting and freezing / The
. . . sap quivers'). The next seven lines generalise the whole
perception further. 'This *is* the spring time,' but not the spring
time of 'time's covenant' (though perhaps of God's), for it is a
spring which, if it stirs men's hearts more intensely than the
most fiery passion, is at the same time icy cold; hotter than
'East Coker's' rustics leaping through their bonfire in a
commodious celebration of natural love but altogether without
the smell of their mortality, the earthy and living smell of
'dung and death.' The hedgerow displays a blossom which
cannot be produced by the natural life of budding and fading
and which is therefore 'not in the scheme of generation' any
more than this heart's passion is. But we are not allowed to
forget the temporal view of this phenomenon even now; 'the
hedgerow / Is blanched *for an hour* with *transitory* blossom,'
with 'a bloom more *sudden* / Than that of summer.'

The last two lines make us suddenly, dramatically aware that
this is not merely a description but the experience of the
protagonist, and perhaps—the anguish of the voice suggests
this—of a particular man. In 'Burnt Norton' the protagonist
had been impatient of ordinary time—

> Ridiculous the waste sad time
> Stretching before and after.

In 'East Coker' he was still thinking almost exclusively of 'the
intense moment / Isolated, with no before and after,' because
'love is most nearly itself / When here and now cease to matter.'
But by 'The Dry Salvages' he has recognised that, though all
this is true, 'the point of intersection of the timeless / With time,
is an occupation for the saint'; 'for most of us, there is only the
unattended / Moment, the moment in and out of time.' It
is such a moment that he apprehends in this first strophe of
'Little Gidding'; now it makes him ask what—if midwinter
spring can be like this—'the unimaginable / Zero summer'
can be like, that 'time' when, simultaneously, midwinter has
become zero weather and spring has become full summer.

The *Four Quartets*' sustained realisation of the incarnation of
the eternal in time may perhaps be suggested by this passage,

but it can only be suggested. The poem as a whole is Mr. Eliot's finest demonstration of his talent for handling a great subject, our perception of reality, in a way that takes scrupulous account of all men's experience and has, at the same time, the authenticity of personal and even specifically autobiographical experience. 'We live,' he has said, 'in an incredible public world and an intolerable private world.' Mr. Eliot's poem conceives a union of them which is both credible and tolerable. It thus realises the ideal he set himself—not perhaps completely understanding at the time all it had to include—at the beginning of his career, 'to transmute his personal and private agonies into something rich and strange, something universal and impersonal.'

Sir Winston Spencer Churchill, K.G.

by D. C. SOMERVELL

David Churchill Somervell is the elder son of the late Robert Somervell, who taught Sir Winston as a boy at Harrow. Sir Winston's debt to him as a teacher of English is generously recorded on an early page of *My Early Life*.
 D. C. Somervell has been a schoolmaster for the greater part of the last fifty years and has found time to write a number of books such as *English Thought in the Nineteenth Century* and *British Politics since 1900*. He is probably most widely known as author of the abridged version of Arnold Toynbee's *Study of History*.

IN 1953 the Nobel Trustees evidently experienced a laudable desire to award one of their prizes to Sir Winston Churchill, and the only question was which prize it should be; for there is no Nobel Prize for Statesmanship. There is, of course, a Nobel Prize for Peace, and a list of its winners makes odd reading today. It consists in large part of persons who, with the very best intentions, proclaimed peace where there was no peace. In the list will be found, for example, the three authors of the Locarno Franco-Anglo-German settlement of 1925, a pretentious sham which artfully concealed the continued activities of the German soldiers who were preparing the way for Hitler.

In any case, to offer the Peace Prize to Sir Winston might seem at first sight a paradoxical proceeding. Here was a man who in his youth had run all over the world—Cuba, Indian Frontier, Sudan, South Africa—looking for wars and thrusting himself into them, so that by the age of twenty-five he had undoubtedly seen a greater diversity of fighting than any other young man then alive. And exactly forty years after all that was over this same man strode to the front of the world stage as one of the greatest leaders of a nation and empire at war that history records.

On this showing, to offer the Peace Prize to Sir Winston might seem rather like offering a beef-steak to the Mahatma Gandhi or a glass of barley water to Falstaff. And yet, has not the great man said, in the preface to that first volume of his biggest book, that the second world war might well be called 'The Unnecessary War.' 'Never was there a war more easy to stop,' he says, and by 'to stop' he means 'to prevent'; and he then proceeds to write half a volume to show how it could and would have been prevented if he had been in control of things from 1933 onwards. Immediately after the war was over the great war leader was excluded from political power once again, and again he saw the menace before most others were aware of it and sounded his warning note at Fulton, Missouri, in the middle of the Middle West, in March 1946. In this speech he forecast the shape of things to come and told both American and British peoples that they would have to get together in defence of the free world against the menace of Communist imperialism. The speech annoyed nearly everyone, much as his anti-Nazi warnings of ten years earlier had done. It particularly annoyed the British Foreign Secretary, Ernest Bevin. But this time the warnings were in due course heeded, and the foundations of N.A.T.O. well and truly laid before Sir Winston returned to power in 1951.

Thus there would be a good case for offering Sir Winston the Peace Prize, not because, like the Locarno statesmen, he proclaimed a sham peace, but because he gave twice over a timely warning of a very real prospect of war. I like to suppose, having absolutely no authority for my supposition, that the Nobel Trustees offered Sir Winston the Peace Prize and that, after he had looked down the list of the previous winners, he said 'Thank you very much, but I would rather not.'

But these admirable trustees, on my supposition, refused to be discouraged, and considered their other prizes. The prize for medicine would hardly do, even though Sir Winston has recorded that he is always prepared to prescribe for his doctor. There is no Nobel prize for painting. If there had been, perhaps this essay would have been written by my old pupil Basil Taylor, or some such person, who would have had the fascinating task of considering just how high our 'Academician Extraordinary' stands among contemporary painters. But there was a prize for literature. Sir Winston had been writing books off and on all his life, and very good books too. He was delighted to accept the Nobel Prize for Literature and add himself as a third to Kipling and Shaw, the only English writers of English prose previously thus honoured. And at this point, having done quite enough preliminary Sirwinstoning, I intend henceforth to call our man Churchill, and to consider his career and his merits as a writer. I trust that this will be more welcome to the reader than yet another brief survey of his immensely long and complicated political career or yet another heartfelt and would-be eloquent encomium upon his services to his country and the world in 1939–45. At least it will be more of a novelty.

Aristotle tells us that 'poetry,' by which he meant fiction, is a higher form of literature than history. This is unfortunate, for we have to record that Churchill's only novel was a failure. Here is his account of the matter in a paragraph from the most delightful of all his books, *My Early Life*. Perhaps it should be added that *My Early Life* was published in 1930 when Churchill was fifty-five and had been a Cabinet minister off and on for nearly a quarter of the century, whereas the novel was the work of a young subaltern in India, aged twenty-two.

Having contracted the habit of writing I embarked on fiction. I thought I would try my hand at a novel. I found this much quicker work than the accurate chronicle of facts. Once started, the tale flowed on of itself. I chose as a theme a revolt in some imaginary Balkan or South American republic, and traced the fortunes of a liberal leader who overthrew an arbitrary Government only to be swallowed up in a socialist revolution. My brother officers were much amused by the story as it developed, and made various suggestions for stimulating the love interest which I was not able to accept. But we had plenty of fighting and politics, interspersed with such philosophisings as I was capable of, all leading up to the *grande finale* of an ironclad fleet forcing a sort of Dardanelles to quell the rebellious capital. The novel was finished in about two months. It was eventually published in *Macmillan's Magazine* under the title of 'Savrola,' and being subsequently reprinted in various editions, yielded in all over several years about seven hundred pounds. I have consistently urged my friends to abstain from reading it.

The advice is, alas, good. The book has, no doubt, touches of Anthony Hope and also of the young Disraeli, but it must be held to fall between these rather widely separated stools. Yet if we refrain from reading it and merely consider the synopsis already quoted, surely significance positively hits one in the eye. A liberal leader overthrows an autocratic régime and is in turn overwhelmed by a socialist revolution—that is the sequence of Tsardom, Kerensky, Lenin in 1917. The 'forcing of a sort of Dardanelles' by a fleet of ironclads—Churchill himself in 1915. This young Hussar was already thinking along twentieth-century lines in the year of Queen Victoria's Diamond Jubilee. But that does not alter the fact that *Savrola* scores very few marks in the Nobel Literature Prize Competition.

Very different was the quality and also the fortunes of *The Malakand Field Force*, which had actually preceded *Savrola*; but before going on to it we should consider Churchill's literary output as a whole and in general terms.

Is he to be regarded as an historian or an autobiographer? The answer is, as both. His method has always been, first to assist in the making of a bit of history, whether as soldier or statesman, and then to sit down and write a book about it. Margot Asquith, the brilliant wife of a former Liberal prime minister, is recorded as saying, somewhere in the early 1920s, 'I hear Winston is writing an enormous book in half a dozen volumes, all about himself, and he's going to call it *The World Crisis*.' *Arma virumque cano*, sang Virgil, 'I sing arms and a Man.' Churchill sings the same, and adds 'and I'm the Man.'

There might seem to be traces of egoism in this procedure, but it all arose very naturally from two facts. The first fact was that Second Lieutenant W. L. Spencer Churchill, having joined the Army, wanted to see and take part in any fighting that there might be. Since the wars of those days were very small and the world very large, and the British Army ramifying over a very considerable part of it, the chances were very much against any particular British soldier taking part in any particular British war of the half-century between the Crimean and the Kruger wars. This was a condition of affairs which Churchill set himself to remedy, so far as his own chances were concerned, by pulling the strings which his aristocratic connections placed at his disposal. There was, for example, General Sir Bindon Blood, a notable performer on the Indian Frontier.

'He was my host's life-long friend. If future trouble broke out on the Indian Frontier he was sure to have high command. He held the key to future delights. I made good friends with him. One Sunday morning on the sunny lawns of Deepdene I extracted from the general a promise that, if ever he commanded another expedition on the Indian Frontier, he would let me come with him.' And less than a year later, though Churchill's regiment, the 4th Hussars, remained sweating and fuming in Southern India, the young hero himself was prancing along the Indian Frontier several thousand miles away, attached to the staff of the obliging General Blood.

The second fact alluded to above was that young Churchill was extremely anxious to become financially independent. His mother (to whom he was devoted) was by this time a widow, and, though rich perhaps by suburban standards, was anything but a wealthy woman by the standard of late Victorian aristocracy, with England on top of the world and income tax at about eightpence in the pound. The generous allowance she made to her elder son made a perceptible hole in her income and Churchill did not want to take a penny more for a day longer than necessary. He already felt the itch to write almost as strongly as the itch to fight. The obvious course was to combine writing with fighting, and in those easy-going days there was nothing wrong in an officer doubling his duties with those of a war correspondent. It might secure the forces a good Press. Of course, if the young officer had ideas of his own which led him to criticise his military superiors, that might prove unfortunate for all concerned, but it was not going to happen under the admirable Sir Bindon.

So readers of the *Daily Telegraph* in the year of Queen Victoria's Jubilee had the privilege of reading vivid accounts of this remote affair—which they might otherwise never have noticed—from the pen of the son of Lord Randolph Churchill. And after that, what more natural than to refashion the whole series as a book? The *Malakand Field Force* records an unimportant affair which would long since have been forgotten but for the place it occupies in Churchill's literary career. Its impact was remarkable. Among the writers of congratulatory letters was no less a person than the Prince of Wales, soon to be Edward VII :

> My dear Winston,
>
>   I cannot resist writing a few lines to congratulate you. . . . Everybody is reading it and I only hear it spoken of with praise. . . .
>
> Yours very sincerely
A. E.

Even more important, for immediate purposes, was the reaction of Lord Salisbury, prime minister for most of the past dozen years and onwards for as long, it seemed, as he cared to stay. He, more than anyone else, had destroyed the career of his brilliant and unwise colleague, Lord Randolph, and now he expressed a wish to meet Lord Randolph's son. The book, he said, had given him a better idea of what had been happening on the Indian Frontier than any of the official documents which it had been his duty to read.

The description of the meeting between the old statesman and the young soldier-author—still only twenty-three, be it remembered—constitutes a striking passage in *My Early Life*. 'He kept me for over half an hour, and when he finally conducted me again across the wide expanse of carpet to the door, he dismissed me in the following terms: "I hope you will allow me to say how much you remind me of your father, with whom such important days of my political life were lived. If there is anything at any time that I can do which would be of assistance to you, pray do not fail to let me know." '

Very touching, but Churchill was already thinking ahead. Lord Kitchener's campaign for the reconquest of the Sudan, a matter of very different dimensions and significance from the little Malakand affair, was approaching its climax, and of course Churchill wanted to be in at the death of the infamous Dervish régime. But Kitchener was a very different proposition from Sir Bindon Blood. He had conceived a strong prejudice against this young upstart, and was determined to keep him out of the Sudan. Churchill approached Lord Salisbury's private secretary, an old friend of his father's. Strings were pulled. It is a complex story, but the upshot was that Churchill arrived on the scene just in time to take part in the famous cavalry charge in the Battle of Omdurman.

Here was material for another book, of a much weightier character than *The Malakand Field Force*. *The River War* is a first-rate piece of historical writing, in which the autobiographical element figures as a brief but brilliantly lighted episode. It tells the whole story of the Nile Valley from the revolt of the Mahdi against Egyptian misrule in 1881, through the tragedy of Gordon, the long years of Dervish anarchy and Anglo-Egyptian preparation, down to Kitchener's campaign, which was a wonder of the world in its day, the break-up of the Dervish empire and, finally, the dramatic and alarming clash with the French at Fashoda. The book was published in 1899 and revised in 1902. My own edition was published in 1933. Perhaps I may be allowed to mention that I bought it at Khartoum, which seems the right place. If ever I find myself in Hell I shall look out for a copy of Dante's *Inferno*.

In this book, published when he was twenty-four, we see Churchill's narrative style fully formed. It is a style which owes something to Macaulay and more to Gibbon, both of whom he had studied with attention while his fellow officers were taking their siestas in Indian cantonments. Occasionally a passage is rather too consciously Gibbonian: 'The first spadeful of sand of the desert railway was turned on the first day of 1897 . . . meanwhile the men of the new Railway Battalion were being trained; the plant was steadily accumulating; engines, rolling stock and materials of all sorts had arrived from England. From the growing workshops at Wady Halfa the continual clang and clatter of hammers and the black smoke of manufacture rose to the African sky. The malodorous incense of civilisation was offered to the startled gods of Egypt.'

Sublime or ridiculous?—whichever you like, it is almost comically characteristic of the strand in Churchill's style which descends from Gibbon, or for that matter from Dr. Johnson. The point we are concerned to make, however, is this—that before Churchill had reached his twenty-fifth birthday, before he had won world-wide celebrity by his escape from Pretoria, before he had entered the House of Commons, he had already laid the foundations of a high position in the world of letters.

Churchill now left the Army. He felt sure he could earn in journalism sufficient to launch himself on the parliamentary career he had in mind. No sooner had he taken this step than the South African War, the biggest thing of its kind in history up to that date, began, and Churchill, of course, attended as a war correspondent. He was captured, before the war was a month old, while assisting the efforts of a ridiculous contraption called 'the armoured train'; was taken prisoner to Pretoria; escaped to Lourenço Marques, and was back with lumbering old Buller, this time as an officer in the South African Light Horse, in time to be among the first to enter Ladysmith. A few months later, after seeing the war through to what looked like its conclusion, he resigned his commission, returned to England and was elected Conservative M.P. for Oldham in the 'khaki election' of October 1900.

The South African War, though it contributed immensely to Churchill's fame, making him perhaps the most famous young man of twenty-five in the English-speaking world, did not add to his literary stature. He collected and published two volumes of his dispatches from the front, but he did not seek to do for this much larger subject what he had already done so brilliantly for the Sudan campaign in *The River War*. For this omission one may suggest two reasons. One reason would be that membership of the House of Commons was opening up before him a host of problems calling for his study. The other would be that, as the war dragged on and he pondered over both its causes and its conduct, he realised that any frank statement of his conclusions on both these subjects might be extremely prejudicial to his prospects as an aspiring member of the political party which had first caused the war and then conducted it. Thirty years were to pass before the publication of *My Early Life*, and from passages in the later chapters of that book we may get an idea of the highly critical and satirical masterpiece of which political prudence deprived us.

However, Churchill soon found that he needed two professions to satisfy his energies, and the result was the publication in 1906 of *The Life of Lord Randolph Churchill* in two substantial volumes. The appetite for detailed records of Victorian party politics has by the middle of the twentieth century so much abated—'a time of great men and small events' as Churchill himself long afterwards called it—that it may be doubted if the book finds many readers today. Yet it was hailed on publication as the most brilliant political biography in the language. Lord Randolph was a good subject, for his career was short. All that matters of it falls well within the decade of the eighties, a most melodramatic decade with Lord Randolph in the thick of it all. He restored the fortunes of the Conservative Party; he deemed himself its master; he put that assumption to the test, and found he was mistaken. The Machine broke the Man. The Conservative Party moved ponderously forward under Salisbury, Balfour and Joseph Chamberlain to its twenty years of assured mastery; the hero of the party in the day of its weakness, the man who tried to realise the ideal of Tory-Democracy, was pushed out of the way; tragic illness completed his ruin. Condemned as a failure at a game where nothing succeeds like success, he was in danger of becoming not only unlamented but unremembered. Here was a challenge to be met by a brilliant son.

As Churchill laboured at the task filial piety had set him the father's story assumed a more and more ominous significance, both for the son and subsequently for his readers. Lord Randolph's story was that of a man who, by reason of family tradition, had joined a 'Die-hard' Conservative Party that did not suit him. Perhaps Gladstonian Liberalism would have suited him still less; and that is only to say that he fell between two stools. So much for Randolph; but what of Winston? He had found himself as ill at ease in the Conservative Party as his father had done. Two years before the book was published he had performed the dangerous operation of crossing the floor of the House. Less than two years after that Balfour resigned, a new Liberal Government won an overwhelming victory, and young Mr. Churchill—for he was still only just over thirty—found himself a Liberal minister, soon to be a member of the Cabinet. In no long time he discovered that the most congenial of his colleagues, the only one whom he could regard as his equal in political drive, was also the most violently detested in the social circles to which Churchill belonged, the Welshman Lloyd George.

So Churchill was launched on the Radical phase of his career, 1905–11, a period he has not embalmed in his autobiographical record, for *My Early Life* breaks off with the first premonitions of his breach with the Conservatives. In these Radical years he established a brilliant record. At the Board of Trade he founded the Labour Exchanges, and also carried through the first effective measure dealing with the evil state of affairs called in those days 'sweated labour.' The best-known document on this subject is still Hood's 'Song of a Shirt' written fifty years before. At the Home Office he began the system of providing entertainment for prisoners—he had been a prisoner himself. As assistant to Lloyd George he saw through the House of Commons the first Unemployment Insurance Bill. Then fate in the person of the prime minister intervened and removed the enthusiastic young semi-socialist from all that fun to the cold grey prospects of the Admiralty.

Some say this was the most important thing that Asquith ever did. It was certainly a turning point in Churchill's career. It meant that as the German menace grew and when war at last came Churchill was in control of incomparably the most important British instrument of war. It looked as if Fate had cast Churchill, at the age of forty, for the rôle of the great British war leader in the 1914 war. For Asquith was bound to go if the war proved long, and who else was there?

Yet it worked out quite differently. Early in 1915 Churchill staked his reputation on a plan (the Dardanelles plan as distinct from the later Gallipoli plan) to break through the straits with naval forces only and bombard Constantinople into submission. The plan failed; for that and other reasons the Conservative Opposition leaders demanded a share in the

Government, and stipulated that Churchill should be removed from the Admiralty. A few months later he left the Cabinet and went to fight on the Western Front. Lloyd George, who ousted Asquith with mainly Conservative support at the end of 1916, soon brought back Churchill as Minister of Munitions, a department of immense magnitude but no longer very exciting. Its teething troubles were long over. When the war ended Lloyd George and his friends secured a further term of office and during the four years 1919–22 Churchill played important parts in a number of exciting postwar activities, such as the support of the anti-Bolsheviks in Russia, the Irish civil war, and much more besides. In the autumn of 1922 the Conservatives broke away from Lloyd George's leadership. The Coalition was broken, and Churchill lost not only his 'party' but, in the ensuing election, his seat. For two years, 1922–4, he was not in Parliament at all.

These facts have been set out, with all possible brevity, to explain the position Churchill set himself to deal with in the first of his two great historico-autobiographical works, *The World Crisis, 1911–18*.*

It would probably be true to say that by 1922, viewing the war in retrospect, British opinion had come to the conclusion that of all the British statesmen involved Churchill had proved the most conspicuous failure. None other had stood so high and fallen so rapidly and so far. He had proved, it seemed, that at forty he was not yet really grown up. He began to manifest his unfitness with that absurd schoolboy prank of the expedition to Antwerp. Then came the Dardanelles. . . . Surely anyone could have told him etc. After that, such great men as Mr. Bonar Law and Mr. Austen Chamberlain decreed that this foolish fellow must henceforth have no finger in the pie of military or naval strategy, and how right they were! Churchill was shut out, and, after a long interval, we won the war. Q.E.D.

That was the climate of opinion which Churchill set himself to change, and the circumstances of 1922 gave him leisure to

---

* Two supplementary volumes appeared later: *The Aftermath, 1918–22* and *The War on the Eastern Front*.

set in order material he had no doubt long been assembling. There are four volumes of the main work, which appeared at intervals during the next few years. The crucial one is the second, which deals with the successive phases of the Dardan-elles–Gallipoli venture in fully documented detail. It is Churchill's *Apologia*, and the general impression left, by this volume and by the others also, upon the average candid reader's mind, a reader probably starting with a prejudice against the author, was that Churchill had understood the making of war much better than any of his civilian colleagues and, so far as a general strategy was concerned, much better than the soldiers and sailors; and that his exclusion from power before the end of the first year had proved an unmitigated disaster.

This may seem an exaggerated statement; and perhaps it is, for it is a drastic simplification, and all simplifications eliminate the qualifying clauses. But if any reader is disposed to dismiss what is here asserted, let him consider the amazingly strong conviction, the *faith*, of the British public in 1940 that to Churchill alone could this new and even more alarming war be safely entrusted. Whence did such conviction come? Very largely, no doubt, from the urgency with which Churchill had warned a wishful-thinking world that the second war was coming, though there is a certain lack of logic in the assumption that the man who is most certain of an oncoming Flood will also be the best man to steer the Ark—that the best meteorolo-gist will be the best navigator. However that may be, behind the prophet denouncing the policy of appeasement lay the author of *The World Crisis*.

The four volumes of *The World Crisis* were condensed in a single volume of 800 pages published in 1930. I have just been refreshing my memory by reading this version, and what surprised me again and again was how much I remembered. Again and again, as I read, I found myself saying 'I know what is coming over the page,' and when I turned the page, it came. Yet I had not looked at the book for twenty years or more. My experience was empirical evidence of the memorable character of the book, both in style and in substance. Many people today seem to think that the first war, compared with the second, was a dull affair. A reading of *The World Crisis* would change their minds on this point.

It was an extraordinary chance that Churchill should have been born at just the date which made it possible for him to be a leading statesman in both wars. If he had been born ten years later he would have been too young for any big career but a military one in the first war. If he had been born ten years earlier he would have been too old for the second. The nation's will might have wafted him up to the position of supreme controller, but he would probably have proved an incubus rather than an inspiration. What is really amazing is that, having written a book to assert that he would have been our best leader in the first war, he was offered by Providence (or improvidence) a second war to prove the truth of his assertion.

Long before all the volumes of *The World Crisis* had reached publication their author had returned to the House of Commons and the Conservative Party as Chancellor of the Exchequer in Baldwin's 1924–9 Government. It was, no doubt, generous of Baldwin to slay so large a fatted calf as he did for this returned prodigal when he offered him the Chancellorship of the Exchequer. Churchill had now presided over seven departments—Board of Trade, Home Office, Admiralty, Munitions, War Office, Colonies and Treasury. It is curious to reflect that one of the few major departments that never came his way was the Foreign Office, though it is with foreign policy that, since the end of the second war, he has been mainly concerned. Suppose that in 1924 Baldwin had sent him to the Foreign Office instead of the Treasury. The man who actually presided over the Foreign Office during those five years was Austen Chamberlain, a man with a conventional mind and a perfect French accent. Substitute the man with an unconventional mind and a French accent of memorable imperfection: would it have made any difference? Let us pass on.

The Conservatives lost the general election of 1929 and Labour (MacDonald) took office for the second time. The Indian problem was coming to a head. MacDonald was arranging by means of round table conferences to let the

Indians have ninety per cent of what they wanted, and Baldwin was leading the Opposition into co-operation with this policy. Churchill would have none of it, and, for the second time in his career, flung out of the Conservative Party, though he did not on this occasion fling himself into any other, no other being available. Thus, when the so-called National Government under joint Baldwin–MacDonald management was formed in 1931 he was not asked to join it. This National Government remained in office throughout the thirties, under the successive premierships of MacDonald, Baldwin and Neville Chamberlain. For ten years, therefore, Churchill was out of office, and only in the latter part of it was his attention monopolised by the Nazi peril. So here we have an admirable opportunity for Churchill the man of letters. Let us consider the use he made of it.

In 1930 Churchill published an account of his first twenty-five (or twenty-six) years under the title *My Early Life: A Roving Commission*. I have already praised this book and quoted from it. I consider it one of the most amusing and delightful books in the language. It has had a large sale, of course, but I am surprised that its sales have not been much larger and more continuous. If publishers and public had both of them more sense there would be at all times a pile of copies of this admirable work in every bookshop in the country and a plain-clothes policeman standing by to see that the copies were not stolen.

This was followed in 1932 by a collection of short essays on a wide variety of subjects entitled *Thoughts and Adventures* and in 1937 by another collection entitled *Great Contemporaries*, being sketches from personal knowledge of some two dozen of the leading figures in the generation that was then passing, or had already passed, from the stage. These last contain some of Churchill's best writing, and, since my subject is Churchill as a man of letters, I shall offer two examples of a particular technique in which he excelled, the technique of building up an idea and crowning the edifice with an epigram. The first example is from the essay on Lord Rosebery, and the point to be made is that this last and most brilliant of Whig statesmen could not adapt himself to the ways of democratic politics:

SIR WINSTON SPENCER CHURCHILL

As the franchise broadened and the elegant, glittering, impos-
ing trappings faded from British parliamentary and public life,
Lord Rosebery was conscious of an ever-widening gap between
himself and the Radical electorate. The great principles 'for
which Hampden died in the field and Sidney on the scaffold,'
the economics and philosophy of Mill, the venerable inspiration
of Gladstonian memories, were no longer enough. One had to
face the caucus, the wire-puller, and the soap-box; one had to
stand on platforms built of planks of all descriptions. He did not
like it. He could not do it. He would not try. He knew what
was wise and fair and true. He would not go through the
laborious, vexatious, and at times humiliating processes necessary
under modern conditions to bring about these great ends. He
would not stoop; he did not conquer.

The second passage of this kind is from the essay on 'the
ex-Kaiser' and is so much longer that I can quote it only in
skeleton:

No one should judge the career of the Emperor William II
without asking the question 'What should I have done in his
position?' Imagine yourself brought up from childhood to believe
that you were appointed by God to be the ruler of a mighty
nation, and that the inherent virtue of your blood raised you
above ordinary mortals. Imagine succeeding, in your twenties,
to the garnered prizes, in provinces, in power, and in pride, of
Bismarck's three victorious wars. Imagine feeling the magnificent
German race bounding beneath you in ever-swelling numbers,
strength, wealth, and ambition; and imagine on every side the
thunderous tributes of crowd-loyalty and the skilled unceasing
flattery of courtierly adulation. . . . Are you quite sure, 'gentle
reader' (to revive an old-fashioned form), you would have
withstood the treatment? Are you quite sure that you would
have remained a humble-minded man with no exaggerated
idea of your own importance, with no undue reliance upon your
own opinion, practising the virtue of humility, and striving
always for peace?
But, observe, if you had done so, a discordant note would
instantly have mingled with the chants of praise. . . . If the
first lesson which was wrought into the fibre of the young
Emperor was his own importance, the second was his duty to
assert the importance of the German Empire. And through a

hundred channels where waters flowed with steady force, albeit under a glassy surface of respect, William II was taught that, if he would keep the love and admiration of his subjects, he must be their champion.

The writer goes on to show that the young Emperor contented himself with warlike gestures for the first twenty years of his reign, and adds:

It was my fortune to be the Emperor's guest at the German Army manœuvres of 1906 and 1908. He was then at the height of his glory. . . .

What a contrast twelve years would show! A broken man sits hunched in a railway carriage, hour after hour, at a Dutch frontier station awaiting permission to escape as a refugee from the execration of a people whose armies he has led through measureless sacrifices to measureless defeat.

An awful fate! Was it the wage of guilt or of incapacity? There is, of course, a point where incapacity and levity are so flagrant that they become tantamount to guilt. Nevertheless history should incline to a more charitable view. . . . It was not his fault; it was his fate.

But two volumes of essays and a light-hearted autobiography were far from satisfying the voracious work-appetite of Churchill during the long opposition years of the thirties. A far more ambitious project was in course of execution.

John Churchill, first Duke of Marlborough, and Lord Randolph Churchill had perhaps nothing in common except that both were in the Churchill pedigree and both had received in some respects less than their due from the established historical tradition. But that was enough. Randolph had been given his literary monument thirty years back; it was now time to tackle the remoter and greater figure. The result was *Marlborough and his Times*, of which the first volume appeared in 1933 and the last in 1938, four large and stately volumes of some 600 pages apiece, bound in red buckram, profusely illustrated and with the Churchill arms on the cover, a stately pile, comparable in its own medium with the stupendous Palace of Blenheim, which Vanbrugh had erected for the great Duke's widow. The book has one advantage over the

Winston S. Churchill

William Faulkner

André Gide

palace that whereas architecture, especially of the Vanbrugh
kind, resembles the traditional Scotsman and 'jokes wi'
deeficulty,' the book, being by Churchill, suffers from no such
inhibition. If the reader wants to know where to find a funny
bit he may be directed to the second chapter of the first
volume, beginning 'Our readers must now brace themselves
for what will inevitably be a painful interlude.'

Probably the first volume, covering the first fifty-two years
of the hero's life down to the death of William of Orange, is
the most enjoyable of the four. It contains more movement
and variety and, for those with sadistic tastes, it is brightened
by the long-drawn-out demolition of the unfortunate Macaulay.
This eminent Victorian had been the most effective populariser
of all the 'evidence' for Churchill's treasonable contacts with
the ex-King whom he had already treasonably overthrown.
Modern research had shown that most of the documents used
by Macaulay were bad evidence and that Macaulay's use of
them had fallen short of the highest standards, but the anti-
Macaulay case had never been presented with Macaulay's
own brilliance. Now was the time to do it, and the man. If
Macaulay in 'another place' was privileged to read, with
withers unwrung, this triumphant trouncing of his former
transitory and erring terrestrial self, he may well have smiled
to himself and ruminated as follows: 'It's my old trick; the
House of Commons style applied to literary controversy. He
trounces me as if I were a malignant minister who had introduced a Denigration (Duke of Marlborough) Bill, and he
were the principal speaker for the Opposition. Still, he does it
remarkably well. I could not have done it better myself, and
I am amused to notice that some of the best (and also some of
the worst) features of his style are obviously derivations from
mine.'

As for the rest of the vast work, there is no denying that the
War of the Spanish Succession was one of the dullest of great
wars. Blenheim was an imaginative stroke, but as for Ramillies,
Oudenarde and Malplaquet, what were they but small editions
of Loos, Somme and Passchendaele in reverse? We won in the
end, but only by sheer exhaustion and after 'the politicians'

had sacked the soldier who won the battles for them—whereas the politicians of two hundred years later never succeeded in sacking Haig. As for Marlborough himself, his pious descendant has cleared all the stains from his portrait; he is no longer the traitor of Macaulay's version or the miser of Thackeray's. But even Churchill could not quite bring him to life. He remains far dimmer than many lesser men, dimmer not only than Wellington but than such one-battle soldiers as Wolfe. Still, the book is a great achievement, a book of such quality and quantity as would furnish a complete reputation for an ordinary donnish historian, yet for Churchill a mere pastime of a few years when political business was slack. Some say that he paid others to do most of his research for him. If that be so, how sensible of him. Several of the greatest artists, Rubens for example, kept a roomful of back-room boys to do all the easy parts of their pictures. If it had not been for this excellent technique there would not have been as many Rubenses in the world, and if Churchill had not been as sensible as Rubens he would hardly have got half-way through his *Marlborough* before Hitler came along and claimed his attention elsewhere.

The second war began in September 1939 and Churchill was at once invited to take charge of the Admiralty, where he had been in August 1914. In the following May, on the very eve, as it turned out, of the German invasion of France, Belgium and Holland, Chamberlain resigned the premiership and Churchill took his place. Thenceforward he enjoyed complete control of the British war effort, with far greater powers concentrated in his hands than had fallen to the lot of any British prime minister. The German war ended in May 1945. Thereupon the Labour members (Attlee, Bevin, etc.) left the National Government. Churchill reconstituted his Government on purely Conservative lines and thus carried on until in the autumn of the same year he was decisively defeated in the general election.

Thus was the material provided for *The Second World War*, on the principle Churchill had illustrated several times over. *Arma virumque cano*; first make a chapter of history, then write it. In *The Malakand Field Force* he interwove the personal adventures of a young subaltern with an estimate of the significance of the Indian Frontier warfare of those days. In *The World Crisis* he both gave an account of his stewardship at the Admiralty and of such further contributions as he was able to make to the war effort and also subjected to devastating criticism a British war policy for which he had not been responsible. Now, after a second world war, he had once again to give an account of his stewardship. The first volume was published in 1948, and five more volumes followed at annual intervals. It is a staggering achievement. There is a character in one of Bernard Shaw's plays who says 'It's trouble enough to live one's life without writing it all down afterwards.' That was never Churchill's view.

The Second World War is naturally today the most familiar of all Churchill's books, and it may be, for aught I know, that it was for this work that the Nobel Prize was specifically awarded. It is the most important—if you like, the 'greatest'—of his books because it is the authoritative account of the greatest of his achievements; but, in spite of its enormous sales on both sides of the Atlantic, it is a tough masterpiece. There is plenty of fine writing in the first volume, but the later volumes are, in large part, receptacles for correspondence, minutes and memoranda, which is exactly the purpose for which they were designed.

If Churchill had wanted to write a general history of the war from the British standpoint he would have done so, and no one else would have done the job as well. But that was not his object; which was, to repeat a phrase I have used already, to give an account of his stewardship. In the very moment of the opening catastrophe the fortunes of England had been entrusted to him. Five years later, after bewildering vicissitudes and hairbreadth escapes, the war had been won. Well, what had been the contribution of the prime minister to that result? The evidence was in the written but for the most part unpublished records. There was the evidence of how, day by day through nearly two thousand days, Churchill had faced each dilemma as it presented itself, made his forecasts, devised his projects, and issued his peremptory orders over the whole field of activity. It was all in the files, and the public should be given as much of the files as they could be expected to digest, served up with as much (that is to say, as little) subsequently written narrative and commentary as was required to show the contexts of the documents. The documents *are* the book, presenting their amazing record, not only of the moral qualities of resilience in adversity and forthrightness of decision but the intellectual qualities as well, the astonishingly wide range of expert knowledge of every topic connected with waging war. The claims made by implication in *The World Crisis* were made good in *The Second World War*. Churchill never seems to have doubted that they would be. Perhaps the most stirring paragraph in the whole book, which contains and was *meant* to contain a great deal of dry documentary stuff, is to be found at the end of the first volume. Churchill has just become prime minister and taken on his shoulders the load under which Chamberlain had staggered and fallen:

> As I went to bed at about 3 a.m. I was conscious of a profound sense of relief. At last I had the authority to give directions over the whole scene. I felt as if I were walking with destiny and that all my past life had been but a preparation for this hour and this trial. Eleven years in the political wilderness had freed me from ordinary party antagonisms. My warnings over the last six years had been so numerous, so detailed, and were now so terribly vindicated, that no one could gainsay me. I could not be reproached either for making the war or for want of preparation for it. I thought I knew a good deal about it all and I was sure I should not fail. Therefore, though impatient for the morning, I slept soundly.

The man who could write that without being ridiculous obviously deserved a Nobel Prize—for literature or what you will.

William Faulkner

by W. S. MERWIN

W. S. Merwin is a poet, but he has long taken a special interest in the work of his fellow countryman, William Faulkner. Born in New York City, Merwin took his degree at Princeton, where he also continued post-graduate studies.

He came to Europe in 1949 as tutor to an American family, but soon made a change and became tutor to the nephews of the Portuguese pretender. Between 1950 and 1951 he tutored a son of Robert Graves in Majorca but then came to England in connection with a play he was writing in collaboration with Dido Milroy. It was called *Darkling Child* and was produced at the Arts Theatre. He has also done much work for the B.B.C., especially as a translator from the Spanish.

His first book of poems, *A Mask For Janus*, was published in the Yale Younger Poets Series. This was followed by *The Dancing Bears* and *Green With Beasts*.

WILLIAM FAULKNER'S speech at his acceptance of the Nobel Prize for Literature in 1949 has in itself become something of a classic. The reputation of his 'life's work in the agony and sweat of the human spirit' now seems as secure as that of any other writer of our century. It took a long time for it to become even generally respectable, and that in itself probably helped to isolate him and his work from the rest of his generation and period. But his individuality, from very nearly the beginning of his career, lay not in his style alone but in his relation to his subject, to human experience as exemplified in the experience of his part of the South. He has made unique use of the themes of time and place—time as tradition, history, the past that influences the present— within several generations of a number of fictitious families who represent the essential composition of a fictitious community (Jefferson, Yoknapatawpha County, Mississippi). Time and place, as he dramatises them, are as much blind urges working from within men and societies as they are incomprehensible circumstances swaying the minds and actions of men from without. He has based his creation of much of this fictitious community on actual people or the legends they left behind them. Above all, the Sartoris family, and to some extent the

Compsons too, present close parallels with Faulkner's own forbears; so it is more than simple biographical curiosity that makes it essential to say something about his family before giving the outline of his own life and career. 'The past,' as he makes one of his characters say, 'is never dead. It's not even past.'

The Faulkners were a South Carolina family, and it was from there that the forbears of the present William Faulkner went west to Knox County, Tennessee, in the first quarter of the last century. There, in 1825, William C. Faulkner, the novelist's great-grandfather, was born. The family in due course moved on to Saint Genevieve, Missouri. There is disagreement between the accounts here: one says that William C.'s father died, leaving the boy in his early teens with the responsibility for the rest of his family, and that he set out then for Ripley, Mississippi, to find his school-teacher uncle, one John W. Thompson. The other is more glamorous, recounting how William C. Faulkner, aged fourteen, got into an argument with a younger brother, hit him on the head with a hoe, and when soundly thrashed by his father ran away and made his way as best he could, mostly on foot, over the several hundred miles to Ripley. He got there only to find that his uncle was in jail in Pontotoc, quite a step from there again. It was nearly night; exhausted and dejected, he sat down on the steps of Anderson's tavern and cried. A little girl saw him, was sorry for him and told the landlord, who took him in, and washed and fed him. Again the stories disagree—one implies that the tavern was in Ripley and that the landlord sent the boy on to Pontotoc the next morning; another that the tavern was in Pontotoc and that the landlord sent the boy back to Ripley. According to the former, the little girl who had found him started to cry as he was leaving, and young William C. Faulkner consoled her by telling her that he would come back and marry her. Years later she did, in fact, become his second wife.

The uncle studied law in jail, acted as his own counsel, was acquitted, returned to Ripley to practise law, and eventually became a circuit court judge. William C. studied law in his uncle's office, and grew up to be a lawyer himself. When he was still in his teens he helped capture a man named McCannon who had killed a local family with an axe in order to rob them; helped, too, to prevent McCannon being lynched once he was captured, in return for which McCannon told him his life story. William C. Faulkner had it printed and sold copies of it on the day of execution, making a profit of over a thousand dollars. He volunteered at the start of the Mexican War, held the rank of first lieutenant in the Tippah Volunteers, saw no action but did see an abortive mutiny, and was wounded by accident but somehow in line of duty, for which he later was awarded a disability allowance. After the Mexican War he went back to Ripley and law practice, and married Holland Pearce, from Knoxville. In 1849 he became mixed up in a weird imbroglio of violence and revenge; a man named Hindman charged him to his face with having obstructed Hindman's admission to a secret society to which Faulkner belonged. Hindman tried three times to shoot Faulkner; the gun misfired twice and before he could pull the trigger a third time Faulkner had killed him with a knife. The town took sides while Faulkner awaited trial; while he was in jail his wife died in giving birth to John Wesley Thompson Falkner (from whom the novelist is descended). Thomas Hindman, the dead man's brother, spoke for the prosecution at the trial, where Faulkner was acquitted, the jury agreeing that he had acted in self-defence. Immediately on his release, Thomas Hindman attacked him, there was a brawl, and Faulkner shot and killed a man named Morris, who had taken Hindman's side. He was acquitted again, and again on his release encountered Thomas Hindman, who drew his gun, but dropped it. The sympathies of the town had turned against Faulkner, and he left for a while, but when he came back the thing started up again. A duel was proposed but prevented, and finally Hindman left for Arkansas.

While all this was going on, William C. Faulkner again met the girl who had befriended him years before, and did marry her. When the Civil War began he raised the Second Mississippi Cavalry and led it at Harper's Ferry and the first Battle of Manassas. His regiment, however, voted to demote him, and placed another man in the colonelcy; whereupon Faulkner returned to Mississippi and organised the First Mississippi Partisan Rangers (later the Seventh Mississippi Cavalry).

After the war he wrote several books, including one best-seller. According to some accounts it was he who dropped the 'u' from 'Faulkner' to avoid any confusion with some local riff-raff of the same name—and it stayed dropped until it crept back in as a printer's error in his great-grandson's first book, and was left there. In politics, he was in on the organisation of the American Party in his state. He and a partner, Richard J. Thurmond, built a railroad from Pontotoc to Middleton, Tennessee. But the partners fell out, it is said, because of 'The Colonel's' grandiose schemes for the extension of the railroad, and the Colonel bought Thurmond out, at Thurmond's own high price. Later he and Thurmond ran against each other for the legislature and he won. The day the election results were made public Thurmond shot the Colonel, who died the next day. Readers of Faulkner will recognise in these particulars the essential scheme of the character of Col. John Sartoris, as he appears in *The Unvanquished* and is mentioned in a number of the other novels and stories.

His son, John Wesley Thompson Falkner, seems to be the basis for the character of the Banker Sartoris of Faulkner's Jefferson, Mississippi. He was known as 'The Young Colonel'—an 'hereditary' distinction. He seems also to have inherited his father's more-than-Southern flair for heroics, but on a smaller scale. He married Sally Murray of Ripley, and they had three children; his son, Murray C. Falkner, was the father of the novelist. Another round of guns and vengeance was responsible for the Falkners moving to Oxford, Mississippi, the model for Faulkner's Jefferson. Murray Falkner had married Miss Maud Butler, of Oxford, and they were living in New Albany, where William Faulkner, the novelist, was born. It is related that a druggist in New Albany had said something to the disparagement of Murray's sister; Murray, confronting the druggist and threatening to thrash him, was shot in the mouth with a pistol, and then, when he fell, shot again in the back with a shotgun.

His father, the Young Colonel, rushed to New Albany when he heard of this, went for the druggist with a horse pistol; but it misfired six times in succession, and meantime the druggist managed to shoot the Young Colonel. Nevertheless, neither he nor his son were hurt very badly. But Maud Butler Falkner, Murray's wife, decided that there had been enough shooting, and that the only way to avoid further outbreaks was to move; and the family moved—to Oxford. The Young Colonel, Faulkner's grandfather, practised as a lawyer, as his father, the Old Colonel, had; was an assistant U.S. Attorney and president of an Oxford bank; he was also active in state politics. Murray C. Falkner (his son and William Faulkner's father) served as a railroad conductor on the line the Old Colonel had built and also as an auditor and depot agent, and later as business manager for the University of Mississippi.

William Faulkner was born on September 25th, 1897, in New Albany. According to local and family testimony he was a fairly good student, active and mischievous apart from his schooling. It is said that he talked his younger brothers and a girl cousin into all sticking their tongues at once to an iron bar one winter. And—with other pranks to illustrate it—that he had more than the normal share of curiosity, and that his propensity for making up stories was so fully developed, so early, that even the other children often didn't know when it was fact he was telling them about and when it was fiction. A bit older, in high school, he seems to have been somewhat more difficult to handle; moody and headstrong, his application to his studies tended to be vague and sporadic; he got his nose broken playing football; in the tenth grade he left school and was given a job in his grandfather's bank. From a very early age he had wanted to be a writer, and for some years he had been writing verse. He read what books were about, and continued to write poems, mainly under the influence of the poets of the Celtic twilight. In 1914, when he was seventeen, he began a friendship with Philip Stone, four years older than himself and a graduate of Yale. Mr. Stone's vocation was the law, but literature was his passion, and he acted as a kind of mentor to Faulkner, criticising his writings and lending him books—the poets of the English tradition, the great novelists, and a number of the modern writers.

In 1918, when the United States had entered the war, Faulkner tried to get into the Army but was turned down for being underweight. Philip Stone was back at Yale; Faulkner went to New Haven, worked at an arms factory there, and attempted to equip himself with British mannerisms and a British accent with which to brave the recruiting officers of the R.C.A.F., which he planned to try next. They accepted him—without troubling about his nationality. He underwent flight training, was commissioned honorary second lieutenant on the very day of demobilisation—December 22nd, 1918; he resigned his commission the next day, and before long was back in Oxford. There he entered on a period of inner bewilderment which took the outward form of a series of poses: a dandy with monocle, neat Empire beard, cane and gloves; a bohemian, barefoot, in dirty clothes, with appropriate beard. He wrote much verse, and in time started writing stories too, to make money. They were typed by Philip Stone's secretary, but were invariably rejected by all the editors they were sent to. In 1919 he enrolled at the University of Mississippi as a special student, did poorly in English, well in Spanish and French, and withdrew a year later. That year (1920) he went to New York and stayed with Stark Young for a time, who—through Elizabeth Prall—got him a job in the book department of Lord and Taylors, from which he was fired before long. He went back to Oxford, did odd jobs around the university campus, including a disastrous (for the Post Office) spell as postmaster of the university, from which job he eventually resigned, under pressure, stating in his letter of resignation that he did so because he was damned if he proposed 'to be at the beck and call of every itinerant scoundrel who has two cents to invest in a postage stamp.' About the same time his first book, *The Marble Faun*, a collection of poems, was published at Philip Stone's expense, but it attracted no notice nor sale to speak of.

But he had saved some money, and decided to work his way to Europe on a ship from New Orleans. In 1924, in New

Orleans, he failed to find the boat but he did find Elizabeth Prall, who had got him the Lord and Taylors job in New York; in the interim she had married Sherwood Anderson, whom Faulkner now came to know. Faulkner saw a lot of Anderson during his six months or so in New Orleans; and apart from encouraging Faulkner to write, Anderson was instrumental in getting *Soldiers' Pay*, Faulkner's first novel, written in New Orleans, published. Faulkner, meantime, was living in the French Quarter—the literary and artistic bohemia—of the city; there he also wrote pieces for the *Double Dealer* and the *Times Picayune*, and collaborated on a book called *Sherwood Anderson and Other Famous Creoles*. *Soldiers' Pay* concerns the return of a young American, wounded as a pilot in the R.A.F., to his home in Georgia—he had been presumed dead—and the effect of his return and subsequent death from head injuries sustained in the war, on the lives of those connected with him: his father, his former girl-friend, and another former soldier and a war widow who had taken up with him on his return journey. The narrative style is elegant, if sometimes a bit stilted; and the dominant tenor of the book is a modish 'lost generation' sadness at a world in which defeat is inevitable. When the book appeared, in March 1926, it was well reviewed but sold poorly.

In the summer of 1925 Faulkner had taken a boat for Genoa. He travelled in Italy, France, and a bit in Germany, spent some time in Paris, and was back in New York about the time that *Soldiers' Pay* appeared. Then he went back to Mississippi to finish another novel, *Mosquitoes*. This book, apparently under the influence of Aldous Huxley, takes for its subject the New Orleans sophisticates of the flapper era. When it was published, in 1927, it too was well reviewed but sold less copies than *Soldiers' Pay*.

Sartoris, his next novel, was written with an eye to commercial success, but Horace Liveright, who had published the first two novels, rejected it; finally Harcourt Brace published it in 1929 but it sold less well than either of the first two. It tells the story of an aviator, Bayard Sartoris, who is haunted by the death of his brother, who had been killed flying in the war. He is driven to tempt death time after time and finally is killed in an airplane, leaving behind him a widow and child. In this novel some of the characters of the later Jefferson saga make their first appearance—the Snopeses, Peabody, Banker Sartoris. It was in writing *Sartoris* that Faulkner first began to find himself, and discover a direction for his writing.

Faulkner now settled down to writing a book that would be good in his own eyes, whether or not it pleased critics or public. His first three books had been written at speed, but he spent three years on *The Sound and the Fury* and 'wrote his guts into it.' It appeared in 1929, published by Jonathan Cape and Harrison Smith. It is surely one of his most important books: its publication marked the advent of a new major talent on the American scene. The book is in four sections, which tell their story in a kind of progression towards objectivity: the first part (covering events on April 7th, 1928, in the Compson household in Jefferson) is told through the person of an idiot— the extreme of subjectivity, fragmentary, discontinuous, timeless, a permanent present of sensation. The second part (June 2nd, 1910) is told through the person of Quentin Compson, the young son of the family, at Harvard—a young man with a blinding morbid obsession which turns on his sister's honour; the immediate events it describes are those which lead to his own suicide. In the third part—covering the events of April 6th, 1928, in the Compson house—the story speaks through the person of Jason Compson, a selfish, degenerate, embittered man, the acting head of the family at that date. The last part is told in objective narrative, and describes the Compson household on April 8th, 1928, focusing on the person of Dilsey, the Negro cook. The bones of the story: Caddy Compson, sister of the Quentin who killed himself at Harvard out of an obscure tangled incestuous feeling for her, had a daughter who was named Quentin after her uncle; the girl grew up in Jason's keeping; he kept for himself the money her mother sent for her, until the girl stole the money from him and ran off with a man from a visiting carnival. The story is about innocence, real, feigned, perverted, rationalised, kept and lost; and about those graces in the human character which endure, and what they endure in spite of—here Faulkner strikes one of his permanent themes. The characters are delineated with mastery, are complex, terribly real, and even at their vilest compel the reader's compassion. Critical acclaim, when the book appeared, was not overwhelming, but there was a pamphlet by Evelyn Scott, *On William Faulkner: The Sound and the Fury*, which attempted to draw attention to his achievement. Still, the book sold less well than *Soldiers' Pay*.

The same year that *The Sound and the Fury* was published, Faulkner married Estelle Oldham; she was two years his elder, with two children by a former marriage, and both families disapproved of the match because of Faulkner's shaky means of subsistence, but he had been in love with her for some time, he did manage to make a living at odd jobs, his books were getting published—and they were married; the ceremony was performed in the College Hill Presbyterian Church, and Faulkner, with his wife and two children, set up house in a little apartment. He took a job tending a furnace in a power plant, working nights, and there between midnight and 4 a.m., with the hum of the dynamo in his ears, writing on an upturned wheelbarrow, he wrote *As I Lay Dying*—'in six weeks, without changing a word.' It is probably the most perfect book he has written (it is the one that he himself likes best)—a kind of grotesque epic, again presenting, in all its contradictions, that undefinable thing that makes men endure, the source of human affirmation which survives the warped actions, the degradations, blunderings, wickedness and mistakes of the human creature. *As I Lay Dying* is about love and selfishness, about human responsibility, which must accept the pain and cruelty and senselessness of circumstances, and which may find love through giving up self and becoming involved in the madness of human action and commitment; and it is about the blind nightmare in which man pathetically persists in painful efforts which are futile except as a kind of series of mirrors which reveal in his garbled actions the enduring if elusive lineaments of his dignity. The story is told in a series of short chapters, each narrated in the person of one of the characters. It tells of the death of Addie Bundren, a former school teacher who had married Anse, a 'red-neck,' a back-country farmer, and given birth to five children, four of them his. She demands that she be buried in Jefferson, and the main part of the story concerns the crazy odyssey of the family, with the coffin containing Addie's body in their wagon, to Jefferson to bury her. To get there they have to cross a flooded river; the bridges are impassable, and they cross at a ford, where the wagon overturns in the current, the coffin falls out and is rescued only with great danger and difficulty, one son has his leg broken and rides the rest of the way in agony, lying on the coffin; a barn in which the coffin is placed for the night—for reasons which by then have become obvious—is set afire by another of the sons, and the coffin is rescued from the flames by still another son, at great risk; all the family pay dearly in fulfilling their promise to bury Addie in Jefferson. And there Anse, taking back the borrowed shovel, after the grave has been made and the body buried, reappears, confronting the waiting family with a new Mrs. Bundren. The characterisation is brilliant, and the mad story is told with compassion, macabre comedy and an unfailing fantasy, in writing of great precision, richness and vigour. Nevertheless, like *The Sound and the Fury*, the book attracted some critical notice, but sold poorly when it was published in the fall of 1930.

According to Faulkner himself, *Sanctuary*, his next book, was written in complete artistic cynicism. (Actually it was written before *As I Lay Dying*, and while *Sartoris* and *The Sound and the Fury* were still unpublished and did not seem likely to be published.) He has said that it had just occurred to him that you could make money from writing, and he thought it would be nice to make some that way. So he speculated as to what would sell, decided, dreamed up 'the most horrific tale I could imagine and wrote it in about three weeks.' The result was *Sanctuary*; he sent it off to Harrison Smith, his publisher, who wrote back that he couldn't publish it—it would land them both in jail. Whereupon, Faulkner says, he himself forgot about it until sometime later when the galley proofs arrived. He was ashamed of the writing, he says, and rewrote the book extensively, but has never liked it much. It was published in 1930 and was an immediate sensation. Critics attacked it, and accused him of being a high priest of a cult of cruelty; they were for the most part hysterically and so quite unfairly harsh, failing entirely even to see what Faulkner was trying to do. *Sanctuary* is about a sensation-seeking girl from Mississippi who is left unprotected by her drunken boy-friend while on a spree; she is raped with a corncob by Popeye, a syphilitic impotent pervert—Faulkner's attempt to create a personification of depravity. She is kept in a brothel and likes it; and a man is killed trying to come to see her there. The book is about these events and their consequences. Its theme is the corruption of values in contemporary society, and it is done not as a two-dimensioned social study, but as a full-blown nightmare, presenting action and scene as projections of the human psyche in the modern world. The writing is sharp and powerful and makes calculated use of complex patterns of imagery; some scenes and passages in *Sanctuary* are among the finest that Faulkner has written. Yet people who came to read *Sanctuary* before reading any other books of Faulkner's are still often 'put off' by it, as the critics originally were. This is probably not only because of the cruelty and depravity of most of the characters and events in the book, but also because these elements are not clearly justified by any obvious allegory, and so seem egregious; and also because *Sanctuary* is a patently serious work in which the action must be taken as morally significant in all its implications, and cannot be simply shrugged off, ignored or laughed at, as it can be in, say, a detective novel, where the violence exists merely as a spring for the plot, and where neither the characters nor the events have the disturbing, recognisable reality of much of *Sanctuary*. In any case, when it was published the critics could not fail to indicate that it was sensational, full of sex and violence, and the book sold and was widely read. Suddenly everybody wanted to use Faulkner's talents. Hollywood bought the novel and made a film of it, and Faulkner embarked on his career as film writer. And as for the magazines, the old rejected stories in Philip Stone's filing cabinet were resurrected and sent off, with prices clearly marked on them. Faulkner was making money.

In the same year (1931) Faulkner published a volume of short stories, *These Thirteen*. Some of these, presumably written during the years when he was at work on *Soldiers' Pay* and *Sartoris*, are woven around a 'lost generation' despair. But there are also stories like 'That Evening Sun' and 'A Rose For Emily,' which are still among the best stories he has done. And in this same volume 'A Justice' and 'Red Leaves' first develop Faulkner's use of the wilderness theme—the world before the white men came, or at least the world they have not yet entirely overrun—which is continued in some of his later work, most notably in ' The Bear.' 'Mistral,' 'Carcassone' and 'Divorce in Naples' presumably were drawn from his sojourn in Europe.

Light in August appeared in October 1932, and the critics took its publication as an occasion for further expatiating their dislike of what Faulkner seemed to them to be doing—by now he was too well known, and was taken too seriously in some circles, for them to be able to simply ignore him. His 'nightmares' were a 'flight from reality'; his creations, one of them claimed, were merely visceral and had nothing to do with 'passionate ratiocination.' *Light in August* is a savage criticism of Southern Calvinist Protestantism. Stiffness of doctrine and vindictive bitterness of spirit, the whole self-justifying, institutionalised paraphernalia which enlists divine retribution on its own side, are seen as kin to and abettors of the most brutal, corrupt and destructive of human passions. The story concerns the chase and lynching of a part-Negro, Joe Christmas. It tells of Joe's life before he performed the action (the killing of Euphues Hines, in self-defence) which called down on his head the retributive wrath of the community. And of Euphues Hines, who manages to persuade herself that whatever act of warped selfishness or embittered cruelty she wishes to perform is God's will, whose instrument she is; she tries to force Joe to kneel to her in prayer, and when he refuses she threatens to shoot him with a horse pistol, and Joe kills her. The other principal character is Hightower, the scion of a family rather like the Sartorises or the Compsons, the preacher whose congregation had forcibly removed him from his church because of the scandalous behaviour of his wife. Hightower is a weak man with a core of strength; capable, *in extremis*, of taking a strong man's decisions, but not of dominating a situation; he is one of the few who takes Joe Christmas's part, and risks his own life and what remains of his reputation to save Joe from the mob. In spite of the bitterness of the book's critique, the situation and action are presented in the round, and Faulkner shows how deeply the evil is embedded in the world of the South, even in much that is good in that world. He is, in fact, attacking virtues which have been corrupted, or cursed with an old guilt, until they have become worse than any vice.

In 1934 Faulkner published *A Green Bough*, his second volume of poems, and *Dr. Martino*, his second book of short stories. The poems are of interest chiefly because they were written by Faulkner. *Dr. Martino* is certainly not as impressive a volume as *These Thirteen*, but there are some fine stories, several of them forecasting some of his later work. 'A Mountain Victory,' for example, is a further exploitation of the Indian material; 'Wash' is a foretaste of *Absalom, Absalom!*; 'Smoke' was later included in *Knight's Gambit*, and 'Honor' looks forward to *Pylon*, the next novel which Faulkner published.

Pylon (1935) is the story of a strange trio of people in a flying circus. Laverne, the girl parachute-jumper, is a kind of symbol of sexual passion; she has run away from a bleak, dreary life and has taken up with Shumann; Shumann himself has become addicted to the homeless hazardous life of a flying circus, at the expense of the medical career he is supposed to be studying for. Laverne also falls in love with Jack, another member of the circus, and takes to sleeping with both men. When it is learned that she is pregnant, the men roll dice to see who will marry her; Shumann wins, and marries her, but the old arrangement continues until Shumann is killed, flying too close to a pylon in order to make money for her second confinement. The story is seen in terms of the trio's relation to a reporter, an epitome of contemporary literary disenchantment, ineffectual, critical of the modern world but incapable of coming to grips with it—a man who has his experience vicariously if at all.

Absalom, Absalom!, published in 1936, returns to the setting and characters of Jefferson. It is one of the novels most central to Faulkner's treatment of the South; in it he attempts to get to the bottom of the compulsion of self-destructive violence which haunts so many of his characters. In so far as *Sanctuary* sets the corruption of the present against the virtues of the past, *Absalom, Absalom!* could be called an 'anti-*Sanctuary*,' for while it continues to make a glamorous legend of the past, it shows in the past the same urges that dog the present, and the same damnation; in fact the past is evoked mainly to show the seeds of the curse that chokes the present. The story is told through the mouth of the Quentin Compson whose suicide preparations are described in the second part of *The Sound and the Fury*. Quentin, at Harvard, tells his room-mate the story—in itself a parable about an enigmatic compulsion, which Quentin feels is an epitome of the South—in an attempt to come to some understanding of himself and of whatever it is that is driving him towards suicide. The story's chief protagonist is Thomas Sutpen, who appeared in Jefferson during the first half of the nineteenth century, out of nowhere, with a small private army of slaves and a French architect, bought a vast piece of land from the local Indian chief, built a house, made a plantation, married, had a son, Henry, and a daughter, Judith. The son, in New Orleans, meets and is drawn to his part-Negro half-brother Charles; Henry ultimately kills Charles to prevent his marrying Judith. Sutpen's plantation is ruined by the war; Henry disappears, an outlaw, and Sutpen tries to sire another son on the daughter of one of his retainers, Wash Jones. But the girl bears him a daughter instead, Sutpen insults her, and Wash Jones kills him with a scythe. Years later, when Henry has returned in secret to die in the house, it burns, with him inside it. *Absalom, Absalom!* is a statement of Faulkner's belief that the institution of slavery left the South under a curse, which must be expiated with much suffering.

Faulkner's next book was *The Unvanquished* (1938). This novel, told as a series of stories, also describes the South during the Civil War period, this time in a straight-narrative medium. It shows young Bayard Sartoris growing up during the Civil

War and, at the end of the war, renouncing many of the old values—symbolised by the vendetta—which he has come to feel are false, melodramatic and destructive.

In 1939 Faulkner published *The Wild Palms*. This book is really two short novels, or long stories, told in alternating chapters. They are alike in theme, but there is no other connection between them; Faulkner has said that he alternated the chapters in this way because neither, by itself, was long enough to make a book. (They were later published separately, however.) They are both about love; one tells of a young wife with two children who forsakes her pleasant but passionless home to run off with an intern whom she meets. After some time together, under harsh conditions, she is found to be pregnant; she urges him to perform an abortion, pleading the penury of their situation, and when he does so she dies of it. The story ends with him in prison, preferring life with only a past to no life at all: 'between grief and nothing I will take grief.' The other story, 'The Old Man,' tells of a convict who rescues a woman during a flood, conducts himself heroically, and gives himself up again at the end.

Faulkner's next novel, *The Hamlet*, deals with the country people of Frenchman's Bend, near Jefferson. It continues with his earlier characterisations of the Snopes family, the unscrupulous white trash, whom he shows among other rural characters. Faulkner makes excellent use of folk material in this book, including the tall story, and the book, while remaining a serious work, is shot through with a raw-boned grotesque comedy. In 1942 he published *Go Down Moses*, a collection of short stories which includes 'The Bear' and 'Delta Autumn,' stories in which the forces of untamed Nature take on a haunting symbolism.

Neither *Intruder in the Dust* (1948) nor *Knight's Gambit* (1949) nor *Requiem for a Nun* (1951) ranks among Faulkner's more important works. *Intruder in the Dust* re-handles much of the same material that he had used in *Light in August*, but with less subtlety and without the urgent reality of the former book. *Knight's Gambit* is a series of detective stories which fall between two stools: they are neither serious Faulkner on the one hand nor plain detective stories with no ulterior purpose on the other. *Requiem for a Nun* continues the story of Temple Drake, some eight years after the events of *Sanctuary*. An irresponsible adulterous decision of Temple's drives Nancy, the coloured girl (a reformed prostitute) whom she has taken in to be her companion and her baby's nurse, to kill the baby. Before her execution, Nancy converts Temple to her own creed: simple belief for its own sake, and the acceptance of suffering. But neither the story, nor the characterisation, nor the interludes describing the history of the jail and court-house, are up to Faulkner's best work. His latest book, *A Fable*, transposes the story of the Crucifixion into a modern situation—the action centres around the first world war. This book is in some ways Faulkner's most ambitious work to date; he spent nine years working on it. Yet he does not seem at home in the mode of allegory which this book attempts, and the work succeeds in fragments rather than as a whole.

With the first considerable money which Faulkner made from his writing, after the publication of *Sanctuary*, he bought a handsome, columned *ante-bellum* house on the edge of Oxford, where he has lived ever since. Some miles away, in the hills, he owns a farm, on which he does a certain amount of the work himself—enough so that he can refer to himself, as he likes to, as 'just a farmer who happens to write sometimes.' And since his first spell in Hollywood, soon after *Sanctuary*, he has returned there from time to time to work on scripts, but he has always rushed back to Oxford at the first opportunity. In Mississippi his chief diversion from family life and work on his farm consists of hunting trips with a few cronies; there is a great deal of yarn-swapping on these expeditions and a lot of whisky is consumed. In general, Faulkner does not take kindly to intrusions upon this way of life: he has had the drive in front of his house ploughed up to discourage reporters and other curiosity-seekers, though there are exceptions to this dislike of visiting strangers. He professes a deep distaste for literary people in general. Perhaps part of it has its roots in the virulence with which most of the critics greeted his work during the first ten or twelve years after he began to be published. In the forties the tide turned; some of the most gifted and influential of the young writers and critics wrote of Faulkner with admiration and perceptiveness, and their work was followed by a growing number of studies which took as a foregone conclusion the premise that Faulkner ranks among the most important writers of the age. But in the years that followed *Sanctuary*, Faulkner had stopped reading the critics at all.

In 1949 he was awarded the Nobel Prize for Literature. His natural shyness, his dislike of public occasions and of being away from home, and probably (another remnant of the years of critical acerbity) a wish to assert his contempt for public approval, made it doubtful, for a while, whether or not he would go to Sweden to accept the award. Finally he agreed to go 'so that his daughter Jill might have a chance to see Paris.'

Faulkner himself feels that he has failed in what he set out to do—to create an indigenous American mode of expression. Yet he is without question one of the major writers of our period, and his whole work, even the failures, contributes to the achievement. More particularly, his reputation is based most firmly on *As I Lay Dying*, *The Sound and the Fury*, *The Hamlet*, *The Wild Palms*, *Sanctuary*, *Light in August*, *Absalom, Absalom!*, and many of the short stories. He is not ultimately a pessimist; his basic perception of human nature goes beyond pessimism to tragedy. For he has faced out the evil of the times, the corruption of the world man has made, the cruelty of man's fate, and through all these he has been able to glimpse and affirm man's rare but indissoluble virtues. It is not only his speech on his acceptance of the Nobel Prize, but his whole work, which celebrates man's capacity for love and compassion and courage, and declares that these things will endure, and that man will endure because of them. His works will endure too, and for the same reasons.

★　　★　　★

The following is a partial list of works on Faulkner, his writing, and his family. I have been indebted to some of them, especially the first two, in the writing of this essay.

WILLIAM VAN O'CONNOR— *The Tangled Fire of William Faulkner* (University of Minnesota Press. 1954).

ROBERT COUGHLAN—*The Private World of William Faulkner* (Harper & Bros. 1953).

IRVING HOWE—*William Faulkner, A Critical Study* (Random House. 1952).

MALCOLM COWLEY—Essay in *The Viking Portable Faulkner* (Viking Press. 1946).

H. M. CAMPBELL and R. E. FOSTER—*William Faulkner* (University of Oklahoma Press. 1951).

LAVON RASCOE—'An Interview With William Faulkner' (*Western Review*. Summer, 1951).

ROBERT CANTWELL—*The Faulkners: Recollections of a Gifted Family* (New World Writing. 1952).

WARD L. MINER—*The World of William Faulkner* (Duke University Press. 1952).

A publication entitled *Faulkner Studies*, a survey of Faulkner scholarship and criticism, has been published periodically since Spring, 1952.

André Gide

by MARTIN TURNELL

George Martin Turnell was educated at Uppingham and Corpus
Christi College, Cambridge. He completed his studies at the University of Paris. Having worked in the editorial department of a
firm of London publishers, he also edited a quarterly called *Arena*.
He served in the Intelligence Corps during World War II and is
now on the staff of the B.B.C.

He has gained a very special place among critics for his approach
to French literature and also as a translator. He prepared the
English version of Sartre's book on Baudelaire, to which he contributed an introduction. He is the author of *Poetry and Crisis, The
Classical Moment, The Novel in France*, etc.

I

ALTHOUGH André Gide is generally recognised in
England as an important writer, it cannot be said that
his work has ever aroused any great enthusiasm in this
country. There was something slightly bewildering to the
English about the immense influence that he once enjoyed
abroad, and about the violent controversies that he unleashed
in France. The intellectuals used to pay lip-service to him in
public as 'the greatest living French writer'; in private many
of them were happy to concur with the common reader who
found him 'unreadable.' This lack of enthusiasm seems to be
due partly to the content of his books, and partly to a fundamental difference between the English and the French approach
to literature.

The English read and enjoy their great writers, but in their
hearts they remain convinced that literature, however great,
can never be more than superior pastime, and that poets, like
soldiers and politicians, need to be kept in their proper place.
They steadfastly refuse to regard the writer as a prophet and
his books as a private bible. If D. H. Lawrence is not yet
accepted as one of the greatest English writers, it is largely on
account of the didactic element in his work and the knowledge
that he considered himself a man with a 'message.'

In France the position is far otherwise. The French are never tired of proclaiming that they are a nation of moralists. French critics seldom quarrel with a writer for having a message; the trouble begins when he is found to be propagating the wrong kind of message. If Lawrence has had far less attention in France than many other contemporary Anglo-Saxon writers of lesser stature it is not because he has a message; it is because his message smacks too much of the nonconformist conscience to be swallowed by a reading public composed mainly of ex-Catholics.

The French use the term 'moralist' in a wider sense than the English. In the French sense Gide was certainly a moralist. He liked to think of himself as a sage in the manner of Goethe, and he certainly had a message. The message was a plea for the emancipation of the individual and for an attitude of non-commitment, which M. Robert Mallet has recently described as 'ambiguity.' There was not, perhaps, anything particularly original about it, but it went to the heads of French youth after the first world war. What I want to suggest here is that we have heard too much about the moralist, that the *Journal*, which is frankly a dull book, has been greatly overrated, and that Gide's reputation will ultimately rest on some of his shorter works of fiction and on his autobiography.

2

André Paul Guillaume Gide was born in Paris on November 22nd, 1869. His father, Paul Gide, was a lecturer in law at the University of Paris, and three years after the birth of his son was appointed to the Chair of Roman Law. He was known to his colleagues as *vir probus* and came of an old Protestant family from Uzès, a town on the borders of Provence and the Midi, which had been a Protestant stronghold since the Reformation.

While spending a holiday in Normandy Paul Gide met Juliette Rondeaux. She had the reputation of being a spoilt young woman who had refused a number of eligible suitors. She fell in love with Paul Gide and they were married in February 1863, when he was thirty-one and she was twenty-eight, but they had to wait six years for the birth of their only child.

The Rondeaux were a prosperous Norman family who traced their ancestry back to the seventeenth century. They were Protestants like the Gides, but their Protestantism had a much shorter history. They had been devout Catholics down to the nineteenth century, but Gide's grandfather, Édouard Rondeaux, who was the son of a Catholic father and a Protestant mother, became a free-thinker and married a Protestant. He began by stipulating that his children should be brought up as Catholics, but changed his mind when the Church did something he disliked and allowed them to be brought up as Protestants, though one of his sons was converted to Catholicism.

It would be difficult to overestimate the importance of the part played by religion in Gide's life and work. Writing of the evolution of his thought, he observed in an entry in his diary for 1931:

> 'Without my early Christian formation (or deformation) there would, perhaps, have been no evolution at all. What made it so slow and so difficult was an emotional attachment to something from which I was unable to free myself without regret. Even today I feel a sort of nostalgia for the mystical and burning atmosphere which produced such a state of exaltation in me at the time. I have never recovered the fervour of my adolescence; and the sensual ardours in which I later indulged were nothing but a ridiculous travesty of it.'

His Protestant upbringing left an indelible mark on him, and his rebellion against it is the key to the real drama of his life.

Paul Gide died of intestinal tuberculosis in 1880 when his son was eleven years old. The child was brought up by his mother and Anna Shackleton, his mother's former governess and the orphaned daughter of a Scottish engineer who had settled in France and helped to build the Paris–Havre railway.

Gide has said in his autobiography that as a child he had no friends. We are inclined to think of him as a lonely, delicate boy surrounded by virtuous and slightly forbidding women like his mother and his aunts, but this is not the whole truth. With so many relatives there was no lack of places that he could visit during the holidays, and he was not entirely deprived of

companions of his own age. At Easter he went to his paternal
grandmother at Uzès. In the summer he went to La Roque-
Baignard, a property in Normandy which his mother had
inherited from her father and which he used as the setting for
Isabelle and parts of *L'Immoraliste*. He spent the New Year
holidays at Rouen with his Catholic Uncle Henri. Henri's
children were too old to be his playmates, but he used to play
with the three daughters of his Protestant Uncle Émile—
Valentine, Jeanne and Madeleine—who also lived at Rouen.
There were visits to Cuverville-en-Caux, where Émile owned
a country house. On his death the house went to Madeleine.
It was to be Gide's home, or rather his base, for many years,
and was the setting of *La Porte étroite*.

Rouen was the scene of an emotional shock which was to
have lasting consequences for Gide. He had begun by preferring
his cousin Jeanne, whose rowdy ways were more in keeping
with his own than those of his other cousins. One evening,
when he was thirteen, he had gone back to the home of his
Uncle Henri, with whom he was staying. His uncle was out.
He returned unexpectedly to his Uncle Émile's to find his
cousin Madeleine weeping bitterly because she had just learnt
of her mother's infidelity, which was to break up the home.
Gide speaks in his autobiography of discovering 'the mystic
orientation of my life.' It was the beginning of a deeply
emotional relationship with his cousin which led to their
marriage. They were inseparable during the holidays, shared
the same interests, read the same books, and when Gide came
across a passage which he thought would interest her he wrote
her initials in the margin.

Madeleine was extremely devout. Gide admitted many
years later that her influence was responsible for awakening
his own adolescent fervour. He became an assiduous student
of the Bible, slept on bare boards, rose to pray in the night, and
washed in cold water in the dead of winter as a mortification.

Gide's schooldays were not among the most brilliant periods
of his life, and he himself expressed surprise that anything
should have emerged from such a 'broken' education. He was
sent at the age of eight to the École Alsacienne, but soon had

to be removed for a term because he had contracted what are known as 'bad habits.' When his father died he spent a year at Rouen, where he shared his cousins' tutor. The next year his mother took him to live at Montpellier, where his uncle, Charles Gide, the distinguished economist, was a professor at the university. He went to the local *lycée* and became aware of the importance of the differences between Catholicism and Protestantism. He was mercilessly bullied because of his Protestantism, and also because his school-fellows felt that he was something of a poseur. He was saved by an attack of chicken-pox, but when he recovered he pretended to be suffering from a nervous illness to avoid being sent back to the *lycée*.

What had begun as a trick seems to have developed into a genuine nervous disorder which seriously interrupted his education during the next five years, and continued to worry him even when he had grown up. He went back to the École Alsacienne in 1887 and became a friend of Pierre Louÿs. The École Alsacienne was considered a good school for the humanities but not for philosophy, and the following year Gide transferred to the Lycée Henri IV. He only stayed three months and then persuaded his mother to allow him to work privately for the *baccalauréat*. He failed in the summer of 1889, but managed to scrape through in October. He thought of studying philosophy at the Sorbonne, but though his name was entered he never worked seriously and did not take a degree.

He had displayed an aptitude for music when he was fourteen, worked under Lanux and other masters, and thought at one time of making music his career. Although he continued to take an interest in music for the rest of his life and played the piano, he had abandoned the idea of making it his career by the time he left school and had decided to become a writer. He found that he was unable to work in Paris, and retired first to the village of Pierrefonds, near the Forest of Compiègne, then to Lake Annecy. In the summer of 1890 he was back in Paris with his first book almost completed. *Les Cahiers d'André Walter* was published anonymously at the author's expense in February 1891. As a publishing venture it was a failure. Gide intended it to appear simultaneously in a de luxe and an ordinary edition, but the ordinary edition contained so many misprints that he was glad to sell it back to the printers for pulping for the value of the paper. A sequel called *Les Poésies d'André Walter*, which was described as a 'posthumous work,' was also published anonymously at his own expense the following year.

Les Cahiers d'André Walter is a work of little intrinsic merit, but it throws considerable light on Gide's emotional development. André Walter is in love with his cousin Emmanuèle—the name Gide used for Madeleine in the autobiography and the diaries—but the match is opposed by his mother. When she is on her death-bed she makes André promise not to marry his cousin. He gives her up and she marries his 'rival,' Allain. In order to forget her he writes the *Cahiers*. Emmanuèle dies; André and Allain contract brain fever and die too.

In his account of the relations between André Walter and Emmanuèle, Gide describes for the first time his conception of love as something spiritualised and disembodied. This attitude was a symptom of the homosexual leanings of which he was at that time unconscious. We must not overlook the importance of the rôle played by Gide's mother either in the book or in his life. He tells us somewhere that his feeling for her was one of 'respectful hatred.' The expression is a strong one, but there is plenty of evidence in his work of a pronounced antipathy towards her. It is a fair inference that his antipathy prevented the homosexual's usual fixation on his mother, and that he transferred the feeling to his cousin, transforming her not merely into a mother-figure, but into what Proust was later to call a *mère profanée*. The transference was helped by the revulsion against physical love which Madeleine experienced as a result of her mother's adultery. It was not in the circumstances in any way an abnormal or unexpected attitude, but it should simply have been a passing phase. Unfortunately, it lent plausibility to Gide's own misconceptions about the nature of love between the sexes and provided him, as we shall see, with an excuse for perpetuating the dilemma.

Gide's aim in writing the *Cahiers* had not been purely or

even primarily literary. He had written it in the hope of persuading his cousin to marry him. In this, too, the book was a failure. He proposed and was refused.

Although his first book brought him neither fame nor the hand of his cousin, his labour was not altogether wasted. Pierre Louÿs introduced him to Mallarmé. The Master complimented him on the book; there were one or two flattering notices by the Master's disciples, and he began to attend the 'Tuesdays' in the Rue de Rome. He had met Paul Valéry at Montpellier at the end of 1890 and his conversations with the poet seem to have inspired his second book, *Traité du Narcisse*, which was published in the autumn of 1891. The influence of Symbolism, however, never went very deep. *Le Voyage d'Urien*, which appeared in 1893, is the first of his ironic works—the last word is a pun on the words 'du rien'—in which he pokes gentle fun at the Symbolist journeys to imaginary lands. In *Le Tentative amoureuse*, published the same year, he set out to prove the superiority of his own disembodied love over normal relations between the sexes.

In October 1893 Gide sailed for North Africa with his friend Paul Albert Laurens, the son of a painter who was studying painting. He felt from the outset that the voyage was to be of momentous importance for him, that it was the first break with the rigid Protestant milieu in which he had been brought up. He had been even by Protestant standards a particularly ardent student of the Bible, but for the first time he left his Bible behind, sensing that it was not through books that the anticipated experience would come.

The outward journey was a hazardous one. A year earlier Gide had been called up for military service, but had been invalided out of the Army almost at once owing to a suspected predisposition to tuberculosis. He fell ill at Susa and a doctor had to be called. He remained there for some days, and it was during his convalescence that he had his first homosexual experience with an Arab child.

The pair decided to spend the winter at Biskra. Whether they realised it or not, one of their main reasons for going to Africa was the search for sexual adventures. Laurens met an engaging Arab prostitute named Mériem. Gide, who had been disturbed by his exploit with the Arab child, clearly hoped that the incident had been a matter of chance and was not the result of an ingrained taste. He therefore agreed to share Mériem with his companion. The experiment was not a success. Thirty years later, he said in his autobiography that he was only able to react by imagining that the Arab boy had taken the place of the girl in his bed.

He was still a sick man. Laurens was badly frightened by a hæmorrhage, and reported it in a letter to his parents, who passed the news on to Gide's mother. Mme Gide hurried to Biskra to look after her son. She discovered Laurens's relations with Mériem, and was profoundly grieved to learn that her son's had been the same. His health gradually improved. Mme Gide returned to France; Gide and Laurens continued their journey, visiting Sicily, Rome, Florence and other Italian cities.

At Geneva he consulted a chest specialist. He was told, greatly to his relief, that there was nothing seriously wrong with his lungs, and that his trouble was nervous. After undergoing treatment he went back to Paris and wrote *Paludes*, a novel about a young man living on a marsh and writing a novel called *Paludes*. It is an entertaining work which treats for the first time the theme of liberation, and the method foreshadows the one which he was to use with much greater effect in the *Faux-monnayeurs*.

In 1894 Gide paid a second visit to Africa. This time he went alone. He found himself at the same hotel as Oscar Wilde and Lord Alfred Douglas. His first impulse was to seize his bags and make for the station, but he felt that it would have been cowardly and decided to stay. He had met Wilde on a number of occasions in Paris in 1891–2, and again at Florence the previous year. On this occasion they became accomplices in the pursuit of Arab boys. Their first exploit together confirmed Gide in his tastes and prompted him to write in his autobiography: 'I had found my own form of normality.'

He began to write the *Nourritures terrestres* at Biskra, but was obliged to interrupt his work in March 1895, when his mother, who was becoming alarmed by his independence, summoned him back to France. He spent some weeks with her and they appeared to get on better. He was hoping to go with her to La Roque in the summer, but in May while he was away staying with friends he received a telegram from her servant saying that she had had a stroke. He hurried home, but she was unable to recognise him and died a few days later.

Gide was distressed by his mother's sudden death, and his distress was probably accentuated by the knowledge that neither his feelings for her nor his conduct in Africa had been those of a model son. Her death had an immediate effect on his work. He was inclined to exaggerate the contradictions of his own nature, but for years each book he wrote appeared to be a refutation of the position adopted in its predecessor. He stopped work for the time being on the *Nourritures terrestres*, which was a reflection of the new freedom he had experienced in Africa, and began to write *Saül*, a play in which he describes the ruin of a soul who had given way not merely to temptation, but to the form of temptation to which he had himself succumbed in Africa.

Neither Gide's family nor the Rondeaux had been in favour of the marriage between the cousins, but the main opposition had come from Gide's mother. She had begun to soften during the last months of her life, and as soon as she was dead he renewed his suit. This time he was accepted. The civil ceremony took place at Cuverville on October 7th, 1895, and the religious ceremony the following day at the Protestant church at Étretat.

Gide has been criticised for marrying in spite of the fact that he knew he was a homosexual. It has been said in extenuation that he did not enter lightly into marriage, but consulted a Swiss doctor, who told him that all would be well once he was married. This has enabled friendly critics to put most of the blame on the doctor, whose diagnosis is dismissed as a crude error of the pre-psycho-analytic age. We may doubt whether Gide himself was really convinced. He obviously had an interest in obtaining the doctor's benediction, but the history of his marriage suggests that he never had any intention of carrying out the doctor's precepts, that he was rather in the position of a solicitor who takes counsel's opinion as a precaution against possible criticisms of his handling of his client's affairs.

After the civil ceremony, which was attended only by members of the families, the couple returned to the house at Cuverville. They spent the evening as usual taking it in turns to read aloud to one another, went for a short walk together, and repaired to their separate rooms. This was not, perhaps, extraordinary, as they were both members of the Protestant Church at the time and the religious ceremony had not taken place. The same scene, however, was repeated the following day on their return from Étretat. There was, in short, no wedding night; there never was to be a wedding night because the bridegroom did not want one, and had convinced himself that women did not have sexual desires.

Although there was no wedding night, there was a honeymoon which was stranger even than the night of the wedding. Shortly after their marriage Gide and his wife set out on a voyage which lasted six months. They spent the autumn in Switzerland, the winter in Italy and the spring in North Africa. It was Gide's first voyage as a young bachelor in reverse. Its real goal was the country which had been the scene of his sexual awakening and his emancipation from the kind of life represented by his marriage to his cousin. Madeleine Gide was the gentlest, the most discreet of wives. We shall never know precisely when she became aware of her husband's tastes, but what she is known to have seen and suffered on her honeymoon would have been more than sufficient to open the eyes of almost any girl born a generation later. Already in Rome Gide had developed a passion for photography. Madeleine found herself at a loose end for hours at a time and without even a room because the bridal chamber had been turned into a studio where Gide was taking photographs of youthful Italian models. In Africa the newly married husband found it impossible to keep his hands off small boys whom he met in the train, and his behaviour was so extraordinary that when they left the train his wife told him that he looked like a criminal or a madman.

On their return to France in 1896 Gide was elected Mayor La Roque-Baignard, and at twenty-six was the youngest mayor in France. All his life he maintained that his civic duties were a matter of real concern to him. In 1914 he took up the cudgels in favour of those whom he considered the victims of the French judicial system in a book called *Souvenirs de la Cour d'Assises*, which was based on his experience while doing jury service. In the two books that he published in 1927 after his tour of French Equatorial Africa, *Voyage au Congo* and *Retour du Tchad*, he attacked French colonial administration for its harsh treatment of the native population; and between the wars he was extremely active on behalf of political refugees from dictatorship countries. There is no reason to suspect his sympathy for the oppressed, but the form it took was evidently intended to counter criticism of less admirable activities or even to provide a cloak for them. That is the importance of his election as Mayor of La Roque-Baignard. It was a sign of public esteem, a sign that his fellow citizens regarded him as a serious young man. For the next twenty years, indeed, his life was outwardly respectable, happy, and by no means unsuccessful.

Les Nourritures terrestres was published in 1897. Although it was to carry French youth off its feet a quarter of a century later, only five hundred copies were sold in the first ten years. It was followed by several minor works, of which the most interesting was *Le Prométhée mal-enchaîné*, but it was not until the appearance of *L'Immoraliste* in 1902 that Gide produced his first major work. *La Porte étroite*, *L'Immoraliste* and *La Symphonie pastorale* are a trilogy dealing with the problems of the human couple in marriage. They describe the failed engagement, the disastrous marriage, and the dying down of love in middle age. Gide has spoken in his diary of the immense difficulties that he experienced in completing the trilogy. Although the three books were originally conceived about the same time, *La Porte étroite*—the first of his books to enjoy a popular success—did not appear until 1909, and the *Symphonie pastorale* did not appear until 1919.

A year before the publication of *La Porte étroite*, Gide had embarked on another important undertaking. With Jacques

Copeau, Gaston Gallimard, Jean Schlumberger and André Ruyters he founded the *Nouvelle Revue Française*. The first attempt to launch the magazine was not an unqualified success, but when it was reconstituted a year later it prospered and by the middle of the twenties was the most famous literary review in Europe. The success of the review led to the foundation of the celebrated publishing house of Gallimard. It would be difficult to overestimate the importance for contemporary literature of this double enterprise, for which Gide must be given a large share of the credit.

The events which were taking place off stage are a less happy story. Gide was and remained all his life *un être de fuite*. It is exact to describe Cuverville as a 'base.' It was the place from which he set out on a hundred journeys, and the place to which he always returned. It was also the scene of the most disastrous episodes of his married life. The African honeymoon was only the first of a number of unfortunate voyages which the couple undertook together. They went to Switzerland in 1897, to Italy in 1898, to Algeria again in 1899, and March 1900 found them at Oran. Madeleine Gide never cared for travel and was only happy when managing her estate at Cuverville. This provided her husband with a convenient excuse for travelling alone. In 1903 he went to Germany. Two years later he was once again in Algeria, but this time he felt the need for companionship and as soon as he arrived he telegraphed for his wife, who hastened to join him. In 1910 he was alone in Spain; in 1912 we find him in Italy with his friend Henri Ghéon, a doctor who was later to enjoy some celebrity as a dramatist and the author of saints' lives, while in the spring of 1914 the pair were in Turkey.

Gide's other memories of the year 1914 were less agreeable. He had first met Claudel in 1895, and a friendship had gradually developed between the two men, who both as writers and as personalities were poles apart. Claudel had certain reservations about Gide's books, but in the correspondence he speaks of them in flattering terms, possibly because he hoped to secure an important convert. Although in later years Gide came to think poorly of Claudel's poetry, he was enthusiastic about it at this time, insisted on his contributing to the *Nouvelle Revue Française*, and undoubtedly did a good deal to bring his work to the notice of the intelligent reader.

Les Caves du Vatican was serialised in the *Nouvelle Revue Française* in 1914. Claudel, who had allowed Gide to use an extract from *L'Annonce faite à Marie* as an epigraph for the book, was appalled by a passage which appeared in the March issue and which clearly pointed to the nature of Gide's anomaly. There was a series of sharp exchanges between the two men, but Gide was defiant and unrepentant. It was virtually the end of one of the most curious of literary friendships. It is true that a few more letters were written in the years that followed, while the publication of *Numquid et tu. . . ?* in 1926 raised Claudel's hopes for a moment and made him feel, as he put it, that he could 'resume his conversation' with Gide. But the hope was illusory; by the time the book appeared Gide had shifted his ground and abandoned the position it describes.

When war broke out Gide, who was unfit for military service, helped to form the Foyer Franco-Belge for assisting Belgian refugees. He worked actively there for some time, but a minor palace revolution brought these activities to an end. At the beginning of 1916 he was back at Cuverville without any war work, and was free to devote himself to writing. It was to be one of the most momentous years of his life, and one of the most disastrous. The agent of disaster was none other than Henri Ghéon. Gide had met him in 1897. They had become what is known as 'boon companions,' taking part together in clandestine exploits. An entry in the *Journal* for 1912 announces that Gide had met Ghéon by arrangement at Pisa and gone with him to Florence, where for ten days they had led 'une prodigieuse vie irracontable'; and there had been the *fugue* in Turkey in the spring of 1914. Frenchmen have expressed surprise that Gide should have remained for so long on intimate terms with a man whom they describe as 'un esprit médiocre.' The reason is not difficult to divine. Ghéon was a large, jovial, daring individual. There can be little doubt that he was the leading spirit in these nocturnal exploits, that it was he who carried the timid Gide with him, did the planning and fixed the rendezvous. He was also, unhappily, remarkably garrulous and immensely indiscreet. In the years before the first war discussion of homosexual practices was almost taboo even in what are known as 'progressive circles,' and a number of French writers have spoken of the embarrassment they felt when Ghéon insisted on recounting his adventures with Gide. On the outbreak of war Ghéon went to the front as an Army doctor. In the spring of 1916 he was converted to Catholicism. At the beginning of May he wrote to Gide to announce his conversion and to bid him follow his example. Although he expressed remorse for the past, he could not refrain from describing some of their more startling exploits in detail. When Gide was away from home Madeleine was accustomed to open his letters, or at any rate the letters from friends whose handwriting she recognised. She read Ghéon's letter. We do not know to what extent she suspected what had been going on, but the letter was unquestionably an appalling shock to her and produced the first open breach between husband and wife. It is impossible not to sympathise to some extent with Gide. It must be said in fairness to him that he had never been a cynical or a hardened sinner, that he had tried his best to shield his wife and preserve his somewhat precarious happiness, and above all that he had never been easy in his mind over what he had done or satisfied with his theoretical separation of love and pleasure. His mental torment at this time is evident from his diary. After the arrival of Ghéon's letter, he had written some twenty pages in which he must have attempted in some way to explain his behaviour. He showed them to his wife, but decided out of deference to her wishes to destroy them.

These revelations occurred at a time when Gide was passing through a major religious crisis. He was certainly very far from Catholicism, and his Protestantism was scarcely orthodox. In the months that followed he tried to come to some conclusions about religion, and wrote the conciliatory *Numquid et tu. . . . ?*, whose publication ten years later was to prove so confusing to Claudel. Although it can be said that he solved his personal problem, the solution was not a religious one. He contrived to give the impression in his diary that though there was a moment when he was near to conversion, it was the behaviour of friends who had become Catholics which finally kept him from the Church. This view cannot be accepted. What turned him away from religion was the effect of Ghéon's letter, the attitude of reprobation adopted by his wife, and the breach which followed.

Gide's new attitude began to emerge the following year. In March 1917 he formed a friendship with Marc Allégret. There was a meeting in Switzerland, and then, in the summer of 1918, when the fortunes of the Allies were at their lowest ebb and Paris was directly threatened, Gide and Marc Allégret spent four months in England. It was the cause of the second great breach between Gide and his wife. He returned to Cuverville in October. In November he asked Madeleine for the key of the drawer where she had kept all his letters to her, so that he could verify a date for a piece of autobiography he was writing. He learnt that the drawer was empty, and that in the state of despair which followed his departure to England she had burnt every letter. In *Et nunc manet in te* Gide has told us that these letters contained the best of himself, that he felt as though Madeleine had killed their child, and that for a week he did nothing but sit by the fire and weep.

It has appeared to some critics that Gide's grief over the destruction of the letters was due to literary vanity. The observation that he had put the best of himself into them certainly lends colour to this interpretation, and the reference to the child was not in the circumstances a happy one. There is, however, another possible interpretation. It is impossible to excuse Gide's treatment of his wife, and the attempt to place a share of the blame on her for the failure of the marriage in *Et nunc manet in te* aggravates the offence, but it must be admitted that in his peculiar way he was deeply attached to her. It is probable therefore that his grief was caused, at any rate in part, by the knowledge that she was trying to obliterate the past, to wipe out the happiness which on her own admission he had given her, as well as the unhappiness his conduct had brought to the home.

The belief that his wife was irrevocably lost to him was almost certainly at the root of the transformation which he underwent during the years that followed. In an entry in the *Journal* for 1927, he observed that throughout history the spiritual adventurer has always been held back by a woman who was 'afraid.' The implication is that he himself should have become a solitary adventurer, detached himself from his wife, and pursued his goal whatever the consequences for her. When we look back on the story of the years that followed the war, it is difficult not to feel that this is precisely what he had done.

The cause of the next upheaval was somewhat unexpected. Gide had for many years been a friend of the painter Théo Van Rysselberghe and his wife. The Van Rysselberghes had a daughter named Élisabeth. Madeleine Gide once remarked that it was a pity that Élisabeth had been brought up without religious principles, and that nothing good could come of it. It was from her own point of view a prophetic remark. Although Gide has declared categorically on more than one occasion that he never felt sexual desire for a woman, he stayed with Élisabeth in the South of France in 1922. The following year a daughter was born. We do not know how much of the story Madeleine Gide discovered or divined. Gide had the impression that she had some mysterious premonition about this and some of his other exploits. He met Élisabeth at Hyères on July 17th, 1922. At that time Madeleine was alone at Cuverville, but on the day of the meeting she gave a friend a gold necklace and a cross studded with emeralds—it was the cross Alissa wears in *La Porte étroite*—which had been presents from her husband and to which she had always attached a great sentimental value. She then wrote and told him what she had done. The effect was only slightly less shattering than the destruction of the letters. Gide interpreted it, no doubt rightly, as a further effort on the part of his wife to detach herself from him.

Gide was always extraordinarily reticent about his relations with Élisabeth and the birth of the daughter, whom he recognised legally after the death of his wife. Some commentators have suggested that *Geneviève* is a veiled account of what happened, but it does not seem to have been a mere passing fancy on either side. In the year in which Catherine Gide was born, Gide and Élisabeth visited Corsica together. After the death of Théo Van Rysselberghe in 1927 Gide established a second and rival 'base' with the family, and in 1930 he and Élisabeth visited Tunisia. The following year Élisabeth married Pierre Herbart, but this did not put an end to Gide's friendship with the family, who were all present at his death-bed.

Although Gide tried to keep his connection with Élisabeth a secret from his wife, he showed no such consideration in his writings. *Corydon*, a defence of homosexuality, which he persisted in describing as his most important book but which is generally regarded as one of the least successful of his works, had been written before the first world war. It is said that Gide was persuaded not to publish it by friends, but it is difficult to believe that he could seriously have contemplated publication during the lifetime of his wife. These scruples had ceased to weigh with him after the rift in his married life, and in spite of strong pressure from Maritain the book appeared in 1924. In 1916 he had begun to write an autobiography. The title he chose for the book, *Si le Grain ne meurt*, was a direct allusion to his state of mind at that time. What he meant to say was that the only way in which he could achieve self-realisation was to free himself from the past, was to kill the past which had hitherto provided him with the material for his work so that new seed would bring forth a different kind of fruit. The book, which tells the story of his life from childhood to his marriage, was not completed until after the war. In so far as it described his sexual experiences in Africa in the first person, it was bound to affect his reputation far more than a theoretical defence of homosexuality, and its effect on his relations with his wife was bound to be far more damaging than anything that he had previously done or written. It may have been these considerations which delayed full publication of the book. It was privately printed in 1920 and 1921, but the commercial edition did not appear until 1926. This was also the year of publication of *Les Faux-monnayeurs*, which Gide described as 'my first novel' and which was his last work of fiction of real importance.

Although Gide lived and continued to write for another twenty-five years, it may be doubted whether anything that he produced, except the *Journal 1889-1939*, added to his reputation as a writer. These years therefore only call for brief mention here. In 1926-7 he visited the Congo, and on his return published the two books which have already been mentioned. The year 1929 saw the publication of the first part of another short trilogy dealing with the problems of an unhappy marriage from the points of view of the husband, the wife and the daughter. *L'École des femmes*, the wife's version, was followed by *Robert*, the husband's version, in 1930, and by *Geneviève*, the daughter's, in 1936. In 1932 Gide became associated with Communism, and in 1935 he visited the Soviet Union in the company of other writers at the invitation of the Soviet Government. Although everything was done to make his visit enjoyable and to give him a favourable impression of Communism in action, he returned sadly disillusioned. In two short books, *Retour de l'U.R.S.S.* and *Retouches à mon Retour de l'U.R.S.S.*, he commented bluntly on the bankruptcy of the system.

Gide spent the war years partly in the unoccupied zone of France and partly in North Africa, where he helped to found an independent review called *L'Arche*. He continued to add to his already bulky *Journal*, wrote a good deal of criticism, some plays, and *Thésée*, which was first published in French in the United States in 1946. Two years after the end of the war he received the Nobel Prize, and the same year was given an honorary doctorate at Oxford. 'Regardez,' he is reported to have said at the luncheon held to celebrate the doctorate, 'regardez, je n'ai pas de rouge à ma boutonnière,' and it was in fact the only form of decoration he ever received.

He died in Paris on February 19th, 1951. He had been the centre of controversy of one kind or another for the last twenty-five years of his life. The end of that life was no exception. He had abandoned any form of religious belief, but except for saying that he was not to be cremated he left no instructions about the manner of his burial. This provoked a clash between his real and his adopted families, and led to some undignified manœuvring. In the event his real family carried the day. He was buried at Cuverville by a Protestant pastor. Martin du Gard protested publicly, and there was a squabble in the churchyard. This was followed by a newspaper controversy about the interpretation of what were practically his last words.

3

One of the best ways of approaching Gide's work is to read *Le Retour de l'enfant prodigue*, which appeared in 1907. In this short book he gives a personal interpretation of the parable of the Prodigal Son. His prodigal returns to the fold not in a mood of repentance, but in a mood of frustration and defiance because he has been driven back by physical privation at the moment when he seemed to be on the verge of reaching his mysterious goal. Gide provides him with a younger brother who sets out on the same errand with the connivance of the prodigal, and the promise to join him when he has made good. Now the prodigal is not merely a partial portrait of the artist; he is the prototype of the prodigals, outsiders, rebels, orphans, bastards and intruders of the other works of fiction. We shall also see that the 'fold' becomes transformed in them into the specifically Protestant community or, as it will be described here, the Protestant cell.

L'Immoraliste, *La Porte étroite* and *La Symphonie pastorale* are all accounts not simply of the human couple in marriage, but of the human couple in the Protestant cell. In *La Porte étroite* Jérôme and his cousin Alissa are in love, and the drama of their love is played out on Uncle Bucolin's property in Normandy. In the first chapter we find ourselves in a walled garden, which stands for the rather stuffy community of uncles and aunts, looking out at the great world which lies, tantalisingly, just beyond its walls. In the second we are told of Jérôme's upbringing and of the docility with which he accepts the Protestant ethic. Although Alissa returns his love, she will not marry him because marriage seems incompatible with the sanctity for which she is striving. It is strange that some critics should have regarded this as a 'religious novel.' Gide himself describes it in his *Journal* as a 'critical book,' and his aim is to demonstrate the destructive influence of a certain kind of Protestant spirituality. The 'narrow gate' does not lead to a fuller life, but to disillusionment and death. Jérôme's faith crumbles, and the spiritual-emotional seesaw kills Alissa. At the end of the book the Protestant cell has disintegrated and Jérôme is left, an unwilling 'prodigal,' contemplating the ruins.

In *L'Immoraliste* the disintegration of the cell begins before the opening of the story. Michel, who speaks of the impact of his early Protestant upbringing in the same terms as Jérôme, has begun to forget the teaching of his dead mother and his education is continued by his father, a distinguished archæ-ologist and an unbeliever, whom he helps with his work. In order to please his dying father, he makes a *mariage de raison* with the Catholic Marceline. He is struck down on his honeymoon by tuberculosis—presumably a symbol of the accumulated sickness of youth—but recovers through the care of his wife, and his life becomes a search for what Gide calls 'the authentic being, "the old man," for whom the Gospels had no use.' He comes under the influence of the sinister figure of Ménalque, who persuades him to neglect his wife when she contracts the same disease from which she has saved him. Once again the book ends with death and disillusionment. Marceline dies and Michel, like Jérôme, finds himself an outcast gazing at the ruins.

In *La Symphonie pastorale* the snow-bound parsonage is an even more potent evocation of the Protestant cell, and the sense of physical and psychological constriction becomes almost painful. The clergyman rescues the blind orphan, Gertrude, and takes her to live with his family. This creates a variation in the usual pattern. Instead of the prodigal, it is the innocent intruder who unwittingly causes the collapse of the Protestant home. Without realising what is happening to him, the clergyman falls in love with his protégée. An operation restores her sight. She 'sees' that they have taken the wrong turning, and that the person whom she really loves is the clergyman's son. Gide is remorseless in his exposure of a smugness which the clergyman takes for liberalism, and determines to punish him as heavily as possible for it. The son and the protégée are converted to Catholicism in record time. Then, with a strange disregard for verisimilitude, Gertrude drowns herself. The clergyman is left praying with his broken-hearted wife amid the ruins of one more Protestant cell.

It will be seen that all three books possess one striking similarity. In each of them the woman is sacrificed to the depravity or the weakness of the man who kills the thing he loves. Michel is a homosexual, and the book describes the symbolical annihilation by the abnormal husband of the normal wife who stands between him and the satisfaction of his desires. Jérôme attempts like his creator to separate love and pleasure. It is a mutilation of the nature of man. Alissa is too much of a realist to accept it, but her own sublimation is another form of mutilation. There is no solution and no escape. She is contaminated and killed as surely as Marceline. *La Symphonie pastorale* is a Freudian 'displacement' of a very different situation, and Gide changed Gertrude's sex as Proust changed Albertine's. The mutilation is both psychological and physical, but there is a momentary recovery before the final tragedy. The innocent intruder is hounded to death, but the real victim is the wife whose happiness is shattered.

Although Gide never ceased to protest against autobiographical interpretations of his fiction and the attempt to identify the author with his characters, he made one interesting admission. He said of *La Porte étroite* that events confirmed what he had foreseen in the book. No one can doubt that the books are a reflection of life in the Protestant cell at Cuverville or that the protagonists bear a strong resemblance to Gide and his wife, but that is not the whole story. They are not autobiographical in the sense that they describe what had actually happened, but they do describe what might have happened, what the author wanted to happen, what in the end did happen. When we examine them in the light of the fresh information which has become available since Gide's death, we are bound to recognise that he was a psychopathic case. Now the primary characteristic of the psychopath is the need to disturb, to disrupt, and finally to destroy. Although Madeleine Gide was over seventy when she died in 1938, her

life had really come to an end years earlier. Gide had brought
about her destruction in precisely the same way that the
protagonists in the *récits* destroy their partners. Jérôme is at
pains to suggest that Alissa was her own executioner; Gide
makes the same suggestion about his wife in *Et nunc manet in te*.

The *Faux-monnayeurs* is a much longer and more elaborate
work, and is essentially an experiment in form. It is an account
of a middle-aged novelist who starts to write a novel about a
coining scandal only to find that the events he is describing are
taking place in the real world. The book is shot through and
through by Gide's personal symbolism, and all his favourite
themes are there. There is the contrast between the 'authentic
being' and the 'counterfeit' which is found in *L'Immoraliste*;
and the circulation of the counterfeit coins by the schoolboys
is evidently a reference to the counterfeit values which they
have inherited from their elders. Bernard is the 'prodigal' who
discovers his mother's lapse, leaves the 'fold,' but returns to it
at the close of the novel. There is, as we should expect, an even
heavier onslaught on the Protestant community than in any
of the earlier works. The *Faux-monnayeurs*, unlike the *récits*, is
extremely easy to read, and the pages in which Gide through
Édouard expresses his views on the nature of fiction are
fascinating. But in spite of the praise it has received, it is
impossible to feel that the book is an artistic success. It does
not possess the shapeliness of the short works, and we have the
impression that the larger canvas does not suit Gide, that his
best qualities appear in dilution. The result is an extremely
interesting experiment that failed.

Gide observed in his diary that the *Faux-monnayeurs* was the
first of his books in which he tried to leave his wife out of
account. The autobiographical element, in the sense defined
above, is as marked in this novel as in the earlier works, but
though there is a good deal of Gide and his wife in Édouard
and Laura the book was the product of a different situation. It
originated in a personal quarrel between Gide and Cocteau
over Marc Allégret which developed into a struggle between
the two men for the intellectual allegiance of French youth.
This is transposed in the novel into the struggle between

Édouard and Passavant, between the 'authentic' and the 'counterfeit' novelist, for Olivier. There are two other very important facts about the book. One is that in spite of the attack on Protestantism, the novelist himself has clearly made his escape from the Protestant cell and is writing about it from outside. The other is that though Édouard and Laura are on affectionate terms she is not his wife. Gide did indeed put himself and his wife into his novel, but he took good care to deprive her of the position which gave her the right to interfere with his designs. Édouard triumphs over Passavant and succeeds with the connivance of the boy's mother, who is a *mère complaisante*, in seducing his nephew.

None of Gide's other works of fiction is of the same calibre as the four books which have just been discussed. *Les Caves du Vatican* has been described as 'a great comic novel,' but though this is an exaggeration it possesses undeniable merits. The account of the miraculous cure and conversion of the free-mason, and his subsequent relapse, is certainly funny. Gide classified the book as a *sotie*—a kind of medieval farce—and the wretched Amédée's journey to Rome belongs to this form of literature. It is a parody of the Christian knight involved in a gigantic swindle. The main weakness is a strain of cruelty and perversity which runs all through it. The *acte gratuit*, which puts an end to Amédée's life, was a theory which could not fail to arouse the keenest interest in a country devoted to the discussion of abstract ideas, but to the rest of us it appears decidedly tiresome, and the sentimentalised figure of its perpetrator is a constant embarrassment. *Isabelle* is a romantic as distinct from a religious parody. It is an unsuccessful attempt to exteriorise the search for the 'authentic being' which ends with the ironic discovery that the real Isabelle—the romantic murderess—is a dreary, uninteresting middle-class French-woman. It is generally agreed that the trilogy *L'École des femmes–Robert–Geneviève* is no more than an exercise by a highly accomplished craftsman. This must also be the verdict on *Thésée*, which on account of the author's advanced age and the moment at which it appeared was fortunate in its reception by the public.

Although Gide was a versatile writer who tried his hand at nearly all the main literary genres, his actual range of experience was far more limited than appears on the surface. It was conditioned by his religious upbringing, his sexual anomaly and his marriage. The conflict which resulted produced three works which deserve to last. *La Porte étroite*, *L'Immoraliste* and *La Symphonie pastorale* belong to the great tradition which began with Mme de La Fayette's *Princesse de Clèves*. They possess the psychological insight, the economy and the linear perfection of the French classic novel. They demonstrate forcibly that the classic form is not merely an æsthetic virtue, but a method of apprehending experience which is as valid today as it was in the seventeenth century. They have, however, one serious flaw. 'I had found my own form of normality,' wrote Gide in a sentence which has already been quoted. In all his work he was trying to set up an abnormal experience as the norm, to argue that the exception was 'natural.' The abnormal element in the three *récits* necessarily prevents them from having the universal validity of truly great art; it also accounts for the repulsion which many people feel for Gide's work and which prompts them to describe it as 'unreadable.'

Si le Grain ne meurt is a remarkable autobiography, and parts of the diaries are indispensable for an understanding of the man and his achievement. His other writings are interesting and stimulating, but they are plainly the work of one who was a very distinguished man of letters rather than a great writer.

Ernest Hemingway

by M. J. C. HODGART

M. J. C. Hodgart was born in Scotland and educated at Rugby and Pembroke College, Cambridge, at which university he took his M.A. He had not long finished there when World War II broke out. He served in North Africa, Corsica, Italy and India, was mentioned in dispatches and made a Chevalier of the Legion of Honour. He returned to Cambridge in 1946 and later became Fellow and Librarian of his old college and University lecturer in English.

His publications include *The Ballads*, and articles in the *Review of English Studies*, the *Twentieth Century*, the *Manchester Guardian*, etc.

He is married, has three children, and confesses that, if it were possible, some of his recreations would be the same as those of Ernest Hemingway. In particular he likes travel in France, Italy and Spain.

He says he has been reading Hemingway since he was seventeen and that he enjoys lecturing about him as much as about Chaucer, Pope, Dr. Johnson, James Joyce and others.

ERNEST HEMINGWAY had already become an institution by 1954, the year in which he was awarded the Nobel Prize for Literature. The year before he had won the Pulitzer Prize for *The Old Man and the Sea*, and the year before that no less than three books about him had appeared. Nineteen hundred and fifty had been another important year in the process of his canonisation: *Across the River and Into the Trees* caused a considerable fuss, a well-known American novelist called him the most important writer since Shakespeare, and Hemingway was the victim of a brilliant piece of journalism, the ribald and unforgettable 'Profile' by Lilian Ross in the *New Yorker*. But even before his stories had been made into movies, even before the glamour of the Spanish War, he had become the symbol of a generation or at least of a way of life. 'Hemingway' had long been an adjective to describe a personality, an attitude, a style. Whatever readers may think of his books a hundred years from now, he is part of the American scene and of the literary history of his age.

This institution has grown up partly from the man and partly from his books. Many of the stories have been about characters whose experience and outlook closely resemble those of their creator; his own life has followed a distinctive and much-publicised pattern, hardly less colourful than his fiction. Hemingway's life work is an intermittent autobiography, partly a confessional undertaken for the sake of self-healing and partly a record of places and people he has loved. Anyone who enjoys his books is forced into contact with this legendary figure; and so a critic who tries to explain why he likes them need have no fear that the author's biography will be irrelevant. Nor need he feel that to summarise this life is the ghoulish business of writing a premature obituary; Hemingway, always preoccupied with death, has written his own death-bed story at least twice, most movingly in *The Snows of Kilimanjaro*, and most revealingly in *Across the River and Into the Trees*.

Ernest Miller Hemingway was born at Oak Park, Illinois, U.S.A., on July 21st, 1899. (He used to give out the date of his birth as a year earlier.) His father was a country doctor and a fine shot, who appears in several of the 'Nick Adams' stories. Hemingway went to high school, from which he ran away several times, but not to university—a unique distinction, it appears, among modern American writers. Before he was eighteen, the U.S.A. had entered the first world war; he tried to enlist, but was turned down on medical grounds. After a short period working as a reporter in Kansas City (like Nick in 'God Rest You Merry Gentlemen'), he was able to join the Red Cross as an ambulance driver in the spring of 1918, and to serve on the Italian front. He was too late for the retreat from Caporetto, and the description of this in *A Farewell to Arms* must not be taken as an eye-witness account. He was wounded on the River Piave, some thirty miles from Venice, went to hospital in Milan, was decorated by the Italian Government, and returned to America in 1919. As a result of his war experiences Hemingway became somewhat psycho-neurotic, or 'shell-shocked' as it used to be called, like his hero Nick Adams in 'A Way You'll Never Be'; and the trauma of battle has remained a dominant theme in all his work.

In 1920 he resumed work as a journalist, an occupation which he pursued with success most of the time until 1926, and at various times later on. In Chicago he met Sherwood Anderson, his first literary master, whose later works he was to burlesque in his parody *The Torrents of Spring*. He next worked in Toronto, then as a foreign correspondent in the Greco-Turkish War, which figures in his earliest stories. While working for the Hearst papers in Paris he came into contact with the expatriate writers, the queen of whom was Gertrude Stein; he was also helped by Ezra Pound and the novelist Ford Madox Ford, and he knew James Joyce. His relationship with Miss Stein was close, and she certainly contributed a little to his characteristic style, but her account of her protégé in her wildly inaccurate *Autobiography of Alice B. Toklas* is not to be trusted. After a few years of poverty in Paris and a year in America, he was able to give up journalism for creative writing. Neither his first work, *Three Stories and Ten Poems* (1923), nor his second, the short-story sequence in *In Our Time* (1925) sold well, but he had a financial success with his first novel, *The Sun Also Rises* (1926, published in England as *Fiesta*). His life in the early twenties supplied the background of this book: a Paris newspaper office, evenings with British and American writers and bohemians, long holidays in Spain.

It was apparently Miss Stein who introduced him to the pleasures of bullfighting, a subject in which he achieved great theoretical expertise. When he came to write *Death in the Afternoon* in 1932, he claimed to have seen over fifteen hundred bulls killed, which would mean an average of about twenty-five fights a year. The experts say that he was unfortunate in his period, too late for Joselito and Belmonte in their prime, and too early for the great Manolete; but they also say that he knows as much about the subject as anyone does. In 1932 Hemingway was considered eccentric and bloodthirsty for saying that a bullfight could be a great æsthetic experience. Today there are thousands of French, British and American enthusiasts; we read that the most popular topic of books borrowed from Bexhill public library in 1954 was bullfighting, and *Death in the Afternoon* has come into its own. It contains material which he uses over and over again, perhaps never so movingly as in 'The Undefeated,' the story of a third-rate bullfighter told with compassion and power. This appeared in his second collection of short stories, *Men Without Women* (1927). He was now able to command high prices from magazines, and had to solve the problem set to all American writers of talent: how to resist the pressure of success and survive to write more than one good book. In 1928 he returned to America, where he lived for the next ten years, mostly at Key West, Florida, and away from New York literary life. In 1929, when he was still only thirty, he published *A Farewell to Arms*, an immense success and perhaps still his best work. Much of his time for the next few years was taken up with shooting in the West and fishing for marlin off Cuba. There were more trips to Switzerland and Spain, and there was big-game hunting in British East Africa, which led to a travel book *The Green Hills of Africa* (1935) and to two famous short stories shortly afterwards. Other short stories were collected in *Winner Take Nothing* (1933), which contains some of his most distinguished, if esoteric, work.

In the middle 1930s Hemingway became involved in one of the most curious cultural trends of the century, the great Leftward swing of the American intellectuals—curious because it has been followed by almost as marked a swing to the Right. Others, like his friend John dos Passos, committed themselves more deeply, but few young Americans of literary talent failed to enter into some degree of friendship with the Communists or their fellow travellers, an historic fact which was to prove embarrassing for many in the 1950s. Capitalism seemed enough of a failure, and Russia just enough of a success to awaken the active liberalism which forms one half of the American heritage. Hemingway's revived 'social consciousness' (to use the period phrase) found an outlet in a novel called *To Have and Have Not* (1937), apparently a hurried recasting of three short stories of different import; it is not a success, but it is at least no worse than most 'social-realist' novels of that time, and the Harry Morgan sections are more readable today than, say, Steinbeck's *Grapes of Wrath*. In the summer of 1936 the Spanish Civil War broke out. Hemingway spent the rest of the year finishing off the novel, before sailing for Spain to support the Republicans, to whom he rendered great services. He covered the front for the North American Newspaper Alliance, wrote the script for an excellent propaganda film, *Spanish Earth*, and raised money for ambulances. After the war he paid a tribute to his defeated friends in his longest novel, *For Whom the Bell Tolls* (1940).

In 1941 he was a war correspondent in China, an experience he has not so far used in fiction. On his return he settled near Havana, where he still lives. From 1942 to 1944 he was submarine-chasing off Cuba in his own motor launch. In 1944 he was back in harness as a war correspondent in the European theatre of operations, at first accredited to the R.A.F., with whom he flew on several operations. For the invasion of Normandy he went with the American Army, first with General Patton's Third Army, then with the Fourth Infantry Division of General Bradley's First Army. He picked up some Resistance troops, organised a private army, and was one of the first to enter Paris, where he rapidly liberated the Ritz. Eye-witness accounts of Hemingway at this time provide some of the most picturesque details of the legend. A court of inquiry was held into his alleged breach of the Geneva Convention by carrying arms while a war correspondent, but he was exonerated and decorated. Later on, he was with the Fourth Division in the east of France and Germany, witnessing an expensive assault in the Hürtgen Forest. Most of this is in *Across the River*, but not completely transmuted into art.

After the war little was heard of Hemingway for several years. It was a time of harvest, when he sold profitably many of his stories to Hollywood. Of the films made from them only two are memorable, the unpretentious *Macomber Story* and the admirable *Killers*. There were some good performances in *For Whom the Bell Tolls*, but the film of *The Snows of Kilimanjaro* is a vulgar distortion of the original story for which Hemingway was not responsible. His health seems to have deteriorated; he caught a serious infection in Italy, and began to suffer from high blood pressure. Once again he wrote a story about his own death, disguised thinly as the death in Venice of an old beat-up colonel. Published in 1950 as *Across the River and Into the Trees* it became a best-seller despite the justified hostility of the critics. He would not, I think, have won the Nobel Prize on the strength of this work, but, not for the first time in his career, a good book followed a bad one. *The Old Man and the Sea* (1952), a short heroic prose-poem, is as moving and as finished as anything he has written, and has been justly followed by the honours paid in the last few years. The legend continues to grow. In 1954 he returned to East Africa and had two spectacular double forced landings in the bush.

That is the well-known 'public' story of Hemingway's life, and it is not easy to get beyond it. I have never seen him, and have only met one who knew him. During the last war I met an elderly and gallant major, who, I was convinced, was the original of 'Pop,' the white hunter in *The Green Hills of Africa*, and indirectly of Wilson in 'Macomber.' On being challenged, the major admitted the imputation with some embarrassment (this, he said, must not be repeated in the mess), and, pressed to describe Hemingway, said with some hesitancy: 'Well, he's not the sort of man you can describe. You see, he isn't anyone like ourselves. . . .' The major's experience had been confined to sahibs and blacks, classes to which Hemingway clearly did not belong, so there were no terms he could find to describe him. To adapt Scott Fitzgerald's remark about the rich, Hemingway is different from us. The critics and journalists have told us about his four marriages, his fist-fights, his hard drinking, his conversation in Red Indian language and in metaphors drawn from baseball and war, his ambition to be the champion of modern literature, and his querulousness at hostile criticism; and much of this seems to fit the portrait of the artist as an old man that can be constructed from his books. This slightly absurd portrait, however, comes mainly from American interviewers, with whom Hemingway is never at his best. The Americans have written too much about him, either in extravagant adulation or half-comprehending hostility, and in front of them Hemingway is inclined to act the tough or the clown. The picture one gets from British interviewers, with whom he is more at his ease, is a different one; we read of a courteous elderly gentleman, scholarly, stoical, industrious, generous, and only mildly eccentric in a way that the British accept as quite natural, especially as it is combined with a love of cats.

Yielding to the demands of a large and athletic frame, Hemingway has spent much of his time shooting, fishing, ski-ing, boxing and drinking and much of his writing is a testament of the pleasure he finds in physical exertion. Gertrude Stein's slander to the contrary, he has shown great physical courage in three wars. At the same time he is an intellectual, knowledgeable about painting, a linguist, and above all a serious student of the novel. Like some of his heroes, he is talkative, ready to interview himself on any topic when no one else will. Of his volubility he seems ashamed, and his heroes are taken to task for being over-explicit about the things that matter. His mentor is Wilson, the white hunter in 'Macomber': 'Doesn't do to talk too much about all this. Talk the whole thing away. No pleasure in anything if you mouth it up too much.' He admires the restraint and laconic speech of the British sahib, like his own friend Captain Dorman-Smith, whose incoherence he reproduces in *In Our Time*: 'It was absolutely topping. They tried to get over it and we potted them from forty yards. . . . We were frightfully put out when we heard the flank had gone and we had to fall back.' What lies behind this is an admiration for the aristocratic-military attitude to life: 'that attitude you get from the best of the English, the best of the Hungarians, and the very best Spaniards,' as he says. This code, part Kipling and part American frontier tradition, has contributed much to his famous style.

Hemingway's books are about places and people; some may think that he has written better about the first. The most memorable parts of his books are the descriptions of country—Navarre in the fishing episode of *Fiesta*, the Italian mountains in *A Farewell to Arms*, the kudu woods in *The Green Hills of Africa*, the Guadarrama in *For Whom the Bell Tolls*, the Big Two-Hearted River, and the sea off Cuba. Most of these concern hill country, to which he always gives strong overtones of meaning. Mr. Carlos Baker has pointed out how in *A Farewell to Arms* there are two sets of contrasting symbols: on the one hand, mountains, with which are associated dry cold weather, peace, love and 'home' (the Abruzzi as described by the priest, the lovers' refuge in Switzerland); on the other, plains, rain, fog, war, hatred, 'not-home' (the flooded plain across which the retreat from Caporetto takes place, the rain that is falling as the book ends). Some such scheme lies behind the apparently casual details of place and weather running through this and the other novels. But there is more to it than symbolism: Hemingway's poetic use of landscape is only effective because he knows about terrain from having looked at it so long and so carefully with a soldier's and, what it much the same thing, a hunter's eye. He sees a landscape three-dimensionally, as an infantry officer does, thinking in terms of fields of fire, dead ground, contours. Take the beginning of *A Farewell to Arms*:

> In the last summer of that year we lived in a house in a village that looked across the river and the plain to the mountains. . . . To the north we could look across a valley and see a forest of chestnut trees and behind it another mountain on this side of the river. There was fighting for that mountain too, but it was not successful, and in the fall when the rains came the leaves all fell from the chestnut trees and the branches were bare and the trunks black with rain.

The whole passage, too long to quote here, presents the landscape first as significant for the war—the offensives were impossible and their failure led to the demoralisation of Caporetto—and secondly, after the seemingly illogical *and* of 'and in the fall when the rains came,' as a metaphor for the demoralisation of the troops and the hero, while 'the rains came' is the first appearance of a theme that is to run through the whole novel. The mountains have yet another meaning, in that they are the setting of the heroic virtue that Hemingway celebrates. The decisive battles of history are fought in the plains, among the turnips and the canals, but these are mass battles, in which the individual matters very little. In the mountains only guerrilla warfare can be effective, and in this every leader and every member of a small band, like Robert Jordan and the Spanish partisans in *For Whom the Bell Tolls*, is faced with the supreme test of his qualities as an individual. Throughout history the traditional ballads have had as their subject the outlaws or 'resistance' in the hills and forests, whether the Borderers, Robin Hood or the Cid, and have sung of their bravery against odds and their defeats with laconic realism; a modern equivalent can be seen in the classic episode of El Sordo's defeat on the hill-top. Hemingway's choice of setting for his actions is, therefore, of moral as well as symbolical intent.

In the main there are two kinds of people in the stories. The first kind are the simple people, of which the classic type is the mountaineer guerrilla. They are seen as fighting against odds, against a better-armed army, like El Sordo; or against a bull, like Manolo Garcia in 'The Undefeated,' or a giant marlin, like Santiago in *The Old Man and the Sea*. In these struggles they have to exercise not only courage but skill, such as are necessary in even a poor torero; the animals, like the lion in 'Macomber,' are admired for brute strength and beauty, but the men for mastery of their dangerous trades. They fail, not because they lack courage, but because they are old or have taken on too much. They accept their defeats with stoicism and dignity, virtues associated by Hemingway with the Spanish notion of *pundonor*: it is a point of honour not to betray their *métier*. A related character is 'the man to whom things happen,' (in Wyndham Lewis's phrase), like the Swede in 'The Killers,' or the Italian colonel shot by the battle-police in *A Farewell to Arms*; unable to cope with the situation, he must meet death apathetically as a wounded animal does. But this kind, although sometimes considered Hemingway's norm, is in fact much rarer than the hero who possesses a skill and exercises it to the last. The stories in which this situation is central are made convincing by a Kiplingesque mastery of the details of the *métier*, and by a true compassion.

The other main kind of hero is the 'Nick Adams' type, who appears under that name in many half-autobiographical stories; Jake Barnes in *Fiesta*, Lieutenant Henry in *A Farewell to Arms*, Robert Jordan and various young men in other stories go to make up this composite person. This hero is far from being a simple man; he is a countryman, engaged in war or sport, certainly, but he is also an intellectual, who has been wounded or shell-shocked, thinks too much at night and is unhappy in his relationships with women. The stories centring on him are about the traumatic experiences of childhood and youth—witnessing a Cæsarian birth, meeting punch-drunk hoboes, and above all the war—experiences to which he keeps returning compulsively in order to control them. Mr. Philip Young, in the best study of Hemingway that I know, quotes relevantly in this connection Freud's *Beyond the Pleasure Principle*. Nick Adams takes part in the elaborate rituals of sport, 'a sovereign opium of the people,' to exorcise the horrors, as in the fishing trip described so minutely in 'Big Two-Hearted River.' He takes drink, 'the giant-killer,' for the same reason, but more significantly he adopts the stoic code of the simple hero, not because it comes naturally to him, but because it seems the best defence against disaster from without and from within. Mr. Young has also shown conclusively that the career and psychological history of both Nick Adams and his author can be paralleled closely with those of Huck Finn and Mark Twain, and has thus proved that there is more than a stylistic affinity between Hemingway and Twain. The finest story on the personal and obsessive theme is 'A Clean Well-Lighted Place,' in which the rôle of Nick Adams is given to an insomniac waiter; haunted by the fear of nothingness, *nada*, his only defence against the Void is order and light, represented by the pleasant café he is unwilling to leave at the end of his day's work. These autobiographical stories are related to the confessional (Hemingway is a Roman Catholic) and to the techniques of psycho-analysis: art itself is a ritual to ward off the terrors of the unknown. Their central point, which always concerns mental suffering, is often so cunningly concealed by understatement and realistic detail that they have been misread by critics, determined to label Hemingway hard-boiled or a lover of brutality for its own sake. The highest point of his art of concealing art is reached in these short fables of human distress, particularly in 'Fathers and Sons,' the last story in *Winner Take Nothing*, in which Nick, now a father himself, comes to understand what his father has meant in his life.

The patterns of these two kinds of character are developed in the longer stories and novels. The first of these, and in some ways still the most interesting, is *Fiesta*. Nick Adams' trauma has here its equivalent in the castration, by a war wound, of Jake Barnes, an American journalist. He is hopelessly in love with Lady Brett Ashley, alcoholic and nymphomaniac, who is engaged to Mike Campbell, an Englishman of her own social set, although she cannot really love anyone. Jake introduces Robert Cohn, a literary friend, to her; she allows him to sleep with her, but becomes bored when he falls romantically in love with her. The first part of the book has as background, now rather faded, the bohemian life of a group of American and British intellectuals in the Paris of the 1920s. Jake and Bill Gorton, an American writer, go off for a fishing trip in the Basque mountains before meeting the others at the Pamplona *fiesta*. The peace and normality of the fishing trip is contrasted with the feverishness of what is to come; at the *fiesta*, the fireworks, daily bullfights and drunkenness work on the lives of these five people, whose characters are brilliantly sketched. Mike and Brett are English upper-class, living on credit, elegant and destructive; Jake and Bill are hard-working Americans on holiday, hard-drinking and tough but still above the moral level of the two English; Robert Cohn is a sensitive and aggressive Jew, amateur writer and amateur boxer, tiresome, wanting to be loved, self-righteous, pitiable but still 'nice.' The crisis comes when Brett takes a fancy to Pedro Romero, a bullfighter of great promise. Jake knows perfectly well that he ought not to introduce Romero to her, since she will undoubtedly ruin his career, and Montoya, the proprietor of the hotel, who has the boy's interests at heart, has trusted him not to do so. But he does.

> Just then Montoya came into the room. He started to smile at me, then he saw Pedro Romero with a big glass of cognac in his hand, sitting laughing between me and a woman with bare shoulders, at a table full of drunks. He did not even nod. . . . I went out. The hard-eyed people at the bullfighter table watched me go. It was not pleasant. When I came back into the café, twenty minutes later, Brett and Pedro Romero were gone.

When Jake has led the cow to the bull, Cohn calls him 'You damned pimp,' and knocks him out. This is justice, and Jake knows it (a point which all the American critics seem to have missed); Jake, not Cohn, has been guilty of a breach of the code by sacrificing the well-being of a bullfighter he admires to his obsession with a woman he despises. This, rather than the epilogue, is the emotional and moral centre of the book. At the end, Jake has gone to San Sebastian to wash off in the sea the *fiesta* dust and his own guilt, when Brett sends for him to fetch her from Madrid. She has decided to leave Romero, for his own good ('You know it makes one feel rather good deciding not to be a bitch'), and Jake can salve the decencies by looking after her, without hope. Despite the sombre title from Ecclesiastes and the notorious epigraph from Gertrude Stein, about the lost generation, this is a gay book, wonderfully comic in dialogue and characterisation.

A Farewell to Arms is a better book in many ways, although it is less rich in plot, characters and moral issues. The plot has been simplified down to the story of Lieutenant Henry, an American in the Italian medical service in 1917, who is wounded, falls in love with Catherine Barkley, an English nurse, takes part in the retreat from Caporetto, deserts, and escapes with Catherine to Switzerland, where after a few months of happiness she dies in childbirth. Apart from the two star-crossed lovers (and Catherine is one of the more credible of Hemingway's heroines), the characters are limited to a number of Italian officers and men and a few others, some brilliantly conceived but none presented from the inside. The element of moral choice is slighter than in *Fiesta*, since the hero does little that is either right or wrong. He has an officer's sense of responsibility, but he sympathises with his men, who after two years of heavy casualties are defeatists. In the retreat from Caporetto he tries conscientiously to save his ambulances, and after they get bogged down to lead his men back on foot. When the battle-police, trying to stop the rout, arrest him and are about to shoot him on the spot as a deserter or a spy, he escapes by diving in a river. From that time on he feels no more responsibility for the war, and no guilt (as Mr. Penn

Warren points out); his only duty is to protect Catherine, and as she tells him, his desertion doesn't matter, since it is only from the Italian Army. The book is remarkable for the intensity of feeling maintained throughout, which makes the young man's passion, his despair, and his longing for happiness seem entirely real. Hemingway achieves it by a series of visual shocks—images of mountains, blasted trees, rain, rivers in flood, casualty-clearing stations—and by the speed of the narrative which itself presents time as the lovers' enemy. Doom is certain; as Frederick Henry bitterly reflects at the end:

> You never had time to learn. They threw you in and told you the rules and the first time they caught you off base they killed you gratuitously like Aymo. Or gave you the syphilis like Rinaldi. But they killed you in the end. You could count on that. Stay around and they would kill you.

But though fatalistic, the book is not nihilistic or inhumane, and some of the most memorable parts are his loving pictures of the Italian soldiers, the drunken surgeon Rinaldi, the young priest from the Abruzzi, the three ambulance drivers, long-suffering, hard-working, once brave but now defeatist, comic, warm, and lost.

For Whom the Bell Tolls, for all its length and scope, shows a still greater simplification. The action is limited to four days in 1937, during which a group of partisans living behind Franco's lines prepare and carry out the demolition of a bridge. Robert Jordan, an American, has been attached to the band for this operation; he has trouble about getting them to co-operate, and because of the treachery of the leader, Pablo, the demolition has to be done by an especially dangerous method. It is finally successful, but during the withdrawal Jordan is injured by a fall from his horse; the others escape, but as the book ends he lies alone in the forest awaiting certain death. There is no serious choice facing him: he is merely a brave man, who has long ago decided to stifle his doubts, join the Communists, and do his duty. Nor is there any conflict between his duty and his love for Maria, the partisan girl who shares his sleeping-bag. Around this plot, Hemingway has built up an heroic prose-ballad about each of the band, telling how he has lived and how he will meet his death. If Jordan and Maria never come quite alive, Pablo, Pilar, Fernando, Anselmo, El Sordo and the others are convincingly shown in their weakness and strength. In a still wider concentric circle, Hemingway has tried to construct an epic of the whole Spanish Civil War, using Jordan's memories and Pilar's anecdotes in a giant series of flashbacks. Although there are wonderful passages, embodying everything that Hemingway has known and felt about Spain—and that is a great deal— although there are the shrewd descriptions of idealistic Communists and cynical Russians, the set piece about the massacre of the bourgeois in a Castilian town, the baroque speech of Pilar about the smell of death, the novel does not hang together as a whole. Like the earlier *To Have and Have Not*, it reads like a set of long short stories, inflated by disquisitions on all the topics that interest Hemingway. If he has failed here, it is not because his vision has been distorted by political passion, for he is admirably fair and well aware that in a civil war neither the abstract rights nor the best men nor human suffering are all on one side. The failure lies in his inability to sustain such an unwieldy structure with his true but limited poetic vision.

This poetic vision is evident even in the least of his novels, which by common consent is *Across the River and Into the Trees*. The quality of this book can be illustrated by comparing it with another novel by a writer of great talent, to which it bears a curious resemblance: *The Desire and Pursuit of the Whole* by Frederick Rolfe, or Baron Corvo. Rolfe's book is about Venice, and its hero is an ill-disguised projection of the author, expressing his views and prejudices at length and sometimes violently, to the point of paranoia; he is exceptionally gifted but a failure, has suffered greatly, and almost dies in Venice. There is an ethereal heroine, very young; there is a whimsical secret order of initiates; the hero takes a violent dislike to some of his compatriots abroad, and knows far better than they how to get on with the real Venetians; admiration is expressed only for aristocrats and the poor; Italian idioms are trans-

Ernest Hemingway

lated literally into English, in a special kind of pidgin dialogue, and there are beautifully written passages about the visual beauties of the city he loves. This could well be an exact description of *Across the River*, except that in the latter there is the actual death of Colonel Cantwell, an old beat-up colonel of the U.S. infantry. It is the one book of Hemingway's that reads like self-parody, but it is redeemed by its true picture of an American professional soldier, endlessly relating his war experiences, and by its powerful evocation of Venice and the lagoon in wintertime.

That would be an ungenerous note on which to end a tribute to a writer who has given so much pleasure to most of us. There is fortunately no need to be sparing in praise of *The Old Man and the Sea*, which, within its self-imposed limits, is a small masterpiece. It is not so much a novel as a lyric on an heroic theme, an allegory of the Crucifixion, based on an anecdote that Hemingway once told in an article about marlin-fishing. There is nothing new in the central situation: we are back to the simple hero, the man of skill who fails but is undefeated. This kind of story has been told by others (notably by William Faulkner in 'Old Man' and in 'The Bear'), but Hemingway brings to it his own expansive feeling, a sympathy between man and Nature, between the old fisherman, the boy, and the creatures of the sea. His style has never been more effective, filed down to an elegiac simplicity in perfect tune with his story. Its cadences create the mythical quality of the old man:

> He was asleep in a short time and he dreamed of Africa when he was a boy and the long, golden beaches and the white beaches, so white they hurt your eyes, and the high capes and the great brown mountains. . . . He no longer dreamed of storms, nor of women, nor of great occurrences, nor of great fish, nor fights, nor contests of strength, nor of his wife. He only dreamed of places now and of the lions on the beach. They played like young cats in the dusk and he loved them as he loved the boy.

It is commonplace to say that Hemingway is a master of fine writing, whose effects are achieved by means of discipline and craftsmanship It is perhaps less usual to claim that he is one of the most poetic of living novelists in English, who cannot

help giving to almost all of his writing a kind of natural magic.
If he has left the usual frontiers of the novel unexplored and
told us little new about men's or women's minds, or about the
society we live in, he has given us the early morning in Havana,
the *paseo* in the Madrid bullring, mallard falling on to the
frozen lagoon, and, in the foreground, an old man, dreaming of
lions.

★   ★   ★

The following are the principal works of Ernest Hemingway.

Three Stories and Ten Poems (Paris and Dijon. 1923).
In Our Time (Paris. 1924).
In Our Time (1925, enlarged edition).
The Torrents of Spring (1926).
The Sun also Rises (1926) (published as *Fiesta*, London. 1927).
Men Without Women (1927).
A Farewell to Arms (1929).
Death in the Afternoon (1932).
Winner Take Nothing (1933).
The Green Hills of Africa (1935).
To Have and Have Not (1937).
The Fifth Column and the *First Forty-Nine Stories* (1938). (This includes 'The
   Snows of Kilimanjaro,' and 'The Short Happy Life of Francis
   Macomber,' both published in magazines in 1936.)
For Whom the Bell Tolls (1940).
Across the River and Into the Trees (1950).
The Old Man and the Sea (1952).

The following are some of the principal books and essays about
Hemingway, to some of which I have been indebted in this essay.

WYNDHAM LEWIS—'The Dumb Ox, a study of Ernest Hemingway,' in
   Men Without Art (London. 1934).
EDMUND WILSON—Essay in *The Wound and the Bow* (New York. 1941).
MALCOLM COWLEY—Introduction to *The Viking Portable Hemingway* (New
   York. 1944).
ROBERT PENN WARREN—Introduction to Modern Standard Authors
   edition of *A Farewell to Arms* (New York. 1949).
JOHN K. M. McCAFFERY (editor)—*Ernest Hemingway, the Man and his Work*
   (Cleveland. 1950. A collection of essays including some of the above).
ARTURO BAREA—'Not Spain but Hemingway?' (*Horizon.* May 1941).
LILIAN ROSS—'How Do You Like It Now, Gentlemen?' (*New Yorker.*
   May 13th, 1950).
PHILIP YOUNG—*Ernest Hemingway* (New York. 1952).
CARLOS BAKER—*Hemingway: The Writer as Artist* (Princeton. 1952).

Rudyard Kipling

by CHARLES CARRINGTON

Charles Edmund Carrington is Professor of British Commonwealth Relations at the Royal Institute of International Affairs (Chatham House). He was educated at Christchurch, New Zealand, and at Christ Church, Oxford. Having gained the M.C. in World War I, he became in turn assistant master at Haileybury College and lecturer at Pembroke College, Oxford. He then served as educational secretary to the Cambridge University Press. During World War II he was a lieutenant-colonel attached to the General Staff.

His books include *The British Overseas, An Exposition of Empire* and, most recently, the authorised biography of Kipling which was a *Daily Mail* Choice.

IN the history of English Literature there are some writers who have established their fame in spite of critical opinion rather than with its help. Perhaps no connoisseur in the reign of Queen Anne supposed that, of all his contemporaries, the disreputable pamphleteer Daniel Defoe would be the writer most highly regarded by posterity. He was 'vulgar,' and the same epithet was applied to Charles Dickens in the reign of Queen Victoria; but Dickens, like Defoe, steadily increased in popularity with the common reader. There are authors whose works are the sensation of a season and soon forgotten; there are authors who are elevated by the critics to the somewhat frigid eminence of a classic reputation, and are read thereafter more as a duty than a pleasure. Some few, and Shakespeare is among their number, ride serenely over the waves of criticism keeping well above water in the trough or on the crest of literary appreciation. Dickens and Defoe and Rudyard Kipling are writers of that order, classics by popular acclaim rather than by official warrant.

Sixty-five years have now passed since Kipling made his first impact upon the literary scene and none of his contemporaries has remained so steadily in the limelight. He is by far the most frequently quoted of modern English authors, and the whole canon of his work has remained in the class which the book trade calls best-sellers, even though his books have never been issued in cheap editions; even though for many years the leaders of literary fashion rarely alluded to his name without a sneer, or at least an apology. Few writers have been so hated, and few so loved.

His sudden appearance in London as a portent from the East was fortunately timed to please a nation avid for information about the Empire which they had found in their possession. India and the men who governed it sprang to life, became real in the imagination of the English, and the short-lived era of Imperialism came into flower. When that political phase had passed away, his rule of life remained as a guide to a whole generation, though many sensitive spirits were so strongly repelled by the political views which he was thought to uphold that they reacted against anything that savoured of Kiplingism. He was an uncompromising writer and never came half-way to meet his detractors.

Kipling had been writing in India for four or five years and his work had already been noticed by a few discerning critics, when, in October 1889, he arrived in London still a very young man. Before the end of the year he made his mark with a spirited ballad that opened with the lines:

> Oh East is East, and West is West, and never the twain shall meet,
> Till Earth and Sky meet presently at God's great Judgment Seat;
> But there is neither East nor West, Border, nor Breed, nor Birth,
> When two strong men stand face to face, though they come from the ends of the earth!

Few lines of verse are better known and few such simple lines have been so misquoted and misunderstood; they took the town by storm. It happened that there was a pause in the flow of English literature, a gap which it was his good fortune to fill. The great Victorians were passing from the scene, though the aged Tennyson down at Farringford was still aware enough of current trends to growl that this young man was 'the only one of them with the divine fire.' The writers of the decadence had not yet publicised their cult, and Kipling's own contemporaries Shaw, Wells, Conrad, Galsworthy, Yeats had to wait much longer for fame and prosperity. His precocity, the 'knowingness' with which he commented on the world at the age of twenty-four, astonished the critics, and they were still more astonished when he reissued the stories and ballads he had written in India at twenty-one. During the early months of 1890 he flooded the market with new and old work, with the series afterwards known as *Barrack-Room Ballads*, by far the most popular book of verse for thirty years, and with eighty short stories, mostly reprinted from Indian journals. Every month there was a new Kipling boom and each bigger than the last. No such sensation had occurred in the literary world since, upon the publication of *Childe Harold*, Byron awoke to find himself famous. The year ended with Kipling's novel, *The Light that Failed*, the book of the season, but, striking though it was, the book was a disappointment. Its many faults of structure and its air of defiant bad taste gave the critics an opportunity to reconsider their verdict. Had this young man, whom a *Times* leader had compared with Maupassant, staying power? Was his work more than 'seeing life by superb flashes of vulgarity,' asked Oscar Wilde (whose own dramatic success and personal disaster still lay in the future)? Kipling's friend and patron, Edmund Gosse, warned him he was attempting too much. 'Go East, Mr. Kipling,' he warned him. 'Disappear! like another Waring. Come back in ten years' time with another budget of loot.' The critics were sure that the boom would be followed by a slump, as one of them cruelly rhymed,

> When the Rudyards cease from Kipling
> And the Haggards ride no more.

He had not yet learned to be as critical of his own work as he became in maturity, and it was an error to reprint so promiscuously no less than to publish new work so promptly. At first he needed the money, but that phase passed and he was soon embarrassed by publishers, who asked and searched for more of this saleable commodity. As a working journalist he had taken no pains to protect the copyright of his early scribblings, which were now available to any unprincipled

printer, especially in America, where foreign authors had little
or no protection under the copyright laws. For the rest of his
life Kipling, like Dickens before him, fought a relentless battle
with the literary pirates, and, like Dickens, he gave way to
occasional outbursts of fury against American publishers and
American copyright laws, with the consequence that he was
often thought to be anti-American. There was a vindictive
streak in Kipling, who did not mince words in a dispute, but
his dislike of publishers who cheated him did not extend to
their whole nation.

During his stay in London he had struck up a friendship,
the closest of his lifetime, with an American journalist named
Wolcott Balestier, who died in December 1891 when Kipling
was away on a long sea voyage. Very soon afterwards Kipling
returned to marry Wolcott's sister, Caroline, and Henry James,
an old family friend, gave away the bride. The honeymoon,
spent in Japan, was cut short by a bank failure in which Kipling
lost the modest savings of his two years' success. There was no
course open for him but to return with his wife to her home
town in New England, where they spent four happy years, and
where their two elder children were born. At Brattleboro,
Vermont, he wrote the books which brought him the most
lasting celebrity: the *Day's Work* and the *Seven Seas*, which
many critics have selected as his best work respectively in
prose and verse; the *Jungle Books*, which from then till now
have never ceased to be best-sellers, not only in England
and America but translated into many foreign languages—not
least in Soviet Russia.

Though written for children in the first instance the *Jungle
Books* promulgated a myth which has powerfully influenced
the habit of mind of the last two generations. In these books
Kipling enunciated—or rather implied, for it is not all explicit
—a principle which he then called the 'Law of the Jungle' and
later, simply, 'The Law,' his stoical substitute for a religion. It
derived from Carlyle and Emerson, the authors who had
influenced his early reading, and required what the trans-
cendentalists called an 'acceptance of the universe,' a willingness
to move with the process of the age, to understand the mech-

anism of life as it is—here and now, to throw all one's energy into operating the machine, to be an actor not an auditor, and within the framework of active life to preserve an absolute personal integrity, to be entirely self-reliant, to take final responsibility for one's actions. 'This we learned from famous men,' he wrote of his schooldays:

> This we learned from famous men,
>   Knowing not its uses,
> When they showed, in daily work,
>   Man must finish off his work—
> Right or wrong, his daily work—
>   And without excuses.

A man's task in the world is to make the machine run efficiently, not to break it. Carping criticism, Utopian dreaming, weak generalising, theory divorced from action, advice without responsibility, were by his way of thinking contemptible, the marks of the *bandar-log*, the monkey-people. In that sense he was always a conservative reformer and never a revolutionary. But he was a writer of fiction in verse and prose, not a systematic thinker, and his reputation has suffered much from critics who suppose that every observation put into the mouth of a fictitious character represents the opinion of the author. As Henry James wrote in 1891: 'for what part of his freshness are we more thankful than for just this smart jostle that he gives the old stupid superstition that the amiability of a story-teller is the amiability of the people he represents. . . . Nothing is more refreshing than this active disinterested sense of the real.'

When the Kiplings left America in 1896, rich, famous and established, it became known that they had departed in high dudgeon. Much publicity was given to a ludicrous quarrel between Mrs. Kipling and her younger brother which had caused a spate of gossip in the small town of Brattleboro, and had ended with a lawsuit in which Rudyard cut a sorry figure. This, however, was not the real reason for his departure. A political crisis over Venezuela had led to a dispute between England and the United States over the Monroe Doctrine and, so violent was anti-British feeling in America, it seemed likely that there would be war. It was politics, not family spite, that drove the Kiplings away. Three years later, when passions had subsided and the British case in Venezuela had been justified by arbitration, he returned to America on a visit which proved disastrous. In February 1899 Rudyard was struck down by pneumonia in a New York hotel and was saved from death only by the efforts of his wife and some American friends. Perhaps there has never been so powerful a demonstration of feeling over the life of a man of letters as over Rudyard Kipling's illness in 1899; it was headline news in all the newspapers of the world, and the congratulations upon his recovery were on a scale that only royalty expects. The congratulations were vain; the pneumonia from which he just recovered was fatal to his infant daughter, whose death was a blow from which he never recovered. The Kiplings could never bear to set foot in the United States again.

He was not half-way through his life, of which the second half was to be mostly spent as a literary recluse in an English village; never again did he adventure far afield or set foot east of Suez. There was now no need for him to write for ready money. His output diminished; all his work was scrupulously revised and edited; and all that he wrote after the tragic year 1899 is infused with a stronger emotion, wrought out from the heart, and accordingly expressed in a richer idiom. Always a lover of technical words and jargon, he tended in later life to a deliberate involution and obscurity. Almost the only great writer who has taken as his topic the world's work and the men who do it, he revelled in professional talk and made few concessions to readers who did not share his taste. This increasing complexity and intensity of style was matched by a deeper understanding of the human heart. The bereavement in the New York hotel had cured him of the slick, smart knowingness of his early days, and not only by a growth of pity. He had always been a good hater, and if he had learned something new about love his power to hate did not diminish.

After some years of house-hunting the Kiplings had settled

at Burwash in Sussex, a village with the merit of inaccessibility. Rudyard had many friends and could be a charming talker, though, in conversation, his talent was rather for making other people talk. There were tales of journalists going to interview him who found when they came away that he had interviewed them. It had been the secret of his art in his younger days to induce soldiers and engineers and civil servants to tell him their own stories; in later life his notebooks were full and his opportunities of making new observation less frequent, with the exception that a stream of visitors came to Burwash by invitation. His possessive wife took good care that snobs and sightseers should not intrude upon his privacy.

The years between 1896, when he left Vermont, and 1903, which saw him settled in Sussex, had seen in world history the first crisis of Imperialism: the partition of Africa and South-East Asia among the Western Powers had been completed; the British Empire had reached its apotheosis at Queen Victoria's Diamond Jubilee and had muddled through the adventure of the South African War; the United States had entered the ranks of the Imperialists by the acquisition of Hawaii, Cuba, the Philippines and the Panama Canal Zone. These were the years of Kipling's greatest influence throughout the English-speaking world, and, both in the British and American Empires, the makers of the age quoted his verses, acknowledging him as their prophet. Cecil Rhodes and Theodore Roosevelt were among his personal friends, and both confided in him; it was for Roosevelt that Kipling wrote the urgent appeal, 'Take up the White Man's Burden,' and did not appeal in vain. What part did he in fact play in the Imperialist Movement, and what message did he give to its supporters? That he approved of the extension of Western civilisation and encouraged the activities of Rhodes and Roosevelt there is no doubt, but to accuse him of 'jingoism,' of militarism, of delight in political aggression is another story. He had appeared upon the scene as a shockingly irreverent young man whose comments on the British Government in India were cynical and *blasé*. The *Barrack-Room Ballads* and the tales of soldiering in India came next, and no one can find in them a glorification of the soldier's life. They had revealed to the British public a new hero, 'Tommy Atkins,' who suffered much and got no credit or reward for serving the 'Widow of Windsor' in campaigns overseas. Never was a military hero with less *panache*, and never did any writer on war expose its seamy side with sharper realism.

> 'What was the end of all the show,
>   Johnnie, Johnnie?'
> Ask my Colonel, for I don't know,
>   Johnnie, my Johnnie, aha!
> We broke a King and we built a road—
> A court-house stands where the reg'ment goed,
> And the river's clean where the raw blood flowed
>   When the Widow give the party.

Kipling's 'Tommies' were revealed as men, 'single men in barricks most remarkable like you,' but not as a conquering caste. Their dim comprehension of the political issues at stake did not go far beyond the necessity of law and order and the promotion of efficiency.

At an early stage he had put all that behind him, 'long ago and far away,' and had turned his gaze upon the men of the sea. Kipling is the poet of the ocean liner, as Dickens the novelist of the stage-coach, and, characteristically, his interest was focused upon the engineers. Not for him to linger lovingly, as Conrad did, upon the passing age of sail; it was his task to sing the song of steam. No part of his message was more striking and original than the poetry of the machines which he elaborated in *M'Andrew's Hymn*, a poem which made him free of the society of sailors and engineers as his soldier ballads had had made him free of their society. The key to this phase of his work is in the set of verses beginning 'Farewell Romance!' and ending with the observation:

> and all unseen
> Romance brought up the nine-fifteen.

It can hardly be imagined today what an astonishing revelation was in those words when they first appeared in 1894.

His power was an ability to speak to the empire-builders in

a language they understood. With him Poetry came down off its winged horse and addressed itself to the soldiers, the sailors, the administrators, the pioneers, the road-makers, the bridge-builders, the engineers in respect of the life they knew, assuring them that deeds were more significant than words, that thinkers and dreamers were useful to society only if they did not make dreams their master or make thoughts their aim. The techno-crats were entering into their inheritance and Rudyard Kipling was their leader. To the men of letters this seemed something like a betrayal of their order, but Kipling was as indifferent to the trends of literary taste as his readers were ignorant of them. His readers multiplied and his sales increased, year by year, decade by decade, long after the critics had written him off, repenting and sometimes forgetting their earlier enthusiasm. No one could now say that he was the 'comet of a season,' and no honest critic could deny that his penetrating observation, his clear-cut expressiveness, were sharper than ever. It was his politics that they disliked.

But what were his politics? He had begun by revealing to the British people the source of their strength and the nature of their obligation in their dominions overseas, teaching them to look outwards, 'East of Suez,' to dream 'of far horizons where the strange roads go down,' and to enter into the lives of those who made this expanding world-wide system. 'What should they know of England who only England know?' he had asked; and had then expanded his outlook by calling on the Americans to come out of their isolation and join in the work of bearing the White Man's Burden. Colour-consciousness did not then dominate the politics of many countries as it does today, and the standards of the 'white man' in the jargon of that day (he always used the colloquial language of the man in the street) meant the code of conduct of what were in plain fact the most civilised, progressive and successful nations.

Not least was he typical of his age in the possession of a puritan conscience, and none of his appeals to his followers omitted a note of warning against national arrogance. The high-water mark of his fame was the publication of the hymn, *Recessional*, written for the old Queen's Diamond Jubilee in

1897. He astonished his cruder admirers and delighted his critical readers by sounding a note of warning:

> Far-called, our navies melt away;
>   On dune and headland sinks the fire:
>
> Lo, all our pomp of yesterday
>   Is one with Nineveh and Tyre!
>
> Judge of the Nations, spare us yet
>   Lest we forget—lest we forget.

Even this celebrated poem contains a contemptuous phrase, and the *White Man's Burden*, which followed it two years later, contains several lines which gave great offence. Kipling, as a preacher, could be something of a scold; and, while he sometimes annoyed his friends, he lost no opportunity of goading his enemies, the radicals and the sentimentalists, into fury. His popularity was so well established that his faults were overlooked by his innumerable admirers, who turned back with renewed delight to his Indian stories, to the *Jungle Books* and to his 'song of steam.' The sale of his books steadily increased, not only in England and America. In France his reputation was as great, partly because his style favoured French translation, and to readers of the other European languages he soon became known. A persistent rumour spread that he had been denied official recognition, as Poet Laureate, because his work had given offence to the Queen, a rumour for which no shred of evidence has come to light. In fact he had been offered and had refused a series of public honours. Entire independence was the first principle of his life and an official personage he would not be. An author who was so irreverent, who defied and despised critical opinion, who habitually wrote in 'cockney' dialect, could hardly expect to earn academic approval, so that it was a triumph when, about the year 1906, the universities began to take notice of him. He had arrived, and was accepted as a literary classic, and it is not surprising that his arrival in the rather frigid Hall of Fame was about the time when the *avant-garde* was reacting most strongly against his ideas and rejecting his claim to literary importance.

In 1906 and 1907 he was invited to accept honorary degrees,

successively from McGill, from Durham, from Oxford, and from Cambridge; and these university honours were closely followed by the award of the Nobel Prize for Literature, the first occasion on which the award had been made to an Englishman. These were honours which did not commit him to any political obligation, and he accepted them without demur.

The climax of Imperialism was past by 1907. During the previous years Kipling had spent each winter in South Africa, on the advice of his doctor; and the winters, he said, had been 'his political times.' After Rhodes's death, he had been closely associated with Milner, who reconstructed South Africa after the war, and with Jameson, the premier of Cape Colony. (The character of Jameson gave Kipling his model when writing 'If—.') Both men were out of office by 1907, their work discredited by the new Liberal Government in Whitehall. The outlook was black for politicians of Kipling's way of thinking, and, in the United States, a similar revulsion of opinion had eclipsed Theodore Roosevelt. If Kipling had been merely an Imperialist, it seemed that his influence was at an end, and his recognition as a world figure at Stockholm a barren triumph. This view of his work was widely taken by the literary critics who supposed that his career was finished. Bernard Shaw (at a later date) dismissed him as an immature, adolescent writer, 'a boy who never grew up.' Meanwhile he continued to write, and for many years more remained a 'best-seller,' though his later work was slighted by professional reviewers in the younger generation.

For more than thirty years he lived in affluence as a country gentleman in Sussex, taking no more than conventional holidays abroad, a comfortable life that was convulsed in 1914, as for all of his generation, by the cataclysm of the first world war. He lost an only son, a blow which deepened his pessimism and lowered his zest for life, but which can hardly be said to have affected his work as did the loss of his eldest child in 1899. Inured to domestic misfortune and aware of the hard blows that Fate can strike, he had no further lesson to learn from sorrow. Kipling's last years were darkened by ill health. From

the time of his son's death he began to suffer from internal
troubles which no doctor could diagnose; for twenty years he
was kept on a regulated diet, was constantly in pain, and on
several occasions very seriously ill. There is little more to say
of his life save that he died in a London hospital soon after his
seventieth birthday. His later work was much concerned with
the problem of pain, and with what he called the 'breaking-
strain,' the load of physical or mental suffering that human
beings can bear.

The books that he published after his recommendation for
the Nobel Prize display a different Kipling from the brash
young man of 1890 who had matured only so far as to become
the Bard of Empire. In 1906 he had published *Puck of Pook's
Hill*, the first of his historical studies, which, like the *Jungle
Books*, were composed on three or four planes, as children's
books in the first instance, secondly for adults, and thereafter
for those who could find a deeper meaning in them. His
detractors, not looking very closely at his work, did not observe
that he had moved into a new dimension, no longer asking
'What can they know of England who only England know?'
but what can they know of England's present who have no
sense of England's past? The future he had seen in terms of the
machines, the creatures of man's brain which would serve man
only if he devoted all his unstinted devotion to them according
to the unswerving Law of their being; the past was something
equally inevitable and absorbing, which controlled the present
by the accumulated wisdom of the ages. He personified it in
the figure of the old countryman:

His dead are in the churchyard—thirty generations laid.
Their names were old in history when Domesday book was made;
And the passion and the piety and prowess of his line
Have seeded, rooted, fruited in some land the Law calls mine.

The 'Puck' Stories show a delicacy of touch that had not
been apparent in the anecdotes of life at Simla which had made
such a stir, fifteen or twenty years earlier. Similarly, his other
stories of the Sussex period have greater range and greater
depth than his earlier work. Like so many of his con-

temporaries he was interested in those psychical phenomena that seemed beyond the margin of the normal. The Viennese psychologists had not yet announced to the world the hypotheses which were to have so profound an effect upon the thinking of the next generation. The mental climate in which they worked was one where novelists and poets were reaching out towards the frontiers of rationality and were explaining the abnormal in terms of the supernatural, whereas their successors would explain it in terms of the subconscious. In the nineties Kipling had written one or two convincing ghost stories in the accepted mode; he had also made some alarming voyages of discovery into the half-world of reincarnation, inherited memory and prophetic dreams. With the development of his own discernment and with the progress of the psychological science he moved to experiments which probed deeper into the recesses of the heart. *They*, his story of child ghosts, a story which may be compared with *The Turn of the Screw*, is written with sensibility and passion; it has not the intellectual force of *The Wish-House*, written twenty years later. But in those twenty years Freud and Jung had made their work known.

Kipling's last important volume, *Debits and Credits*, was published in 1926. In addition to *The Wish-House* it contains at least five other stories which no critic should overlook. If he had written nothing but *The Janeites*, *A Madonna of the Trenches*, *The Bull that Thought*, *The Eye of Allah* and *The Gardener*, on that reputation alone he would rank as one of the world's great story-tellers. All of them are highly characteristic; his style with its concrete images and forcible words, his biblical mannerisms, and elaborately built-up scenes, his sense of atmosphere, which is so strong that action seems hardly necessary, is unmistakable. Yet many of the lesser stories, and even these in some passages, are so involved and obscure as to be hardly intelligible. Some, too, are exceedingly unpleasant. In the whole range of Kipling's work there is not to be found a single obscenity, and rarely an erotic suggestion, but coarse language and brutality of conduct are common in his work, as they are common in life.

It will be noticed that there are few young women in his cast of characters, and few great lovers among them. A man's man when young, he differed from most other writers by dealing with every other aspect of a man's life more willingly than with his love-life. In maturity he wrote much of women, and some critic may yet think fit to make a study of them; but they are unloved women or unrequited lovers or women inaccessible and remote like the faint and charming 'Mrs. Bathurst,' who attracted all men, not by her beauty or her intelligence but by the indefinite quality to which Kipling first gave the name of 'It.'

Subtle and complex and sophisticated as his later stories were, they failed to catch the mood of the 1920s. There was no doubt that he was an old-fashioned writer, left behind in the march of progress and most unwilling to thrust himself into the van. Above all, his politics were outmoded, when sentimental liberalism was in vogue. Even when his cousin, Stanley Baldwin, became prime minister in a Conservative Administration there was little that Kipling could find to approve in his policy. It was the tone, the direction of the new age that he most disliked. The prophet of adventure, self-reliance, efficiency and independence found little to please him in an age devoted to the deplorable doctrine of 'safety first,' to the cautious restrictive habit of the trade unions, to the gutless moralising of the League of Nations. He made no concession to changing fashion in conduct but stood firm upon his stoical creed. The 'Gods of the Copy-book Headings,' as he assured his readers, would reassert their sway.

An address that he gave to the University of St. Andrews in 1923 gave offence to some who looked for smoother words. 'The power of the tribe over the individual,' he said, 'has become more extended, particular, pontifical, and, using the word in both its senses, impertinent, than it has been for many generations. Some men accept this omnipresence of crowds; some may resent it. To the latter I am speaking. Nowadays, to own oneself in any decent measure, one has to run counter to a gospel, and to fight against its atmosphere.'

The world, which had once accepted his words and followed

him, had now swung away to run in a contrary path, leaving him—exactly where he had always stood. Nothing that had happened led him to suppose that courage and self-reliance had ceased to be the master virtues or that the four-square principles of 'the Law' had ceased to be the conditions of human life. No mere words or wishes could charm away the consequences of indolence and folly. He did not live to see the second world war, which he had long thought inevitable.

Thomas Mann

by EDMOND VERMEIL

Translated by L. J. LUDOVICI

Edmond Vermeil was born at Vevey in Switzerland of a French father. He went to school at the Lycèe of Nîmes and afterwards studied at the Universities of Montpellier, of Freiburg in Breisgau, Germany, and of Munich. He completed his studies at the Sorbonne under the instruction of the famous Charles Andler.

He taught at the University of Göttingen and then at the Alsatian School in Paris. During World War I he served three years in the trenches as a captain but in 1917 was called to a post in the Deuxième Bureau, France's M.I.5.

After the war he held the Chair of the History of German Civilisation at the University of Strasbourg and came to the Sorbonne in 1934. During World War II he was flown out of France and arrived in London to join General de Gaulle's organisation.

He is the author of numerous books about Germany. *Germany's Three Reichs* and *The German Scene* are two of these which have been translated into English and published in London.

WHERE in modern times can we find a literary output like that of Thomas Mann, showing such force and clarity, such a constancy of effort towards perfection and the strict observance of those rules which great art always obeys?

I

In his *Reflections*, which appeared in 1917, Thomas Mann offered us the most exact and most profound definition of high German culture. In particular he cited the case of the incomparable Johann Sebastian Bach. To him Bach's was an ardent and spontaneous genius, allied to solid craftsmanship and a most scrupulous attention to rules.

Moreover, we must not forget that Thomas Mann was always a faithful disciple of Nietzsche and Schopenhauer. There is no more perfect writer of prose in the whole of German literature than Nietzsche, no writer with a greater respect for his mother tongue, no writer more dedicated to purifying his style and capable of lighting up the treasures of the national language. At the same time he kept close to the Greek model. As for Schopenhauer, venerated by Nietzsche himself, did he not enrich the splendours of his prose with deep meditations about what the fertilising illusions of great art mean to human life, to the struggle against despair and pessimism, to the mastery of the self and the triumph over the betrayals of destiny?

To these two names, so frequently mentioned by Thomas Mann, we must add that of Richard Wagner. We only have to re-read Nietzsche's fourth 'Unseasonable Consideration' and Thomas Mann's own essay on Wagner—which has remained famous—in order to convince ourselves that Wagner's extra-ordinary perseverance in the face of the thousand obstacles which confronted him during his pursuit of the higher aim he had set himself from his youth exercised a kind of fascination over Mann.

Under the steady influence and guidance of such masters, his work as novelist and essayist progressed with a regularity and amplitude which evokes the admiration of the world's literary *élite*. Following the astounding novels counting among his major works: *Buddenbrooks*, *The Magic Mountain* and *Doctor Faustus*, the whole of his vast production is finally linked up with his more recent efforts. These drew nourishment from the inexhaustible springs of the Bible. I believe that in France only Proust and Claudel can sustain comparison with Mann, with his fascinating train of novels, with their wide canvases, in which he reverts to the most ancient myths of human history, inter-woven with a symbolism that he found appropriate to the problems of our epoch.

2

Thomas Mann earned that shade of touching gratitude which is mingled with so much justifiable admiration through his own evolution, through the profound modifications that circumstances have produced in his judgment upon humans, upon nations, upon the diverse cultures of Europe which have borne fruit in other continents. To be capable of reorientations, to be able to break with a certain past, to seek unceasingly for the truth—be it at the cost of the stiffest trials and bitterest renouncements—in order to be able to tell it to his misguided countrymen without equivocation or meanness of spirit, was to gather in the best of the Nietzschean heritage. To my way of thinking, nothing in Mann's life and work more fully qualified him for the Nobel award reserved for those who have endowed humanity with the most useful and glorious discoveries.

Along his road, and especially during his exile, Mann encountered the wealth of the Western mind, its highest traditions. But reorientations did not bid him part company with the land of his birth. Indeed he never dreamt of it. His ties with German culture bound him so closely that they would not have allowed him to do so. On the contrary, did they not enable him the better to understand and reveal to the world the true greatness of European culture? And he mastered this 'Europeanism' only after the direst of struggles. In this lies his merit.

To recall Mann's position at the time of World War I is not to diminish his stature; it is a true point of departure. He was convinced that Germany alone possessed the secret of real culture, that she alone could overtake the artificial, mechanised civilisation of our day and reach up to the heroism which sustained the living order, everlastingly threatened by the violence of passions. He seemed to adopt an exclusively critical attitude towards the nations of the West like Britain, France, Italy and the Russia of the Tsars. Had he forgotten Nietzsche's vehement diatribes against the Germany of Bismarck, and had he thus been led to think of his country as the Great European Centre, destined to ensure the fertility and stability of the Old World, at a time when his country was bent on its destruction?

In his defence let us say that from the commencement of the nineteenth century German thought had created an ideology which radiated from every corner of the Germanic horizon and culminated in an idea of this sort, in the notion that Germany was specially predestined, and that a providential rôle had fallen to her. Nietzsche himself had believed this and built his hopes upon it in his own times. However, he had turned his back on his country because, in his judgment, it suffered from an irremediable lack of culture.

For a moment, therefore, Mann had believed in a German victory, in the rightness of Germany's final triumph. The defeat and collapse of 1918 could but lead a mind of this scope to reflect afresh upon Europe and its future. At this stage Mann wrote *Buddenbrooks*, a novel at once so German and so European. In it he is hardly lenient towards his compatriots, towards the industrial materialism and the nationalism they had falsely exalted. It is odd that he was not unduly surprised by the dissolution of Bismarckian Germany, not that he viewed the downfall of his country as desperate. He did not modify his conception of real culture in any detail, but he now dared to accuse Germany, placed between the rationalism of Poincaré and Lenin, of having plunged into arid intellectualism, into technical mechanisation and into Teutonising pan-Germanism, when there was comfortable peace. He also prophesied the impending collapse of the Weimar Republic at an early date. He understood only too clearly the game of the right-wing reactionaries. Far from understanding their mission and saving democracy, they thought only of destroying it, of preparing German youth for Caesarism and the war of revenge and of conquest.

3

Here then was the first point: to return in all sincerity to a criticism of the whole without in any way sparing Germany. Mann wrote his *Magic Mountain* in order to set his conception of German democracy within its natural framework. Doubtless it is the most artificial book that he ever wrote. It took up again—though in new keys—his definition of Western culture, now contrasted with Russian Communism; that is, a definition of the opposites between which Germany was naturally placed while she was endeavouring to bring about the revival that in the future had to be brought about.

It was an attitude quite in conformity with his mentality. It is in itself an explanation of the kind of symbolism the informed reader discovers in him so readily. The structure of the whole book is eloquent. It evokes for us the human body viewed from the standpoint of analytical rationalism and the science of medicine; the mountain eternally wrapped in its white shroud, propitious to meditations upon universal life and death, the vast plains where a variety of Philistine activities are carried out, mechanised by sovereign industry and grown bellicose on account of Western ambitions.

While Settembrini embodies the rationalist optimism of the French and Italian Left, the stubborn philosophy of the Enlightenment so mistrusted by Germans, with its superficial and outmoded though generous jargon; in short, the pseudo-mystical republicanism of Freemasonry; the Jesuit Naphta, a strange figure forged all of a piece, represents at once Catholicism and Communism, brothers and enemies. In Mann's eyes the crime of these doctrinarians was the sacrifice of individual personality and of normal communal institutions to an ideal of perfect, tyrannical uniformity.

The period which opened with the Armistice of 1918, and took in the years immediately preceding the Nazi explosion and the Third Reich, was notable because Mann did not cease in all loyalty to perfect his definition of German neo-Liberalism and his conception of real democracy. In his mind this conception had to become identified with real culture. Having once gibed at the facile dreams cherished by the eighteenth century, and having condemned them in the almost untranslatable term *Wunschbarkeit*, he in his turn took himself with bowed head into Utopia. Reverting to an entirely untranslatable term, the perfect *Volksstaat*, he solicited with complete sincerity the national State worthy of this name and now placed at the service of the whole people and the living nation.

What Thomas Mann saw in future democracy was not the *Volksstaat* alone and the 'Politicalised People,' but above all a kind of 'Directorial' State. Thus he returned to the Nietzschean idea of the selection of the finest, of a carefully chosen *élite*, of a new-model aristocracy. Walter Rathenau and Hermann Keyserling returned to this very idea at the same time as Mann. This chosen *élite*, it appeared, would have to form the bridge between ancient territorial monarchy and democracy inspired by the West. And it would have to govern a Germany that had once again become the Great European Centre.

4

At the same moment, however, the real people, people in the concrete sense, were in Germany being subjected to a process which, since the appalling inflation of 1920-4, had been making a wholesale proletariat of them. Meanwhile the traditional *élite* consisting of the old ruling classes repeated their former mistakes, their brutalities. Could Thomas Mann then believe that Germany was on the way towards choosing and guaranteeing economic stability, of favouring the free development of her creative energies under the control of the State, of constructing a hierarchy of rights founded upon a perfect technical education, of maintaining at home a sort of middle way between the imperfections of the West and the dangers of Communism?

He was certainly not the first to declare that the people should not be identified with the State, that the nation in movement should not be enclosed within the political, administrative and military machinery. Taking all in all, he dreamt generously of a democracy which ensured the bond between personal values in their proper order, and the social categories; of a democracy which ultimately suppressed the privilege of wealth and culture. This was harking back to romanticism rather than preaching an organic union between individual energies and collective forces.

How can we fail to be grateful for Mann's attempts to define the most desirable type of German democracy from the standpoint of Europe's future during the Weimar Republic? Yet Mann along with other writers had forgotten that no effective selection could be made among a people bereft of political maturity and afflicted by a bankruptcy which summed up its entire history. This people could not be ripened for the tasks awaiting them in the future by the surging chaos of four war years and of defeat. Under the guise of democracy lurked industrial and military dictatorship, as well as secret rearmament, which asserted itself with growing vigour from 1930 to 1933.

5

With Marshal Hindenburg in power the Hitlerite party was carried forward by its own irresistible *élan*, and Thomas Mann was not slow to understand the then inanity of his generous dream, to foresee that Teutonising barbarism was to blaze forth from social and financial disaster, from unemployment among the workers, from the despair of the ruined middle classes. He turned with insurmountable horror from the Government whose accession to power he witnessed. He did not hesitate. With rare courage he raised his indignant protest in his forever famous address given in the Salle Beethoven. He pleaded solemnly with his countrymen, evoking in his turn the terrible crisis of unemployment and want.

Should the electoral success won by the Nazis on September 14th, 1930, then be interpreted as an explosion of spiritual forces lying dormant and neglected by an ineffectual democracy? In which quarter would it be held that that barbarism stemmed from recent humiliations? Mann did not overlook the fact that the Allies had left Germany her industry, her political unity; that they had even allowed her a professional army and, what is more, a Balkanised Europe that could be overthrown by a rearmed Germany.

It was too late. The tide flowed on and broke all barriers. The chosen *élite* dreamt of by Thomas Mann was there in the terrifying form of Nazi leaders issuing from a desperate people; leaders sustained by the gifts and the prestige of industrialists and country landowners as well as by Westerners who saw in Hitler the future conqueror of Stalin. For Thomas Mann it meant exile, together with the loss of his most precious possessions.

6

Courageous when faced with the Nazi peril in Germany, he remained courageous when as a citizen of the United States he was put in contact with Western resistance. He spoke directly to his countrymen in broadcasts. He attacked the Hitlerite régime anew, beseeched his compatriots to revolt from it and not to allow themselves to be submerged by a Satanic barbarism; he opened their eyes to the prospects of a different future, and his moving pleas did him honour, for far from wishing to avenge himself he wanted to cure Germany of her ills and bring courage to her frenzied population.

Thomas Mann employed the inexhaustible resources of his literary virtuosity in nailing the leaders of the Third Reich to the pillory before German and world opinion.

The disgust Hitler inspired in him was limitless. 'Out of his mouth so many unclean things came forth,' he wrote, 'that I experienced veritable repugnance that my name should have been mentioned by him.' Mann noted, moreover, that Hitler had betrayed two essential principles in his doctrine. First he betrayed his anti-Bolshevism by concluding the Russo-German Pact. Secondly he betrayed his racialism by his alliance with Japan. Mann saw Hitler simply as the unconscious instrument of a fatal destiny. To him the pretence of a Nazi revolution was merely a shocking reaction. Did it not claim to wipe away with Christianity the whole heritage of the French Revolution? In addition Mann prophesied at any early date the bankruptcy of the diabolical régime which made of Germany a nation isolated from all others.

In Mann's opinion the real tragedy—the collapse of Nazism kept apart—was the fate reserved for the German people. On this issue irony was tinged with warning. What was to befall the master race, the race which, according to pure Hitlerite doctrine, had been chosen to regenerate Europe and the world? He did not delude himself; like Friedrich Meinecke he saw that Nazism reached down into the very roots of German life. Yet he did not intend that it should be confused with the true German spirit in its very highest traditions. He was pained to see this true German spirit thus debased. His concern was that the wholesale destruction of Nazism should not involve the wholesale destruction of Germany should the country fail to break its bonds with the Third Reich. He realised the extent to which his country had repudiated its eighteenth century. Who could save her if she was incapable of saving herself?

There was some hope if she displayed modesty and reserve, if she abandoned her false notions of superiority inculcated in her by false masters.

He described the new world in which Germany could take her place after the inevitable expiation with a trace of optimistic enthusiasm. He admired Roosevelt, authentic representative of a working democracy. How far we have travelled from the former diatribes against the Anglo-Americans! Mann had learned that the Anglo-Americans never consider war as normal, that this was just where they differed from the Germans.

In fact the war could have been avoided. The nations which fought Hitler bore a heavy responsibility for the world-wide misfortunes of our time. 'Never will humanity forgive itself for allowing what happened to happen,' exclaimed Thomas Mann, 'what could happen again.' He knew the extent to which the cause of humanity had been betrayed in the West. 'In the face of such danger,' he added, 'it was not an easy matter for an American of German origin to owe his birth to a country which attacked and pillaged Europe by unleashing forces of such cruelty and fury.'

Mann thus plainly carried out the duty that had fallen to him. He had to make the prospect of a better world shine before German eyes, a world in keeping with humane laws. We can thus see in him the type of German who understood the demands of an international order and realised the place his country should tomorrow occupy within it—provided she could make herself worthy.

7

Since those days, Mann's chief masterpiece, *Doctor Faustus*, has renewed and prolonged his incontestable fame as a writer beyond catastrophe itself. It provides an admirable sounding-board for the soul, the character, the spiritual and intellectual history of Germany. Not without reason has this book been described as 'very German' in its psychological content; in its profound views upon art and culture revealing the author's passionate love of music; in its deliberately charged and frequently archaic style, its highly studied composition.

Through a minute description of a complex environment, its dangers and its excesses, Mann analysed the culture which in 1917 he had set against that of the West so as to demonstrate its superiority. Adrian Leverkühn's destiny, his demonic nature, his musical genius, strangely calls to mind that of Nietzsche himself, that of the most disquieting genius ever produced by Germany; even to his local origins, even to his Lutheran background, even to his tragic testimony of bourgeois decadence in Germany and in Europe itself. The final lament of this new-style Faust, more tragic than Goethe's, the living embodiment of Germany's destiny in an epoch whose horrors the Sage of Weimar could not have predicted, concludes with an apocalyptic vision that recalls with gripping exactitude the disasters of 1945.

Thomas Mann started writing it in 1943. 'If my works have assumed a monumental character,' he recorded concerning this subject, 'it was without my having foreseen it or wanted it. *Buddenbrooks*, *The Magic Mountain*, *Joseph and His Brethren*, *Lotte in Weimar*; all these works are explained by the modest desire to tell a story. In the event—and for the first time—things turned out differently. It became the work of my old age. For once I knew what I wanted; the task with which I grappled was no less than to undertake the novel of our times. It had to be clothed with the highly precarious and dubious life of an artist.'

In this, Mann, with Dr. Aderno, Professor of Frankfurt University, returns to that profound philosophy of music held by Schopenhauer, Wagner and Nietzsche. Human genius itself is in jeopardy, in its most irrational, troubled and disquieting aspects; in its sinister and awful relationships with lower, infernal Powers. It is the career of a man endowed with higher gifts which unfolds itself before our eyes from one stage to the next. It all takes place not in the North, homeland of trade, but in the South, land of the Germany of dreams and ideals. There music and theology are inextricably mixed. Is it

not significant that men like Bismarck and Nietzsche developed
in this orthodox and pietist background? And are not the
addresses of a Schlappfuss on demonology, on the relative
power of God in the face of Evil, infinitely revealing to us
Westerners?

For it is before the Demon that Leverkühn appears (Chapter
25, climax of the novel), to be told of what his own genius
consists. A simple bottle of champagne and the German
becomes intoxicated, like the students in the famous Auerbach
Tavern in Goethe's *Faust*. He then takes himself for a god, later
falling from the heights of dazzling illumination into wretchedness and mediocrity.

Yet what belongs to God is inspiration, enthusiasm joined to
intelligence, to reason. The only diabolical thing is inspiration
in disarray. Here was the problem that Nietzsche had treated
with genius in his first masterpiece while still in the flush of
youth. In it he saw the human tragedy as born of the spirit of
music.

Not without motive does the Demon remind Leverkühn at
the conclusion of their nocturnal meeting of the mystery of
death. It is the climax of the novel. Faust's final plaint mingles
with the plaint of the author himself, certain about the fate of
Hitlerite Germany. It links up with the pleas lavished upon the
German people by Mann in his broadcasts at a time when all
was in doubt, and, above all, Germany herself. It seemed as
though collective intoxication is like the momentary intoxication and enthusiasm of the artist, of the Devil, of the Demon,
when these are not controlled by sovereign reason. *Alles
Ausdruck ist Klage*, states the text. Man can open his mouth only
to groan under his fate. But he shuts it in death, for there are
no words, no possible means of expression suitable for death.
Silence alone is obligatory.

After 1945 German public opinion turned against Thomas
Mann with unnecessary severity, for reasons evidently concerned with politics. But it had badly understood and falsely
interpreted *Doctor Faustus*. Time had to pass, there had to be
reflection before this misunderstanding was dispelled. Some
years ago in France the Sorbonne gave Thomas Mann a

triumphant welcome. Not long afterwards the enlightened inhabitants of the great Hanseatic city of Hamburg honoured him. The latest chapters of his most recent novel, *Felix Krüll*, created a great impression there. In 1955 he talked about Schiller in Weimar and in Stuttgart, in East Germany and in West. Here was a symbolic situation. For Germans spiritual unity alone is possible.

.   .   .   .   .

Thomas Mann is dead. His mortal remains were placed in Swiss soil. In *Doctor Faustus* he imagined a nocturnal encounter between the hero, Adrian Leverkühn, and the mysterious personage who could pass for Mephisto in this second version of Faust. When Adrian questions him finally about death, the enigmatic personage replies there are no words in any language to describe or explain its mystery. Therefore silence; silence alone is suitable. Let us remain mute now that a great writer has gone, and let us contemplate soundlessly the living message he has left us.

François Mauriac

by MARTIN TURNELL

I

INTERNATIONAL celebrity comes more easily to some writers than to others. It depends partly on differences of national psychology and partly on imponderable factors which are not always readily explained. The England which had acclaimed Marcel Proust even before his own countrymen and had paid grudging tribute to Gide, took much longer to make up its mind about François Mauriac. For a time, indeed, it looked as though his work might have to be labelled not perhaps 'For home consumption only,' but 'Not for export to Anglo-Saxon countries.'

Mauriac's most famous novel was published in 1932. The following year, at the age of forty-eight, he was elected to the French Academy. In spite of a few dissenting voices and a good deal of abuse from his fellow Catholics, he was widely regarded in his own country as the most distinguished living French novelist. *Le Nœud de vipères* was translated into English in 1933 and was a failure. Its gloomy angular religion and sultry passions made no appeal to intellectuals who were fretting themselves about 'the people,' flirting with Communism or on the point of engaging in amateur soldiering in Spain. They were utterly incomprehensible to the stolid, unimaginative middle-brow public who expected their literature to be 'cheerful,' to foster instead of undermining their social and moral complacency.

It needed something little short of a spiritual revolution to turn the unsaleable author of the thirties into the Book Society Choice of the forties. A generation which had lived through a second world war and seemed already on the brink of a third, a generation for which the greatest sporting event of the period was not Wembley, Wimbledon or Lord's but Bikini, was much more disposed to give Mauriac a hearing. The nature of the change which had taken place is well suggested by Mr. Peter Quennell.

'Catholic novelists,' he said, 'have this great advantage—that, since they are conscious of the tremendous moral implications of an isolated word or gesture, their vision of life has a heightened quality, an intense dramatic relief, which is often beyond the reach of the matter-of-fact agnostic, whose standards, though possibly more rational, from a literary point of view are sometimes far less stimulating. Everything counts—nothing is trivial or insignificant—in Barbey's curious universe; and it is his art to bring out the dramatic intensity, the moral light and shade, of every subject he touches on. Lust is elevated to the height of passion; it becomes a ruling motive that carries all before it, not a desultory experiment made by indifferent partners.'

Although this was written in 1947 of a novelist who had been dead for practically sixty years, it applies almost word for word to Mauriac. It also helps to explain his vogue. The readers of the Age of Fear had had enough of 'rational standards' and 'desultory experiment[s] made by indifferent partners.' They wanted to be convinced of 'the tremendous moral implications' of their actions; they wanted, in a world in which the individual seemed to count for less and less, to be assured that everything 'counted,' that nothing was 'trivial' or 'insignificant'; they wanted 'dramatic intensity,' wanted to find that lust *could* be 'elevated to the height of passion.' Above all, in a world threatened with physical annihilation, they wanted to be told that if man had a body which could be blown to pieces he also had a soul which could be saved or damned *by his own actions*.

2

François Mauriac was born at Bordeaux on October 11th, 1885, and was the youngest of five children. One of his three brothers became Dean of the Faculty of Medicine at the University of Bordeaux, another a barrister, and the third a priest.

Mauriac comes on both sides of prosperous middle-class families. They owned extensive properties in the Bordeaux area which were to provide the setting of some of the most impressive of his novels. One of his earliest recollections is the sight of his paternal grandmother sitting, with her handbell and a box of lozenges, in the vestibule of 'the depressing house at Langon which I used in *Genitrix*—a vast building with shaky foundations which trembled when the trains on the Bordeaux–Cette line passed during the night.'

He lost his father when he was only twenty months old. Death came suddenly, even violently to certain of the menfolk in the family. The father had spent the day visiting a property which he had just inherited from an uncle. On his return home he complained of a severe headache. The next day he was dead. The grandfather died when François was five. His end was equally sudden but more dramatic, and recalls some of the deaths in his grandson's novels. He, too, had spent the day inspecting his land. Then, after dinner, he went to the house of a woman friend for his usual game of boston. When the game was over, she asked him to go with her to Benediction. Although the old man had been a notorious anti-clerical all his life and never went near a church, he accepted the invitation. In church he appeared to be profoundly recollected. On the way back he collapsed. He was carried home to bed, had time to murmur 'We are saved by faith,' and died.

Although Mauriac's father had been an unbeliever, his mother, whom he portrays as Mme Dézaymeries in *Le Mal*, was a deeply religious woman. Her faith was coloured by a marked strain of Jansenism which left its impress on her son's character and contributes to the gloomy atmosphere of the novels.

'As soon as the clock struck nine,' he wrote in *Commencements d'une vie*, 'our mother knelt down, and we huddled round her. My brothers fought for "the corner" between the *prie-Dieu* and the bed. The one who occupied this privileged place buried his head in the curtains, which hung down from the canopy, and could drop off to sleep at the first words of the prayer: "Prostrate before Thee, O my God, I thank Thee that Thou hast given me a heart capable of knowing and loving Thee . . ."

'Our nightshirts were so long that I should not even have been able to scratch my feet. We knew that the Infinite Being demanded that children should sleep with their hands in the form of a cross on their chests. We went to sleep with our arms crossed and our palms clamped to our bodies, clutching the holy medals and the scapular of Mount Carmel which we were not allowed to take off even in the bath.'

When he was five he was sent to a kindergarten run by nuns where his brothers had been before him. There is an amusing glimpse—or was it simply a tale?—of one of the lay sisters. 'My brothers maintained that, when an unusual noise was heard in the classroom, the sister went round sniffing out little behinds until the smell betrayed the culprit.'

He was a highly impressionable child. 'Never,' he wrote, 'have I had such a taste for solitude as in those early years. When I was ten, I suffered so much from the promiscuousness of school life that I remember spending a whole hour in the appalling lavatories simply because I could be alone there. I enjoyed roller-skating enormously because it was a game which could be played without the assistance of any of my schoolfellows.'

In another passage from *Commencements d'une vie* he describes his childhood hardships:

'It was still dark during those gloomy winters when the servant, Louis Larpe, came and knocked on our doors at half-past five. In those days there was nothing unusual about a servant being up at five in the morning. I used to get up, shivering with cold, by the light of a Pigeon lamp. We never had fires in our bedrooms, not for reasons of economy or even of austerity, but on account of the theory that "our toilet would be finished long before the room could get warm." . . . The long day stretched ahead of me with its ambushes and traps; the martyrdom of feet swollen with chilblains being thrust into damp shoes was already beginning. Our toilet was soon over; it would have needed heroism to wash. After a hurried cup of cocoa, we paraded up and down in front of the door waiting for the *parcours*; it was our name for the school bus which went round the town picking up other little boys who were as sleepy and as ill-washed as ourselves.'

When he left the kindergarten, Mauriac joined his brothers at the Collège Grand-Lebrun which belonged to the Marist brothers. He has paid tribute to the ability of his clerical schoolmasters, but he makes one striking observation on their educational methods which throws some light on his own work. 'Our masters,' he says, 'excelled in creating about us a celestial atmosphere which bathed every moment of the day: they did not form Catholic intelligences; they formed Catholic sensibilities.'

He went from the Collège Grand-Lebrun to the *lycée* at Bordeaux, where he was remembered as a brilliant pupil with a taste for Pascal and Racine. He passed the *licence ès lettres* at the University of Bordeaux. Then, in 1906, he went to Paris to study at the École des Chartes.

'The École des Chartes,' he has told us, 'was only a pretext. It was not that I had the slightest interest in historical research, but it was the only one of the great schools where mathematics was not a compulsory subject. I was hardly there before at the end of six months I had made my escape "in order to embark on a literary career," as our relatives put it.'

He was in the same fortunate position as the young Gide had been. He did not have to work for a living or to curry favour with editors and publishers. If publishers were not prepared to risk their money on his books, he was perfectly well able to finance them himself. Soon after leaving the École des Chartes, he began to publish verse in two magazines called *Temps Présent* and *La Revue de la Jeunesse*. A friend, who was later to become a Benedictine monk, ran a small publishing house. He brought out Mauriac's first collection of poems, *Les Mains jointes*, in November 1909. The book was published at the author's expense and cost him five hundred francs—'no trifling sum in those days,' as Mauriac later remarked.

On February 8th, 1910, Mauriac received a letter with a black border and the monogram of the Chamber of Deputies. It was from Maurice Barrès.

'You are a great poet [it began] whom I admire, a true poet, measured, tender and profound, who does not attempt to force his fragile voice in order to move us to tenderness over our

childhood. I should like to say so in public. That is why I have
been slow in writing to thank you for this precious little book
which has been read and re-read every day of the last fortnight.
I am deeply delighted to discover that we have a poet.'

The young Mauriac was not unnaturally overwhelmed. He
had like his fellow townsman, Jacques Rivière, an immense
admiration for Barrès. 'In 1910 I set Barrès so high that, owing
to one of those complications which belong to our twenties,
I had not sent him *Les Mains jointes*, so unworthy did the little
book seem of so great a master, and also because I was afraid
of his contempt or his silence which would have left me
inconsolable.'

Although he had not sent Barrès a presentation copy, he
remembered being asked by a Bordeaux bookseller for a de
luxe edition for Monsieur Barrès. For Barrès had been shown
the book by Paul Bourget, to whom Mauriac had sent a copy,
and had been so impressed that he decided to buy it.

Mauriac's reply led to a second letter written on February
19th:

'My dear Poet,

When I was your age I confess that I should have fretted
myself while waiting for the reviews of my first book to appear.
So I am writing to tell you that I have mentioned the *Mains jointes*
in an article which I have written for the *Écho de Paris* and which
may appear any day now, and that in about ten days' time I am
going to write a whole article about your charming little book.
And there is no need to thank me. It is for me to thank you for
giving me some verse that I can enjoy.'

Maurice Barrès was an unbeliever with a great admiration
for the Catholic Church who had been waging an enthusiastic
campaign for the preservation of historic churches since they
had been handed over to the faithful, at the time of the separation of Church and State, 'to maintain or to allow to fall into
ruin as they saw fit.' In an article characteristically entitled
'L'Esprit et la Bête,' which appeared in the *Écho de Paris* on
February 21st, Mauriac found his little book bracketed with
Péguy's *Jeanne d'Arc* and a work called *La Splendeur catholique*

by Pol Loewengard as 'one of the favourable signs in recent literature.'

Two days later Mauriac was present at a public lecture by Barrès. In spite of black looks from the chair, he jumped on to the platform after the lecture with the words: 'I am François Mauriac.' 'Well,' came the rejoinder, 'so you're not a little seminarist after all.'

Barrès's article appeared on March 21st. It was all that the young Mauriac could have hoped for. Although he retained a affectionate admiration for Barrès, it does not seem to have been reciprocated, or rather, like many celebrated writers, Barrès was inclined to be fickle. *Les Mains jointes* had caught his attention. He undoubtedly overrated it, lost interest in its author, and failed to acclaim his real achievement when it came. At one of the last meetings between the two men in 1922—Barrès died the next year—Mauriac asked him if he had read *Le Baiser au lépreux*, 'the first of my books which does not make me blush and which after twelve years justified his confidence in me.' Barrès's only reply was 'a vague gesture.' It did not really matter; he had given Mauriac a splendid send-off from which he never looked back.

A second volume of poetry called *Adieu à l'adolescence* was published in 1911. Mauriac has spoken harshly of these early verses, but the poet in him has always remained alive. A third volume of poetry, appropriately entitled *Orages*, appeared in 1925 in the middle of his richest period as a novelist, and a fourth under the title of *Le Sang d'Atys* in 1940.

Mauriac's first two novels, *L'Enfant chargé de chaînes* and *La Robe prétexte*, were published in 1912 and 1913. In the latter year he married Jeanne Lafon, daughter of a civil servant, and became the father of four children—two sons and two daughters.*

On the outbreak of war he was called up in the auxiliary medical service and took part in the Salonika campaign. The first war seems to have made little impression on the man or his work. As soon as it was over, he settled down to his career as a

---

* His son Claude enjoys a considerable reputation as a literary critic, and has written a remarkable study of André Gide called *Conversations avec André Gide*.

writer. He wrote two excellent novels, *La Chair et le sang* and *Préséances*, which both appeared in 1920. *Préséances* showed clearly the direction in which he was moving; it was the first of many biting attacks on the provincial bourgeoisie.

'I was not made for failure,' Mauriac observed, a trifle petulantly, when the success of one of his plays seemed to hang in the balance. He had no grounds for complaint. Few contemporary writers have begun their careers in more favourable circumstances, have had a better send-off, or have reached the front rank of their profession more quickly and with less opposition than Mauriac. The ten years from 1922 to 1932 were a period of almost unbroken success. They produced five novels whose chances of survival, as one critic has recently pointed out, are at least as good as any other works of fiction written in our time. They are *Le Baiser au lépreux* (1922), *Genitrix* (1923), *Le Désert de l'amour* (1925), *Thérèse Desqueyroux* (1926), and *Le Nœud de vipères*. He also wrote four other novels during the same period which possess many of his characteristic merits: *Le Fleuve de feu* (1922), *Le Mal* (1924), *Destins* and *Ce qui était perdu* (1927). He was awarded the Grand Prix du Roman for *Le Désert de l'amour*. In 1932 he was elected President of the Société des Gens de Lettres and the following year, as we already know, he entered the French Academy.

Mauriac is the author of some twenty-five volumes of fiction, but none of the novels and stories which have appeared since *Le Nœud de vipères* is of the same calibre as the finest work done up to 1932. *Le Mystère Frontenac* (1933) has been described as a sort of 'oasis' in his work, and it undoubtedly marked a *détente* after the growing violence which culminated in *Nœud de vipères*. It has been said with considerable truth that his range is narrow. The later novels do, indeed, give the impression of a master craftsman who has begun to repeat himself, to use a formula instead of exploring fresh regions of experience. The criticism applies equally to *La Fin de la nuit* (1935), which was a sequel to *Thérèse Desqueyroux*, *Les Anges noirs* (1936), and *Les Chemins de la mer* (1939). *La Pharisienne*, published in 1940, is an uneven book; it contains pages which recall the author of *Le Désert de l'amour* and *Le Nœud de vipères*, but unhappily most of it belongs to a lower level. The three short novels which have appeared since the last war, *Le Sagouin* (1951), *Galigaï* (1952) and *L'Agneau* (1954) are clearly the work of an expert craftsman, but they add nothing to the novelist's reputation.

It may well have been the fear of repeating himself and the belief that renewal would come through a change of *genre* which prompted Mauriac to turn to the theatre. *Asmodée* was given its première at the Comédie Française in 1938, and enjoyed a considerable success. It was the only play that he wrote before the war, but three more were produced after the war—*Les Mal aimés* in 1945, *Passage du malin* in 1948, and *Le Feu sur la terre* in 1951.

Although Mauriac's reputation will ultimately rest on his novels and to a considerably lesser degree on his plays, he is like many Frenchmen a highly versatile writer with a number of volumes of criticism and biography to his credit. Books like *Dieu et mammon, Le Romancier et ses personnages* and *Le Roman* are primarily skilful apologias for his own particular form of novel, but in the short essays reprinted in a series of volumes rather misleadingly entitled *Journal* he has shown himself a penetrating critic of literature. The most notable of his biographical studies are his *Vie de Jean Racine* (1928), which is important for an understanding of his own achievement; *Trois grands hommes devant Dieu* (1931), which contains three interesting essays on Molière, Rousseau and Flaubert; *Blaise Pascal et sa sœur Jacqueline* (1931), *Vie de Jésus* (1936), and *Sainte Marguerite de Cortone* (1945). His more specifically religious writings include *Souffrances et bonheur du chrétien* and *Le Jeudi Saint*, which both appeared in 1931. Mention should also be made of his delightful autobiographical essays, *Commencements d'une vie, La Rencontre avec Barrès*, and *Journal d'un homme de trente ans*, which were first published between 1931 and 1948, and reissued in one volume under the title of *Écrits intimes* in 1953.

It is well known that Mauriac was one of the intellectual leaders of the French resistance movement during the German occupation, and was obliged on one occasion to go into hiding in order to escape from the Gestapo. The war also brought a widening of his activities through the outspoken articles which he wrote in *Le Figaro*, and continued to write after the end of hostilities, as well as the launching of a review with an implicit Christian outlook, *La Table Ronde*, in 1948.

On November 6th, 1952, he was awarded the Nobel Prize for Literature. The citation spoke of 'his penetrating analysis of the soul and the artistic intensity with which he has interpreted human life in the form of the novel.'

3

There is no better introduction to Mauriac's art than his own critical writings. In books like *Le Romancier et ses personnages*, *Dieu et mammon* and the occasional essays in *Journal* he has described his aims with a perspicacity which is rare in an imaginative writer.

'I cannot conceive a novel,' he says, 'without the house which will be its setting being present to my mind down to its tiniest nooks; I must be familiar with the most obscure of its garden paths, and I must have a knowledge of the whole of the surrounding country—not a superficial knowledge either. Colleagues have told me that they choose, as the scene of a novel that they are thinking of writing, some little town which up to then was unknown to them, and that they take a room at an hotel there for the whole of the time that they are working on the book. That is the very thing I cannot do. It would not help me in the least to settle down, even for a considerable time, in a part of the country which was unknown to me. No drama can begin to come to life in my mind unless I set it in places in which I myself have always lived. I must be able to follow my characters from room to room. Their features often remain blurred in my imagination; I only see their silhouettes, but I smell the damp in the corridor along which they are walking; I am ignorant of nothing that they hear at a particular hour of the day or night when they cross the vestibule and go on to the steps.

'This necessity condemns me to a certain monotony of atmosphere which is the same from one book to another. It forces me to make use of all the houses and all the gardens where I have lived since I was a child. But the homes of my family and friends are not sufficient; I have to invade the homes of neighbours. In this way I have, in all innocence, unleashed in imagination the most terrible of dramas in those decent provincial houses where, at four o'clock in the afternoon in dimly lighted dining-rooms which smelt of apricot, old ladies used to offer me, when I was a little boy, not Thérèse Desqueyroux's arsenic but the finest muscadine grapes, cream cakes, quince pâtés, and a large glass of rather sickly syrup.'

'I am a metaphysician who works in the concrete,' he says in another place. 'Thanks to a certain gift of atmosphere, I try to make perceptible and tangible, I try to give the smell of the Catholic universe of evil. I make incarnate that sinner of whom the theologians give us an abstract idea. . . .

'Often, impressed by my critics, I have dreamt of writing the story of a saintly little girl, a sister of Thérèse Martin*. . . . But as soon as I set to work, everything takes on the colour which is my eternal colour. My finest characters become enveloped in a sulphurous light which is proper to me. I do not defend it: it is simply mine.'

'The hero of *Nœud de vipères* or the poisoner, Thérèse Desqueyroux, horrible as they appear to me, are free from the one thing which I hate in this world and which I can hardly tolerate in a human being—complacency and self-satisfaction. They are not satisfied with themselves; they are aware of their wretchedness.'

There is a pleasant irony about the comment on one of the familiar types who people the novels:

'Why should I not bestow on this man, whose type obsesses me and who is continually reborn, even if I have killed him off at the end of a book, what it is in my power to give him: a new life, children and grandchildren if he has not had any? I give him another chance. . . . I admit that with me, this isn't saying very much. . . .'

In these passages Mauriac shows us how the novelist sets about his business, how people and places take possession of him. He touches on some of the main themes of his work— the setting which is an organic part of each novel; the religion which seems to act as a ferment of destruction; his horror of

* Thérèse Martin became St. Thérèse of Lisieux—'The Little Flower.'

the smug provincial bourgeoisie. He even hints at the fratricidal family feuds which fill the books.

'Families, I hate you!' cried Gide in the *Nourritures terrestres*. There are strange antithetical resemblances between the lives and work of Gide and Mauriac which illuminate the achievement of each of them. They both came from prosperous middle-class families; they were both deeply marked by religion; and they both rebelled against their environment. It is at this point, however, that divergences begin to appear. Gide's life and work were a continual oscillation between two worlds, between 'the Protestant cell' and the world of moral freedom represented for him by North Africa. Mauriac is a more ruthless, a more penetrating critic of the bourgeoisie than Gide; his hatred of its religious hypocrisy, as we can see from the best pages of *La Pharisienne*, is at least as strong as Gide's, but he chose a different method of attack. He does not offer an alternative world on the human level; he offers another dimension of life, a spiritual world which opens to the gravest of sinners, or the most hardened of hypocrites, once they can free themselves from the form of living death which he depicts.

The same divergences are apparent in the two writers' attitude towards religion. For Gide religion was a shirt of Nessus which clung to him and never ceased to torment him in spite of his claim to have allayed his spiritual unrest and attained serenity. Mauriac never attempted to break with religion, but his conception of religion is as different as it could be from Gide's. He sees the Christian's life not as a state of serenity, but as unending tension. He speaks enviously of converts like Maritain for whom Catholicism had been a free *choice*:

'That is my drama. I was born into Catholicism; I did not choose it. This religion was imposed on me at the time of my birth. A good many others were born into it who lost no time in making their escape. But it is because the faith which was inculcated into them did not "take." I, on the other hand, belong to the class who are born into Catholicism, who understand when they have barely reached manhood that they can never get away from it, that it is not in their power to leave it and come

back to it. They were inside; they still are; they will stay there
for ever. They are filled with light; they know that it is true.'

Religion is not for Mauriac, as it was for Gide, primarily
a moral system, something that you carry round in a book as
Gide carried his Bible about with him. It is something absolute;
it is the wholly other, the disruptive force which suddenly
wrecks the smug complacency of the provincial landowners
and exposes not merely their false values, but their sham
religion.

Mauriac's environment has the same compulsive force as
his religion. He has told us that he loved and hated Bordeaux,
that he tried to get away from it and never could. Bordeaux
and its surroundings are woven into the very fibres of his being
and his books, so much so that one sometimes feels tempted to
describe him as a regional novelist. In all his finest work we are
surrounded by the desolate *landes*, the pines and the sand, the
sand and the pines. We smell the cinders in the air when fire
has destroyed acres of pine forests, or hear the thunder growl
as the enormous hailstones come pelting down and flatten
out the precious vineyards. We see, too, a people for whom the
dread disease—the hereditary disease—in spite of the pines is
tuberculosis.

From this setting Mauriac has extracted a dry, gritty poetry
which is peculiarly his own:

'The plain, which stretched away in front of us, lay open to the
sun in the midst of a silence which was as deep as when it sleeps
in the moonlight. On the horizon, the *landes* formed an immense
black arc under the metallic sky.'

'The cinders on the pathways, the dry crackling fields, the smell
of parched geraniums, the sight of a girl eating her heart out on
an August afternoon, no other plants—there was not a single
detail which Thérèse did not find again in her heart.'

'Beyond, a black clump of oaks hid the pines; but their resinous
odour filled the night; Thérèse knew that they surrounded the
house like a hostile army, invisible but close at hand.'

It is the setting that contributes very largely to the
'monotony' of which Mauriac himself has spoken. It also

throws into high relief the violent actions of the characters. What we find in the novels is a passion at the centre of a silence. For the atmosphere at the centre is alive with suppressed passion, with smouldering hates which are always on the point of erupting and destroying innocent and guilty alike. We see far more than the tortured face of a lovesick girl on a torrid August afternoon. In one of the sombre houses standing in the middle of the silent desolate *landes*, we catch a sudden glimpse of a wife furtively slipping poison into her husband's medicine glass; we see a jealous mother turning a deaf ear to the cry for help of a sick daughter-in-law, returning to her own room and leaving the woman to die; and we hear the anguished murmurs rising from the bed of a hideous young man and a ravishing young woman joined together in holy wedlock.

A homely image provides further insight into the nature of Mauriac's world:

'A pine planted in the rich earth of a field enjoys a rapid growth; but very soon the heart of the tree goes rotten, and it has to be cut down in full maturity.'

This world is a diseased world. It is a world which presents the outward appearance of health and strength, but its heart is rotten.

Although Mauriac has expressed a special affection for Balzac, Baudelaire and Rimbaud, the most important single influence on his work has been the influence of Racine. It is often said that there is a family likeness between Racine's principal characters, who, with their savage passions, all belong to the same stock. It could be said with even greater truth of Mauriac. He does not give the impression of being any fonder of families than Gide, but families are at the centre of his work. His interest is twofold. He is interested in the family as a social unit, and he is interested in the resemblances between the members of certain groups which form what might be described as psychological families in the manner of Racine. There are in fact three main groups. There are the complacent, avaricious middle classes; there are the saintly figures like

Lucie de Villeron, Mme Dézaymeries, Noémi d'Artiailh and Yves Frontenac; there are, finally, and most important of all, the sinners.

In Mauriac's provincial families with their distinctive names—the Fondaudèges, the Blénauges, the Desqueyroux, the Péloueyres—there is an overlapping of the social and the psychological, of the 'family' in the accepted sense of the word and the psychological group. They pay lip-service to religion, but their real religion is the cult of the family, their social position, their pines, their vineyards, and their cash.

'It was the cult of a class,' says Louis of the Fondaudèges, 'to which I felt proud to be promoted, a sort of ancestor worship adapted to the use of the bourgeoisie, a collection of rites whose only significance was social.'

That is not how members of the families see themselves. 'The family is not a thing we joke about,' says Bernard Desqueyroux pompously to his wife. He cheerfully commits perjury not to save Thérèse, but to save the honour of the family. Worship of the family name, the family position, the family properties becomes a form of idolatry to which the things that really matter are unhesitatingly sacrificed. It seems perfectly natural to them to sell their daughters to disastrous husbands in order to restore their tottering fortunes or to maintain their social position:

'I shall never forget the surprise I felt when I saw your sister, Marie-Louise, whom you called Marinette, who was a year older than you and looked younger with her gracefulness, her long neck, her slightly top-heavy mass of hair, and her child's eyes. The old man to whom your father had handed her over, Baron Philipot, filled me with horror. But since his death I have often thought of this man of sixty as one of the unhappiest men I have ever known. What a martyrdom the imbecile must have suffered in order to make his young wife forget that he was an old man! He wore a corset which was done up so tightly that it nearly suffocated him. The tall, wide starched collar hid the folds of the fallen cheeks. The dyed moustache and side whiskers emphasised the ravages of the violet-coloured flesh. He scarcely listened to what was said to him because he was always looking for a mirror;

and do you remember how we laughed when he had found one if we caught the wretched man looking at himself, going through the perpetual self-imposed scrutiny. His dentures prevented him from smiling. His lips were sealed by a will power which never let him down. We had also noticed the curious movement he made when he put on his top hat, to avoid disturbing the extraordinary lock of hair which began at the nape of his neck and spread out on the top of his head like the delta of a small trickle of a river.'

This is the account of the wedding night of Noémi d'Artiailh, who has been married off by her impoverished family to Jean Péloueyre through the well-intentioned but disastrous intervention of the parish priest:

'In the cretonne curtains the figures of two guardian angels veiled their faces in shame. Jean Péloueyre had a long struggle first against his own mirror, then against a dead woman. At dawn a feeble moan marked the end of a battle which had lasted six hours. Jean Péloueyre, who was drenched in sweat, dared not move, he looked more hideous than a worm beside the corpse which was at last abandoned.'

In spite of the expression of sympathy for the old man in the first passage, Mauriac dwells with a savage glee on the physical ravages—'ravages' is a favourite word—of the old and the ugly; and there is a sinister inflection about the word *livrer* when it is used to describe impoverished parents disposing of a virginal daughter to a wealthy but physically revolting man.

'The reason why I have known people who had lost their faith,' said Mauriac in *Dieu et mammon*, 'is because an uneasy conscience like mine finds satisfaction in trouble, and therefore seeks our similar types of conscience.'

The middle-class property-owners and the saints are people who are free from tension because they have solved their problems according to their different lights. They provide the setting for the sinner who lives in a continual state of tension. He rebels against middle-class complacency and is drawn, without realising it, in the direction of the saint but is distracted from his goal by temptation, usually by sexual temptation. It is, indeed, his horror of the cold complacency of the middle classes which drives him to rebellion, but it also drives him to sin and crime before he can find the true path. Thérèse Desqueyroux loathes the smug self-satisfaction of the family into which she marries and tries to poison her husband. Louis, in the *Nœud de vipères*, is driven into hatred of religion and of his family who practise this religion for the same reason. His son speaks of 'the reasonable, moderate religion which has always been honoured in our family.' That is not how his father sees it:

> 'What I detested beyond everything was this crude caricature of Christianity, this mediocre infusion of Christian life. I had pretended to take it for an authentic representation of Christianity in order to have the right to hate it.'

This is a crucial passage for the understanding of Mauriac. In one of his books he quotes, with approval, some famous words from the *Apocalypse*:

> 'I know thy works, that thou art neither cold nor hot. I would that thou wert cold or hot. But because thou art lukewarm and neither cold nor hot, I will begin to vomit thee out of my mouth.'

What redeems the sinner in Mauriac's eyes is precisely the fact that he is not 'lukewarm,' that he is capable of passion. For in the long run to be capable of passion means to be capable of love. Disaster occurs when the sinner's love is focused on the wrong object, on the creature instead of the Creator. It also occurs when he allows his exasperation over 'this crude caricature of Christianity,' over 'the reasonable and moderate religion which has always been honoured in our family' to change his love into hatred, when in short the faults of the complacent middle-class family drive him into exercising one of the most destructive emotions known to erring humanity.

A great deal of the tension in the novels springs from the principal characters' claustrophobic sense that they are prisoners. Their prison is both physical and psychological. They are the prisoners of the arid, frightening *landes*, and they are the prisoners of the no less frightening materialism of the family circle. For Thérèse Desqueyroux, as we remember, the pines 'surrounded the house like a hostile army, invisible but close at hand.' In another passage we read:

'The family! Thérèse let her cigarette go out; with staring eyes she saw the cage with its innumerable and living bars, the cage filled with ears and eyes where, motionless, crouching, her chin resting on her knees and her arms round her legs, she was waiting for death.'

This is Louis:

'As soon as I am made helpless by illness, the family circle closes in on me. You are there, watching me.'

The 'outsider' and the 'prisoner' are two of the most significant of the many symbolical figures to be found in modern fiction. The 'outsider,' the man who does not fit into contemporary society and ends by disrupting it, has had a long and successful career since Stendhal created him; and no one has expressed more powerfully than Proust the terrors of the man trapped in a psychological prison. Mauriac's particular contribution is to have shown that the 'outsider' and the 'prisoner' are, or can be, complementary aspects of the same personality. It is because they do not fit in and because they are a threat to the sacred family that Thérèse and Louis are turned into prisoners with the 'family circle' watching them, closing in on them. He has also given a fresh dimension to the concept of the 'outsider.' For Mauriac's sinners correspond in the Order of Grace to the 'outsiders' of a Stendhal or a Gide in the order of Nature. 'La vraie vie est absente,' wrote Rimbaud in *Une Saison en enfer*. It is precisely the dilemma of Mauriac's sinners. The smugness and banality of 'the family circle' thwart their unconscious spiritual longings and because they have not found the path to 'la vraie vie,' they are suspended perilously on the brink of the abyss.

'I always make a mess of my virtuous characters,' Mauriac once said. It is only too true, and it has led to a twofold criticism of his work. Critics who do not share his beliefs have accused him of 'rigging' experience, of introducing artificial and improbable conversions in order to give a religious aura to novels which are at bottom anything but religious. His fellow

Catholics have put it in another way. They have made his well-known indulgence for the sinner the basis of a charge of complicity. This is the seduction scene in *Le Fleuve de feu*:

'It was the delicious and desperate moment when two beings, though still making a pretence of resistance, know that they are lost. The abyss has not yet swallowed up their mingled limbs, but they are leaning sufficiently far out over its depths to be sure that henceforth no power on earth or in heaven can snatch them back.'

The tone is undoubtedly equivocal. It is also characteristic. For what gives the novels their distinctive flavour is precisely the mixture of sorrow and fascination that we find here. There is less direct autobiography in Mauriac's novels than in those of almost any other contemporary novelist, but the characters of every novelist must to some extent be a projection of the tensions and conflicts in his own mind. The nature of the conflict underlying the novels is not difficult to discover. It is a conflict between two forces pulling in diametrically opposite directions, between the claims of God and the fascination of the creature. It is reflected in the titles of some of the books like 'God and mammon,' 'the desert of love' and 'the river of fire,' or in phrases like 'la minute délicieuse et désespérée' and the 'fatigue délicieuse et criminelle.' This use of antithesis is a persistent feature of Mauriac's style. 'Fire' clearly stands for passion, for an immense thirst for life. 'Water' is usually the living water of religion which alone can quench the thirst of passion. 'Sand,' 'cinders' and the 'desert' are images of frustration. Pleasure turns to dust and ashes, love creates a 'desert' round the lover, when the creature tries to slake his thirst at the wrong source or focuses his passion on the wrong object.

These observations provide us with a short answer to the charge of complicity. There is no complicity in the sense of the deliberate exploitation of sin, and the moral orthodoxy of the novels is not in doubt. At the same time, the drama of the characters is a reflection of the personal drama of their creator. This alone can guarantee the authenticity of the experience, and provide an answer to the charge that the experience is 'rigged.' If the characters are in some degree a reflection of their creator, he must necessarily identify himself with them. That there are occasions like the seduction scene in *Le Fleuve de feu* when a wrong step provides both the author and his readers with a vicarious satisfaction is perhaps inevitable.

Mauriac speaks disparagingly in *Le Romancier et ses personnages* of the artificiality of the French classic novel. All art forms make use of a certain number of conventions. The *tirade* of the French classic dramatists is one. Mauriac's use of the flashback in *Thérèse Desqueyroux* or the diary in the *Nœud de vipères* is just as artificial—and, in its own way, just as effective. The truth is that in spite of his criticism, Mauriac himself is directly descended not simply from the French classic novelists, but from the French classic dramatists. It is precisely the fewness of the characters, the economy and simplicity of design, and the tautness of construction which make his novels so brilliantly effective and give them their extraordinary explosive force.

'The heroes of the great novelists, even when the authors claim that they are not trying to prove or to demonstrate anything,' he wrote at the end of his study of the novel, 'contain a truth which may not be the same for each of us, but it is for each one of us to discover that truth and apply it to himself. For what no doubt provides us with our *raison d'être* and justifies our strange and absurd profession is the creation of an ideal world thanks to which living men see more clearly into their own hearts, and are able to show one another more comprehension and more pity.'

The pursuit of truth and the desire to see more clearly into their own hearts has been the constant preoccupation of French writers from Montaigne down to our own time. Mauriac possesses the seriousness, the single-mindedness, and the insight which belong peculiarly to the French tradition. His range may be narrow, but he goes deep. It can justifiably be claimed for him that his religion gives his work another dimension which sets him apart from most of his contemporaries, and his superb craftsmanship should be a lesson to them all.

PART TWO

Science

Albert Einstein.

Albert Einstein

by J. BRONOWSKI

Dr. Jacob Bronowski was born in Poland and educated at Jesus College, Cambridge. From 1934–42 he was Senior Lecturer in Mathematics at the University of Hull, taking an active part in the organisation of adult education classes in Yorkshire. He was responsible for the introduction of a new type of science class emphasising the historical and social development of the sciences and their relation to general culture. His chief personal interest lies in the relation of the arts and science.

In 1942 he was head of a series of mathematical and statistical units planning the economic bombing of Germany and later Japan. In 1945–6 he was scientific deputy of the Chief of Staff's Mission which reported on atomic damage in Japan. His first broadcast was made on the night of the Bikini explosion and was called: 'Mankind at the Crossroads.'

He has worked for U.N.E.S.C.O., has been Carnegie Visiting Professor at the Massachusetts Institute of Technology and is now Director of the Coal Research Establishment of the National Coal Board.

His books include *The Poet's Defence, William Blake, A Man Without a Mask, The Face of Violence,* and *The Common Sense of Science.* His broadcast on Einstein created great interest, and he is well known to a large public through his appearances both on radio and television.

I

THE death of Einstein has closed an heroic age in science. His was an heroic age in two ways. First, its scientific discoveries reached to the roots of our conception of the world, and made a revolution in thought. In Einstein's lifetime the concepts of large-scale and of small-scale physics were made over and created afresh, and much of this creation was his own work. He helped to make his an age which profoundly changed our view of the relation between man and nature.

And second, in Einstein's lifetime the scientific tradition was challenged more persistently perhaps than at any time since Galileo died. The unwritten axioms of free speculation and open discussion on which the scientific method rests were attacked first by militarism, then by intolerance, and then by secrecy. To the end of his life, Einstein defended his fellow scientists against these, not because they were special beings, but because they were human beings. What he loved in science was the play of the human mind conforming to no limits except the facts of Nature. To Einstein, science lived by the breath of democracy.

These two sides of the man combine in the picture the world still has of him, which is rounder than that of a great specialist. The world has seen and seized in Einstein's thought some gift of imagination which has leapt from his mind to ours, and which has shown us Nature not as a ready-made machine but as an exciting and largely unread book filled with unforeseen speculations. Einstein remade the outlook of his age and of those that will follow as I think it has been remade only twice before in the history of Europe since the Renaissance: once by Isaac Newton, and once by Charles Darwin.

There are of course people who do not see science in this way, as an intellectual force which has exploded and is now remaking the beliefs of men. These people find in science only the technical inventions, the comforts which brighten and the gadgets which threaten their morning shave and their evening drink. Educated in a language in which science is not understood, they still regard the work of scientists as a crust on our commonplace living and thinking. But what Newton did, what Darwin did, what Einstein has done, is to penetrate our lives to the core by a process of intellectual discovery far deeper, and more radical, than the invention of the aeroplane, or even of printing.

The great revolutionary thinkers in science have been what I have called them, thinkers even more than inventors and experimenters. And it is not the complexity, but the simplicity of their thought which made it, and makes it, a challenge to everything that the rest of the world has taken for granted; which makes it a challenge which three times now has conquered the thinking world.

Newton, Darwin and Einstein were none of them in any sense brilliant thinkers. None of them was quick at academic research, or crackling with the fireworks of invention. All three were fairly slow boys at school and at college. All three made their discoveries outside the universities, in solitary and rather forbidding work. And all three brought to the study of Nature the searching simplicity which hermits once turned on their visions.

2

Albert Einstein was born in a Jewish family in South Germany on March 14th, 1879. His father did not do well in business, and moved to Switzerland and later to Italy, always in search of better luck. The boy Albert was left behind at school in Germany and ran away. Later he went to college in Switzerland, but he did not distinguish himself, because (as he himself tells) he could not become interested in much of the university curriculum even in his own subject, which was physics. When he had taken his degree he had no university prospects and he had to take a job as a minor official in the Swiss patent office. He did his own thinking in the evenings, and he was still working in the Swiss patent office when he published his first great papers in 1905.

This was the *annus mirabilis*, the wonderful year in which the young man of twenty-six wrote three papers which made outstanding advances in three separate branches of physics. They were a paper on the nature of light, a paper on those small movements on the trembling surface of liquids or in tobacco smoke which are called (after the nineteenth-century botanist who first observed them) the Brownian movement, and the famous paper which formulated the Special Theory of Relativity. To the world at large Einstein's name is now linked simply with Relativity. This is not unfair, because certainly Relativity is his largest achievement, in the intellectual revolution which it set off, and in the solitariness with which Einstein worked on it. Relativity is the monolithic thought, and the most adventurous. By contrast, Einstein's other early work of which I have spoken was related to the new quantum physics, and was therefore based on ideas which had been published by Max Planck in 1900, and on which then and ever since numbers of bright young physicists were working. Yet we must not forget that in these early papers, and for ten or fifteen years afterwards, Einstein was also a leader in framing the concepts of quantum physics. Everything he did that year has the same simple intellectual grandeur. It looks into the heart of physics.

3

Let me play the doctor as well as the historian for a moment and lay bare the heart of physics as it was in 1905. The heart seemed sound, but it had developed a small murmur which was nagging at the peace of mind of more thoughtful scientists. That is, the triumphant laws in which Newton, more than two hundred years before, had given order to Nature could still be tested, day in and day out, and found right almost everywhere. But only *almost* everywhere. There was a small murmur of exceptions. The planet Mercury was not quite keeping time; the speed of light refused to behave as classical physics expected; and the electrons which had been discovered recently, in 1897, seemed to change their mass as they changed their speed. These could of course be taken as three minor irregularities, and although physicists could not ignore them, few of them were looking for more than minor ways to tinker with Newton's laws in order to make them cover these exceptions.

The minor adjustments were not getting physics forward, and it is characteristic that Einstein never had any truck with them. From the outset he looked for no ingenious gloss on the laws of physics, and for no minute error of formulation. He set himself to reach the unwritten assumptions on which the laws themselves were built, and asked whether it might not be there that the flaw in the physics of the nineteenth century was hidden.

These unwritten assumptions had been clear to Isaac Newton in 1666 when he had made his great discoveries as a young man of twenty-three. I have already said that Newton had just that directness of mind which Einstein now exercised. Newton knew what assumptions he was making: he had simply found them unavoidable. The lesser scientists who followed him, however, had rarely spared these assumptions a thought.

Put in scientific terms, Newton's assumptions were that space and time are given to us absolutely. They are, as it were, fixed boxes in which the events of the world occur, and they are the same for every observer. Put more generally, the assumptions take for granted a sharp division between the observer and the natural world which he observes. Classical physics saw Nature as a chain or network of events which unrolls itself in imperturbable sequence, and of which the observer is a witness but not a link. The observer since Newton's day had been a god, altogether outside the machine of the physical world.

What Einstein, from the beginning of his thinking, asked about this majestic view was not whether it is true, in some abstract sense—whether it can be metaphysically held—but whether it is practical. Does science in fact record impersonal events? Can it separate the fact from the finding, and distil the event from our observation of it? Once the question is asked, the answer is plain; and the answer is No. Physics as we actually practise it does not consist of events; it consists of observations. And between the event and those who observe it there must pass a signal, a ray of light perhaps, a wave or an impulse, which simply cannot be taken out of the observation. Event, signal, and observation: this is the relationship which Einstein saw as the fundamental unit in physics. Relativity is the understanding of the world not as events but as relations.

4

Something like this had been said by philosophers for some time: that science must get rid of abstractions and make its system only out of what is in fact observed. Einstein himself acknowledged his intellectual debt to philosophers of science, Ernst Mach in Vienna, Henri Poincaré in Paris, and the first and greatest sceptic about our habits in and outside science, the eighteenth-century British philosopher, David Hume. But it is one thing to lay down a philosophic dictum how science should or should not be carried out, and another to persuade the man in the laboratory, or the man working with a slide rule and pencil and paper. Einstein was the first practising scientist who took this philosophy of science seriously, as something more than a pious impractical hope. He put it into equations, and within a few years physicists were astonished to find that it explained the erratic behaviour of Mercury, and predicted the bending of light near the sun. It had linked mass and energy from Einstein's first papers.

I want to underline the content of these ideas, because they go beyond the field of physics. This is a view of science, and indeed of all knowledge, not as a mechanical record, but as an activity. Einstein had not asked himself what space and time are, abstractly; he had asked how physical observers carry out the process of measuring them. For example, how do two observers at a distance apart compare their times? They can do so only by sending a signal from one to the other, and the signal itself takes time to travel through the space between them. It follows that there is no way in which we can define 'now' for all observers everywhere, at once. Every observer has only his own 'here and now.' In our experience of the physical world, space and time cannot be wholly separated from one another; each is part of a single reality.

And this is not an abstract background like Euclid's space. Einstein's space-time is a real medium in which physical processes act and are observed. It is given its structure by the matter which it contains, and this matter bends and shapes it because the function of space and time as scientific concepts is just this—to enclose matter.

These are the deep and challenging ideas with which Einstein revolutionised large- and small-scale physics from 1905 onwards. And it will now be plain why their influence has been so much wider than science. They are universal ideas; they reach below the methods of mathematics and the laws of physics, to our basic conception of the relationship between man and the world.

These ideas do not apply only to space and time. I have already said that one puzzle since 1897 had been the relation between the mass and the energy of a fast-moving electron. Several men (Poincaré among them) had been feeling their way towards the answer which Einstein found in his first paper on Relativity in 1905. Again Einstein asked: Can we define the mass of a body without allowing for its motion, and therefore for its energy? And again the answer is No. These two Nos—the No which denies that space can be separated from time, and the No which denies that mass can be separated from energy—are related. Our physical experience is more of a piece than our pigeon-holing minds had let us think.

5

The new concept of mass has become famous because it underlies the conversion of matter into energy, which was demonstrated spectacularly in the explosion of the atomic bombs. This has made the formula, that energy is equivalent to mass multiplied by the square of the velocity of light, that is

$$E = Mc^2,$$

familiar and moving to millions who know no other mathematics. And we should be moved by Einstein's equation, but not because it has helped to kill more than a hundred thousand people. We should be moved because the equation gives a new unity to Nature, no less deep than those which the imaginative artists and poets have tried to find. Energy is mass, mass energy, is a unity of the same kind as Keats created in the closing lines to the *Ode on a Grecian Urn*,

> Beauty is truth, truth beauty,—that is all
> Ye know on earth, and all ye need to know.

Einstein's preoccupation and achievement was the search for these unities, of which those which involve mass are of particular interest. Few people talk about the mass of a body, and indeed Newton had great difficulty in framing a definition of mass, and failed. We always talk about the weight of a body. And for the next ten years Einstein asked himself a new question: Why is it that mass and weight are always related? Why do we experience mass as weight? When I throw a ball, I overcome its mass; when I lift it, I overcome its weight. Why are the two actions linked? Einstein answered this question in the General Theory of Relativity which was published in 1915—published, that is, in Germany early in the first world war.

For answer, Einstein gave a new picture of the field of gravity round a body. A massive body, he said, distorts the space-time in which it lies; it forms, as it were, a hollow round itself. When I drop a ball and it falls, it is really rolling like a marble into the hollow made by the earth. And the earth itself is like a larger marble which flies round the hollow in space-time made by the sun.

This is an attractive formulation which can be seized and pictured at once. But if it is to be an effective picture, if what it describes is truly a distortion of space and time, then everything which crosses the sun's hollow must be drawn inwards: not only a ball, but a ray of light as well. So, in 1919, two expeditions went out to watch the eclipse of the sun in the spring of that year, in order to see whether light which passes near the sun curves into its hollow. The expeditions, headed by Arthur Eddington, announced their findings in November 1919, at one of the most dramatic meetings ever held at the Royal Society. The findings tallied with Einstein's forecast. Light does bend towards the sun, and by approximately the amount which the General Theory of Relativity predicted. Einstein had made gravitation a behaviour of space and time.

6

I have drawn attention to one wartime date and I must underline the other. The success of the General Theory of Relativity in uncovering a new and strange phenomenon of Nature, the curvature of light within space, was announced to the world in 1919. This was barely a year after the armistice, and while the peace treaties were still being wrangled over at Versailles. The accident of date had, I think an influence on Einstein's later outlook and career. Before I consider the scientific work of his last years, therefore, I will return briefly to his biography, which I left when he was twenty-six, in 1905.

In the next years, he became both a leader and an *enfant terrible* of physics. Einstein first appeared before a large gathering of physicists in 1909, and here and at a famous Solvay meeting in 1911 he made a deep impression on his fellow scientists. What impressed them was his ability to unite his own ideas of Relativity with those of quantum physics, which were then being hammered out by them all. He was offered and accepted a chair in Prague. A little later he went back to become a professor in Switzerland. By 1914 a special post had in effect been created for him as Director of the Kaiser Wilhelm Research Institute for Physics in Berlin.

At this moment the first world war broke out. The German Government was anxious to muster intellectual support for its ambition, and put pressure on its leading men to speak for it. Eighty-three of them were persuaded to sign a manifesto addressed 'an die Kulturwelt' in support of Germany's actions in the world war. The list of those who signed makes sad reading: it includes Paul Ehrlich and Gerhart Hauptmann, Max Reinhardt and Wilamowitz, Röntgen and Planck and Ostwald, Sudermann and Humperdinck and Siegfried Wagner. Einstein did not sign. He and three others issued a counter-manifesto against militarism. He was then, as he was afterwards, fearless in his love of peace; and then as afterwards, German patriots did not forgive him.

Even as a young man, Einstein had chosen Swiss in place of German nationality when he had the chance, because the regimentation of Germany had outraged him. He chose to become a German again after 1918 as a gesture of support to the new Weimar Republic. But the Weimar Republic did little to save him from attack when after 1919 the fame of his work had made him a public figure. He was attacked on two flanks.

On one flank were the rising Nazis. To them Einstein and his theories were, in the phrase of that day, simply 'un-German'. The ancient phrase has an unhappy ring, for in the years between such phrases have become common in many countries to describe whatever intellectual dissent is disliked there. Thus the Nazis hated Einstein as a Swiss Jew with un-German ideas.

Meanwhile men across the Rhine, with bitter memories of the long and bloody war, resented him as a German scientist of whom too much fuss was being made. In the face of these feuds, Einstein received the Nobel Prize for Physics in 1921—with a citation in which the cautious awarding committee, however, made no reference to Relativity. When soon after he went to Paris to give some lectures, he had to be hidden from French nationalists there for fear that they would demonstrate against him. Twenty years later the demonstrators were collaborating with the Nazis, and Einstein had been forced to flee across the Atlantic out of reach of both. I ought to add that those who remember his visit to Paris in 1922 recall with pleasure, when they speak of it, that Einstein brought his violin and played quartets with his fellow scientists.

He went to America when life had been made intolerable for him in Germany in 1932, and he worked at the Institute for Advanced Study in Princeton from then on. Up to this time he had been a pacifist. Now it seemed to him that, like other doctrines, pacifism had to be looked at afresh to see whether it fitted the facts of the world as it then was. On August 2nd, 1939, Einstein broke with a lifetime of pacifist belief as only he could have done. He wrote to tell President Roosevelt that recent work in atomic physics which had been disclosed to him privately made it probable that an atomic bomb could be constructed. And he advised Roosevelt that, since work on atomic fission was in progress (ironically, at the Kaiser Wilhelm Institute) in Berlin, it must be feared that the Germans would try to make such a bomb. The marvellous youth who at twenty-six had first equated mass with energy, now at sixty saw the equation threaten the world.

7

A new war did not stop Einstein from thinking, working, learning. His ambition remained what it had been from boyhood. He who had braided together so many strands of experience, time with space, mass with energy, gravitation with space-time, wanted to braid the whole of our physical experience into a single theory. He went on looking for the unity within all Nature. One field in physics still stood apart: the field of electric and magnetic forces. Einstein spent his life from about 1930 in trying to link this with the field of gravitation.

It is pertinent that when Einstein wrote about his boyhood, he recalled two events as turning points. At the age of four or five, he had been fascinated to see a magnetic compass needle turn steadily towards the north, wherever it was held, and at that moment he realised that the laws of Nature are universal. And at the age of ten or thereabouts, he learned some geometry and was excited by discovering a proof of the theorem of Pythagoras for himself. This mixture of magnetism with geometry became in a sense the guiding method of his later work.

There have been other attempts to unite electro-magnetic forces with the other physical forces in a single picture of the world. Einstein himself made several. He made the last early in 1953. This was essentially an extension of the work by which Clerk Maxwell in the 1860s linked electricity and magnetism with light, and so showed that light is an electro-magnetic wave—and incidentally foretold the existence of radio waves. In the same way, Einstein's own work in General Relativity had already connected gravitation with light, and indeed had implied that gravitation is a wave which travels at the speed of light.

Einstein's attempt to forge this last link between the physical forces differed from the attempts of others. I can put the difference in this way, descriptively: that Einstein looked not merely for a formal combination, but for a fusing together of the two opposed kinds of symmetry which Clerk Maxwell's equations and his own Relativity equations have. He looked once again for an underlying structure, below the equations, to give unity to all the physical phenomena of the world.

In one respect Einstein's recent theories were at odds with those of other physicists. The new generation of physicists who have grown up in quantum physics have, for the past twenty-five years, abandoned the hope of making a model of the small-scale world in such a way that every effect has a cause. Instead, they have accepted a Principle of Uncertainty which says that there is an essential limit to our prediction of minute events, because there is an essential limit to our description of these events. We can never know exactly which of two alternative paths one of the tiny units of Nature, an electron, a light quantum, or part of a nucleus, will take. This is because we can never describe fully the state in which it is—say, its position and its speed at the same time.

Einstein is almost the only great physicist who steadfastly opposed this view, and refused to believe that Nature deals in chance and probability. Perhaps his refusal was not based altogether on intellectual grounds, but was a personal conviction which as a young man he might have called prejudice. The theories which Einstein proposed to the end of his life are all strictly causal theories. Rather oddly, his last equations can be shown to lead to contradictions when applied to very small units of matter, if these units can be chosen arbitrarily. Einstein held that the contradictions must resolve themselves because the units as they actually occur in Nature must somehow arise out of, and be fixed by, the equations themselves.

That is, if Einstein's last field equations are to be true, they must contain within themselves the conditions which make them applicable only to matter in the precise sizes in which matter ultimately occurs. Einstein held that the fundamental units of Nature have not been fixed arbitrarily. True, his equations are continuous—they contain no basic jumps to fix the size of a natural unit of energy or matter. Yet in his seventies he cheerfully set about a task which to others seemed hopeless, of finding whether the quantum jumps can be made to grow out of his continuous equations. He hoped to show that the proton, the quantum and the electron, and all the other building bricks of matter, of energy, and of electricity, are determined in their natural sizes by some internal limitations in his field equations.

In his own words, Einstein would have no truck with discontinuity and chance in the equations of Nature. The occurrence of chance, he held, is only a confession of our own failure to see to the heart of things. Because at the heart of things, he believed, there must stand a rational god and not, in his telling phrase, 'ein würfelnder Gott'—a god at dice. It is a powerful idea, but I ought to say that it is shared by no other great physicist now. I suspect that the younger men think it as old-fashioned, with the smack of an outworn metaphysic, as Einstein once thought his own elders.

8

Einstein lived his last years quietly in a suburban house in a suburban street in Princeton. He was saddened by the events in which the last war ended and which followed it. Towards the end of his life he said of his letter to Roosevelt which initiated the atomic bomb, 'Had I known that the Germans would not succeed in producing an atomic bomb, I would not have lifted a finger.' He refused the presidency of Israel because, he said, he had 'neither the natural ability nor the experience to deal with human beings.' Yet he was endlessly good-humoured and modest with them. He was patient even with the many strangers who sneaked up to his front porch and had their wives photograph them as if they were just coming out of the great man's house. If Einstein had any impatience left, it was to the end, as it had always been, impatience with authority.

Einstein was one of the intellectual heroes of history; and such heroes, like Newton and like Darwin, are always two-fold —rebels in their work, and heretics in society. He prized the integrity of man's personality more highly than man's science. Back in the 1920s he said, in some desultory interview, that two discoveries might destroy mankind: atomic energy and universal thought-reading. The wry prophecy sums up Einstein's passions. He saw deeply into Nature, her promise and her threat, but he was not too abstracted to remember the fallibility of men. For him the key to the world lay in the minds of men. He fought for freedom of the mind from his rebellious schooldays and the manifesto of 1914 to his dying day. In his last years he spoke out constantly against the inquisition which then darkened America. But even his love for science and for freedom was not abstract. These were for him the high places of the human mind, and he loved those; he loved people.

His richness of sympathy made him a symbol to an age. It carried his ideas beyond their scientific setting so that, more profoundly than the work of any philosopher, they changed the outlook of philosophy. All his ideas grew from one conception: that the world is not given to us absolutely, but is something which we actively observe and thereby shape. For Einstein was a practical thinker; to him, truth was that which is experienced in action. When he died, on April 18th, 1955, Einstein had created a new empiricism, as revolutionary and as lasting as that with which Galileo laid the foundation of science.

Sir Alexander Fleming

by L. J. LUDOVICI

Having come down from Oxford, L. J. Ludovici joined a firm of publishers in London 'to learn the business.' Later he was literary and publicity director of a publishing house which he helped to found.

When the war came he joined the R.A.F. as an aircraftman and was demobilised with the rank of squadron leader. At the end of hostilities he transferred to the Air Historical Branch of the Air Ministry and wrote a narrative concerned with one aspect of the R.A.F.'s contribution to the war.

He later combined work as editorial consultant to a publishing firm with writing. His books include biographies of Sir Alexander Fleming, discoverer of penicillin, and of Sir Alliott Verdon-Roe, the air pioneer (called *The Challenging Sky*). He has also translated from the French Professor Edmond Vermeil's famous study of contemporary Germany entitled *The German Scene*.

IT is said that all the world knows the manner in which Alexander Fleming discovered penicillin. Yet fanciful journalists still persist in mingling fact and fiction. A story written in a well-known magazine soon after his death in March 1955 gave its readers an affecting picture of the inevitably pretty but lachrymose young nurse whose tears put the scientist on the road to his great discovery!

There is, however, one remarkable and curious aspect of Fleming's life which is far from widely known. Woven into it were a series of apparently unrelated events, yet without any single one of them it probably would not have achieved the climax it did. 'There were so many of these events and they were all so purposive that we feel driven to deny their being due to mere chance,' said Professor C. A. Pannett, his old friend and colleague, in the address he delivered at St. Paul's Cathedral on the day Fleming was buried there.

It is these mysterious workings which give Fleming's life story a perennial fascination.

I

Alexander Fleming was born at Lochfield Farm, near Darvel, in Ayrshire on August 6th, 1881. His father had married twice, and Alexander was the third of four children by his second wife, Grace Morton, of Darvel. The Flemings were a family representative of many like them who inhabit the Scottish countryside. They were farmers from time immemorial, and handed on from generation to generation the same persistent characteristics: a profound sense of independence, limitless tenacity, patience and industry, a clear-headed grasp of reality and a taciturnity which concealed an essential warmness of heart. His father died when he was seven. His mother at once assumed the responsibility of running the farm and maintaining a large family. She stood at the centre of the affections both of her own and her stepchildren, between whom no division existed, and this was perhaps the best testimony to her qualities.

Alexander began his schooldays when he was five. Daily with his sister and two brothers he tramped a little over a mile across the fields and through Lochfield Glen on his way to Loudoun Moor School. This 'wee school up on the hill' was a single classroom in which a succession of teachers imparted the rudiments of knowledge to him. According to his brother, Robert, 'he took easily to his lessons and certainly had an alert intelligence and excellent powers of observation.' These powers of observation were sharpened by his preoccupation with Nature. Every spare moment of his boyhood was spent tramping the remote uplands surrounding Lochfield Farm. The habits of birds and beasts enthralled him, and he enjoyed the freedom of a world of his own.

At the age of ten he began attending the big school at Darvel. He now walked four miles downhill into Darvel at eight o'clock each morning and four miles uphill into Lochfield each afternoon at the close of the school day, winter and summer. Sometimes he was soaked to the skin, but he tells us how he revelled in drying himself before a peat fire. At Darvel School he first made contact with town-dwelling boys. 'Living as we did at the end of the road and on the edge of the moor,' he observed, 'we considered ourselves a bit better than the boys in the town. They did not know how to climb, they did not know how to guddle trout in the burn and they did not know where to find peewits' eggs.' Constant roaming in the open air and the performance of various tasks on the farm laid the foundations of a sturdy frame and of the health and stamina which were afterwards such an asset to him.

When he was twelve it was decided that he should continue his studies at Kilmarnock Academy. Kilmarnock was sixteen miles away and a daily journey to and fro was out of the question since there was no transport available. He therefore boarded out in Kilmarnock, attended school during the week and returned to Lochfield at weekends. Each Friday evening during term-time he strode home from Newmilns station, a distance of over six miles. On Monday mornings at cockcrow he repeated his march in the opposite direction, though he was sometimes able to catch the old horse-bus into Darvel. 'Nowadays,' he has said in describing this phase of his life, 'it would be regarded as a crime to allow a schoolboy to walk six miles. But it certainly kept me fit.' His memories of Kilmarnock Academy were of a 'very big school on the top of a hill, a very good school then, where a system of constant examinations kept us boys always at it.'

2

After about eighteen months in Kilmarnock Academy Alexander went south. In 1895 he came to London to his brother Thomas, who was practising as an oculist in the Marylebone district. Once in London he resumed his schooling at the Polytechnic, where, according to him, 'I found that the work which the boys were doing was just what I had done two years before.' In 1897, when he was about sixteen, he left the Polytechnic ('forced on me by economic reasons'), and began work in the office of a shipping company in Leadenhall Street, where his wage packet was as unexciting as his prospects. During this period he devoted himself to spare-time soldiering and joined the London Scottish Volunteers. It enabled him to spend his leisure in the open air and to improve his skill as a marksman. He represented the London Scottish in team-shoots at Bisley and carried off several prizes. He was also an excellent swimmer and won a place in the regimental team.

One day he played water polo for his team against St. Mary's Hospital, and it was a sporting encounter which provides a unique example of the opportune interventions of destiny in his life. When he was about eighteen he received a small legacy and considered how he might improve his circumstances. 'My brother Thomas pushed me into medicine,' he tells us. He then had to choose a medical school and there were twelve of these in London. 'I did not know any of them,' he continues, 'but I had played water polo against St. Mary's so to St. Mary's I went. The choice of a school for this very insufficient reason had a great influence on my career, for at the time I joined St. Mary's as a student, Almroth Wright joined as a teacher in bacteriology.'

Of course it was not simply a matter of being pushed into medicine. First he had to matriculate and then sit for a hospital examination. He easily won the Senior Entrance Scholarship in Natural Science. His career in medicine had begun, whether selected for him by some wayward concatenation of events, by some deeper intuition within himself, or by the operations of a transcendental Power. And he had lighted upon a vocation perfectly suited to him. Professor Pannett has given a vivid account of his first meeting with Fleming at St. Mary's Medical School, where they appeared as competitors for a scholarship:

He was a little older and more mature than the rest of us, a quiet man with alert grey penetrating resolute eyes. From that day we became friends, and with the possession of the scholarship, his future as a doctor was decisively settled. For the first few years we were rivals but afterwards our paths diverged, yet never was this bond of friendship strained, for Fleming had that steadiness and steadfastness of character that gave the quality of security to the friendship that lasted unsullied until his death. This constancy of the man was outstanding and inspired a confidence in his friends and companions which was never misplaced. He was simple in outlook and reticent by nature, almost shy, but undeviating in pursuit of the line of conduct he thought was right, though he never ran into trouble if it could be avoided. He was often inscrutable and hid his real thoughts, but that was when he had not come to a decision in his own mind. When he made a pronouncement it was nearly always wise and certainly well considered.

On that early autumn morning how far it was from our thought that we were in the presence of one of the greatest men of the century.

At first Fleming was set on becoming a surgeon, and in 1909 was made a Fellow of the Royal College of Surgeons. Meanwhile he was offered a job in Sir Almroth Wright's laboratory soon after he qualified on August 5th, 1906, the day before his twenty-fifth birthday. Gradually he fell under the spell of Wright, a great scientist and man of culture, and he remained to work in that laboratory until the day of his own death in 1955.

It was the era of immunology, of vaccine therapy. Wright had begun preventive inoculation against typhoid by using heat-killed cultures, and proclaimed a theme which rang new in medicine. Metchnikov of the Pasteur Institute in Paris believed that the cause of immunity from infectious disease was the white corpuscle in the blood, the phagocyte. The phagocyte, is a living cell that attacks and ingests invading microbes. This is known as phagocytosis. However, Wright and his assistants showed that it was not enough for phagocytes and microbes to come together, the microbes had in some fashion to be 'prepared' before the phagocytes could swallow them. They concluded that this 'preparation' was brought about by some property in the blood serum which they named opsonin, a derivation from the Greek word *opsono*: I prepare victuals for. Bernard Shaw, who was inspired by the discovery to write his *Doctor's Dilemma*, said the microbes had to be 'buttered' for the phagocytes. It now seemed that the measurement of a man's opsonic power would make possible the development of vaccine therapy against microbic disease. If his opsonic power could be restored to normal by an appropriate dose of vaccine, then his phagocytes could deal with the invading microbes.

Dr. Leonard Colebrook, Wright's biographer, has called this 'a fundamental discovery of the first importance,' and he regards vaccine therapy as the idea which dominated medicine for almost twenty years.

Thus it was in a tonic mental climate, charged with expectations and excitements, that Fleming began his life as a bacteriologist.

3

By April 1909 Fleming had produced two fruitful pieces of research. First he suggested how Acne vulgaris (a disease marked by disfiguring pimples) could be treated by vaccines, and he also devised a simple method of serum diagnosis in syphilis which was usually diagnosed by the more complex Wassermann reaction. Oddly he was almost the first person in Britain to try out Ehrlich's salvarsan, which may also be described as the world's first chemotherapeutic remedy. Wright knew Ehrlich and it was to his laboratory that Ehrlich sent an early sample of his celebrated cure for syphilis.

The progress of Fleming's early endeavours was shattered by the outbreak of World War I a couple of days before his thirty-second birthday. Soon he was in France with Wright and a team whose business it was to investigate the appalling problems of sepsis, which was the cause of numberless casualties. They settled down in Boulogne, living in a house which Wright had taken in the Boulevard Daunau. They improvised a laboratory on the roof of the Casino, which had been the headquarters of a fencing club. Soon the halls of the Casino were lined with rows of wounded soldiers on stretchers placed close to each other.

At this time medical men were pinning their faith to chemical antiseptics which were poured into wounds 'according to the fancy of the medical officer.' Soon campaigns were started in favour of particular types of antiseptic. But how effective were these antiseptics which were being poured into wounds with such careless rapture? So far as Fleming could see soldiers treated with carbolic showed a higher percentage of gas gangrene cases than the general run of the wounded, while soldiers treated with iodine showed almost no better results than those treated in other ways. When antiseptic pastes became the fashion, wounds were plugged with these pastes, drainage was blocked and gas infection developed. Thus antiseptic pastes had to be abandoned.

Fleming viewed antiseptics with gathering scepticism, and his scepticism was intensified by two beautiful experiments he did which today rank among 'classics of the lab.' By employing a device called a slide-cell, he proved that carbolic acid in fact made a first-class culture-medium of blood. It had this effect because it killed leucocytes in a concentration at which it did no harm to bacteria. With the protective leucocytes out of the way, the microbes could grow unhindered. 'By this method,' said Fleming, 'I found carbolic acid and all other common antiseptics used in former days killed leucocytes more easily than they killed microbes. They were not likely to be very successful in the body. And they weren't.'

Taking a glass tube, he drew out several small processes to represent the diverticula which exist in all serious and recent gun-shot wounds. He then reproduced in his tube the conditions arising in a primary infection and tried to sterilise it with some of the antiseptics in common use. He was convinced that it was impossible to sterilise a wound with such an antiseptic even if it were possible to keep the substance in the wound for a long time without dilution. Wright and his team advocated the use of hypertonic saline, which caused a prompt flow of lymph from the tissues into the cavity of the wound. By this means they felt Nature's immediate response to injury could be stimulated.

This recommendation involved Wright in acrid controversy and divided the medical world against itself. On the one hand was the 'physiological school' which concentrated upon aiding the natural protective agencies of the body against infection. On the other hand was the 'antiseptic school' which aimed at killing microbes with some chemical. The problem before medical science was to discover an antiseptic which was harmless to the tissues of the body, in other words, one which did not kill the leucocytes and leave the microbes unmolested.

Fleming's experiences in France made him—to use Professor Pannett's phrase—'reticent, dour, acutely perceptive, more aware than anybody else that antiseptics were quite hopeless as therapeutic applications.' Fleming himself remained deeply interested in the natural defences of the body. 'Early in my medical career,' he said, 'I learned the real value of natural antiseptics.' Again: 'Experiments I made convinced me that probably the most effective anti-bacterial agents in the body are the cells themselves.' Nature soon recompensed him for his close study of her by revealing to him the presence of one of her most extraordinary creations whose presence in the body fends off microbic invasion.

On February 13th, 1922, Sir Almroth Wright forwarded to the Royal Society a paper by Fleming entitled: *On a Remarkable Bacteriolytic Element Found in Tissues and Secretions.* 'In this communication,' wrote Fleming, 'I wish to draw attention to a substance present in the tissues and secretions of the body, which is capable of rapidly dissolving certain bacteria. As this substance has properties akin to those of ferments, I have called it lysozyme.' Behind the deceptive formality of the words, however, lay the strange story of its discovery. It stemmed from Fleming's inquisitiveness. He was suffering from a cold and started to investigate his own nasal secretions. On the fourth day when he examined one of his cultures he noted a bright yellow microbe. But as he made the examination a tear from his eye fell upon the culture plate. The next morning when he again looked at the culture plate he found a clear space where the tear had fallen. Instantly he made the correct deduction. His tear contained a substance hostile to the microbe. At that moment his profound scepticism about antiseptics vanished, for here, revealed to him, was an antiseptic lethal to microbes yet harmless to human tissue.

Lysozyme was the essential prelude to penicillin.

4

Fleming was forty-one when he discovered lysozyme. Only a year before he had married an Irish lady, Sarah Marion McElroy, who was said to be as gay and volatile as he himself was reserved. A son was later born to them, who, when he grew up, followed in his father's footsteps and became a doctor. When Fleming was forty-seven, he was appointed Professor of Bacteriology in the University of London. He had thus reached the highest position open to him in his profession. At about the same time he discovered penicillin.

The summer of 1928 was cool and damp, encouraging the presence in the air of mould spores. We know how in damp seasons mould settles on bread, on shoes or any other object left lying about the house. Fleming was engaged upon some routine lab work which involved the periodic examination of his culture plates with a dissecting microscope. At each examination he had to remove the covers of the plates for a moment, and while the covers were off a mould spore directed by we do not know which of the winds of Heaven landed in one of them. Note that this culture plate (known as a Petri dish) was a shallow glass dish only four inches in diameter, and that it stood among others on the bench of his small laboratory. As he himself has put it: 'There are thousands of different moulds and there are thousands of different bacteria, and that chance put the mould in the right spot at the right time was like winning the Irish Sweep.'

As he looked at the culture plate in which the mould had fallen, he noted that the microbes he had been cultivating, which happened to be near the mould, were dissolving. Once again he instantly made the correct deduction. A clear space round the place where the mould had fallen meant that the mould was giving out a substance lethal to microbes. Since the mould was later identified as a penicillium, he called this substance penicillin. 'But for that previous experience [with lysozyme],' he said, 'I would have thrown the plate away, as many bacteriologists must have done before. Instead of casting out the contaminated culture with appropriate language, I made some investigations.'

He published the result of these investigations in the *British Journal of Experimental Pathology* (Vol. X, p. 226) on May 10th, 1929. His paper was soberly headed: 'The Antibacterial Action of Cultures of a Penicillium, with special reference to their use in Isolation of B. influenzæ.' He reported that penicillin had the power of arresting the growth of microbes, it had the power of dissolving them and of destroying them. Moreover, it was not toxic to animals and harmless to the body cells. 'It was this non-toxicity to leucocytes that convinced me that some day it would come into its own as a therapeutic agent,' he has written.

He tells us also how he 'collected a couple of juniors in a lab' and did 'a little bit of work' and 'got as far as we could.' Then 'we got stuck—short of chemical knowledge.' The difficulty was that penicillin behaved erratically, and is what scientists describe as 'labile.' It was a cruel paradox, but Fleming could not produce it for use as a therapeutic agent, intensive and brilliant though his investigations were. He therefore let penicillin rest and went on to other things. Meanwhile the remarkable success of sulphanilamide had brought chemotherapy into the foreground, and vaccine therapy was for the time being compelled to take second place. The two modes of treatment seemed incompatible, yet Fleming, with his acute gift for synthesis, advocated that they should be used in combination. These views he communicated to the *British Medical Journal*.

Nineteen thirty-seven is a year worthy of mention, for then Professor H. W. Florey and Dr. E. B. Chain of the Sir William Dunn School of Pathology at Oxford completed their researches on lysozyme, the substance Fleming had discovered in 1922. And now came the wholly unforeseen move by the hand of destiny which led to the resuscitation of penicillin. Dr. Chain was searching for agents with powers similar to those of lysozyme, and accordingly conducted a thorough examination of all the literature he could find on the subject. What he found was a number of papers dealing with microbes able to produce substances which inhibited the growth of other microbes. As a biochemist his interest in this field of research impelled him to read through these papers. By the sheerest chance he came across Fleming's paper on penicillin which had appeared in the *British Journal of Experimental Pathology*. Moreover, the close link between the departments of chemistry and pathology, which at Oxford then existed under one roof, encouraged

Alexander Fleming.

Thomas Hunt Morgan

H. J. Muller

Chain to pursue the subject. At last he made up his mind that penicillin might provide a fruitful field of investigation. He talked it over with Florey on their way home one evening, and it is said they made up their minds to start work on penicillin just as they passed beneath a great elm at the entrance to the park.

What must be made clear is that neither Florey nor Chain had anything in mind other than a piece of academic research; they had no idea that their consummation of Fleming's work would lead to so great an alleviation of human suffering. In August 1942 *The Times* devoted a leader to the subject of penicillin and drew from Sir Almroth Wright this rejoinder:

> In the leading article on penicillin in your issue yesterday, you refrained from putting the laurel wreath for this discovery round anybody's brow. I would, with your permission, supplement your article by pointing out that, on the principle *palmam qui meruit ferat*, it should be decreed to Professor Alexander Fleming of this research laboratory. For he is the discoverer of penicillin and was the author also of the original suggestion that this substance might prove to have important applications in medicine.

When honours were showered upon Fleming and he was almost everywhere acknowledged as the discoverer of penicillin, certain critics, among them the science correspondents of some newspapers, persisted in claiming that he was extremely lucky, that far more should have been heard of Florey, Chain and their 'Oxford team,' who made penicillin available to all as a therapeutic agent. But nothing can change the facts. One September day in 1928 Fleming discovered penicillin, correctly deduced its significance and was responsible for naming it. However, it would have been invidious to select any single person for particular honour in a case like this. Fleming, Florey and Chain were jointly awarded the Nobel Prize, and Fleming and Florey were knighted. Each had made a vital contribution in presenting a great remedy to the world.

> I might have claimed that I came to the conclusion as a result of serious study of the literature and deep thought, that valuable antibacterial substances were made by moulds, and that I set

out to investigate the problem. That would have been untrue, and I preferred to tell the truth, that penicillin started as a chance observation. My only merit is that I did not neglect the observation, and that I pursued the subject as a bacteriologist.

So Fleming said modestly in his Nobel Prize Lecture which he delivered in Stockholm on December 11th, 1945. Moreover, he hardly ever failed to draw attention to what he himself described as 'the brilliant work of the Oxford team.'

The consummation of Fleming's work by Florey, Chain and others does, however, raise the problem of due financial reward. They received nothing but the money from their Nobel award. It has long been a tradition in science that its discoveries should be given free to the world. This tradition was decisively broken in the case of prontosil, a drug produced by the chemists of I. G. Farben, the great German combine. 'Before announcing the merits of prontosil,' Fleming has written, 'the industries interested in its production perfected their preparation and covered it with patents. Fortunately for humanity, Trefouels and his colleagues in Paris demonstrated that prontosil in reality acted only after having been broken down in the organism, and that its action was entirely due to the liberation of sulphanilamide. This last, more simple, could do all that prontosil did, and was not covered by patents.' Clearly Fleming was on the side of the long-established tradition.

But when penicillin was being developed, efforts were again made to patent certain of the processes involved in its production. 'I have heard that patents have been taken out both in England and America,' Fleming remarked in New York in 1945, 'but when the basic information has been given free to the world, it seems a pity that people should seek to make capital out of matters of detail. But perhaps it is a necessity in our present social system.' Then he added with a hint of distaste: 'Fortunately I am not concerned with this aspect of penicillin.'

We are therefore left with the reflection that what the men of science gave free has been a limitless source of profit not only to patentees but to all those concerns which have been making penicillin. And we can wonder also whether drugs like penicillin should not in future be manufactured under the auspices of the State, on behalf of the whole community, and on a no-profit basis.

Fleming was himself aware of the amazing thread of chance which ran through his life. 'The story of penicillin,' he once said, 'has a certain romance in it and helps to illustrate the amount of chance, or fortune, or fate, or destiny, call it what you will, in anybody's career.' It is exquisite irony that the militant disbeliever in antiseptics should discover one of the most perfect antiseptics of all, and that his mind should so curiously have been prepared for it when he found lysozyme.

Yet among such speculations we must not forget that Fleming was 'a great technician of the lab,' as one of his colleagues has described him, and that he had reached the heights of his profession before he became renowned as the discoverer of penicillin.

Fleming's first wife had died in 1949, but in April 1953 he married Mrs. Amalia Cotsouris (Vourcka), a Greek bacteriologist who had worked in his laboratories at St. Mary's Hospital. In September 1954 he announced his retirement. He did not intend to be idle; he declared that he would probably concentrate on trying to discover more about immunity to human diseases. He was indeed returning to those great themes in medical research which Wright had enunciated in the earliest days of his career, though they could never have been far away from his thoughts at any time.

He died suddenly in March 1955, and was buried in St. Paul's Cathedral on the 16th of that month. In a very moving funeral oration, his old friend Professor C. A. Pannett said: " . . . by his work he relieved more suffering than any other living man, perhaps more than any man who has ever lived."

Can a nobler epitaph adorn the memory of anybody who has lived among us?

Thomas Hunt Morgan

by S. C. HARLAND, D.Sc., F.R.S.

Sydney Cross Harland was educated at Scarborough High Schoo and King's College, London. He became Assistant Superintendent of Agriculture of St. Vincent in the British West Indies, and later Professor of Botany and Genetics at the Imperial College of Tropical Agriculture in Trinidad. He has also acted as general adviser to the State Cotton Industry, San Paulo, in Brazil.

He was elected a Fellow of the Royal Society in 1943 and is now Professor of Botany in the University of Manchester, and a member of the Agricultural Research Council.

Very appropriately his chief hobby is gardening. And of course travel.

THOMAS HUNT MORGAN, zoologist, embryologist and geneticist, was born on September 25th, 1866, in Lexington, Kentucky, being the elder son of Charlton Hunt Morgan of that State and of Ellen Key Morgan, *née* Howard, from Baltimore. At the age of twenty Morgan graduated B.S. from the University of Kentucky. After a short period of postgraduate work in that university he took up studies at the Johns Hopkins University, Baltimore, proceeding to the degree of Ph.D. in 1890. His career subsequently may be divided into three convenient periods. The first period from 1891 to 1904 was spent as Professor of Zoology at Bryn Mawr College for Women. He then became Professor of Experimental Zoology at Columbia University, New York City, from 1904 to 1928. Finally from 1928 to 1945 he was Professor of Biology at the California Institute of Technology, Pasadena, being director of the William G. Kerckhoff laboratories.

In common with other biologists of his time, Morgan as a boy was keenly interested in natural history and at a tender age collected fossils, birds and birds' eggs. At the age of twenty-one, just after graduation, he visited the marine laboratory of Alpheus Hyatt at Annesquam, Massachusetts. He did research work in the summers of 1888 and 1889 at the U.S. Fish Commission laboratory at Wood's Hole. In 1890 he was awarded the Adam Bruce Fellowship, which enabled him to visit Europe. At Naples he met Hans Driesch, whose influence perhaps led him into the domain of experimental embryology. Naples saw him again in 1899 and 1900. From 1902 onwards he was actively associated with the Marine Biological laboratories at Wood's Hole.

Towards the end of his career he set up a private laboratory at Corona del Mar, California, but died in 1945 before he could enjoy the slower tempo of retirement.

Early in his career as a student Morgan was noteworthy for his critical scepticism and his forthright and independent views on controversial matters. By the time he moved to Columbia he had published eighty-four papers, many of them important contributions to experimental embryology, as well as two books; one of the latter, a now almost forgotten work, had the significant title *Evolution and Adaptation*.

Had Morgan not left Bryn Mawr for Columbia his career would doubtless have continued in his favourite field of embryology. But at Columbia he ran into a group of workers who had greatly been inspired by that brilliant cytologist E. B. Wilson, and when at the suggestion of Castle and his colleagues he began to use *Drosophila melanogaster*—the fruit fly—as experimental material he founded a school of genetical research unparalleled in its fecundity and in the richness of the ideas which it has contributed to modern biology. It is not too much to say that the school founded by Morgan, associated with the names of his chief colleagues, Muller, Bridges, Sturtevant, has played a predominant rôle in the establishment of genetics as the most quantitatively exact branch of biology which it is today.

It is worth while returning for a moment to the situation in Columbia during the first years of the twentieth century. The chromosome basis of heredity was supported strongly by E. B. Wilson, who from 1905–12 had contributed a series of classical studies on chromosomes. Other students of Wilson, namely Montgomery, McClung and Stevens, had also made important contributions. 'The thrill of these new discoveries,' says Muller, 'inspired even the undergraduates studying biology at Columbia College, and a crop of them growing up under the influence of the courses given by Wilson's former students were attracted into the Drosophila work which

Morgan, thanks to the suggestion of Castle *et al.* had found to provide so fruitful a lead for the investigation of these questions.'

Here at Columbia were the leading cytologist (Wilson) and the leading experimental morphologist (Morgan) of the United States. Wilson had the bolder mind. He believed that the Sutton-Boveri conclusions regarding the cytological basis of the mechanism of Mendelian heredity were sound. In 1909 Wilson wrote a paper entitled 'The Cell in Relation to Heredity and Evolution.' In 1911 he defended the chromosome theory in a public lecture, 'The Physical Basis of Heredity.' Later in the same year he advanced the fundamental concept that in the production of every character the entire germinal complex is concerned.

Morgan was slower to accept these new ideas, although ultimately he became the leading protagonist of the chromosome mechanism of heredity. In 1909, five years after he went to Columbia, he was still sceptical about the concept of Mendelian factors or hereditary determiners. As a substitute he proposed a theory of alternative states of stability of the protoplasm. And in 1910 he attacked the chromosome theory of heredity in the following words: 'Our general conclusion is, therefore, that the essential process in the formation of the two kinds of gametes of hybrids, in respect to each pair of contrasted characters, is a reaction or response to the cells, and is not due to a material segregation of the two kinds of material contributed by the germ cells of the two parents.' In the same paper he adopted the attitude of suspended judgment in regard to the chromosomal basis of sex determination. 'I could, by ignoring the difficulties and by emphasising the important discoveries that have been made, have implied that the problem of sex determination has been solved. I have tried rather to weigh the evidence, as it stands, in the spirit of the judge rather than in that of the advocate. One point at least I hope to have made evident, that we have discovered in the microscopic study of the germ cells a mechanism that is connected in some way to sex determination; and I have tried to show, also, that this mechanism accords precisely with what the experimental results seem to call for.'

From this it will be seen that Morgan was cautious, sceptical, and indeed ultra-conservative. He distrusted speculation. In the words of Muller, he took part as a leader in a wave of scepticism whose adherents 'doubled the doubt till they doubted it out.' But Morgan's scepticism was only a part of the experimental approach with which he tackled controversial questions. He had a passion for experiment and exact observation which led him to throw overboard his preconceptions when the facts called for it.

So it was that in the same year, 1910, in which he had suspended judgment about sex determination, he made the fundamental and basic discovery of 'sex-limited,' later known as sex-linked, inheritance of white eye in Drosophila. He put forward the hypothesis that a factor for red eyes, paired with a factor for white eyes, was associated with a factor for femaleness. The mode of inheritance of white eye was essentially similar to that of haemophilia or colour blindness in human beings. In 1911 he gave an account of other 'sex-limited' characters in Drosophila such as yellow body and miniature wings.

From these studies of sex-linked inheritance Morgan (although anticipated by Goldschmidt in 1910 through his study of sex-linked inheritance in other organisms) gave whole-hearted support to the concept of dual determiners and the chromosome theory, especially as the genetical data were supported by the chromosomal pattern elucidated by Miss Stevens.

Morgan then proceeded to his greatest contribution to modern genetics—the elaboration and demonstration of the genetical facts required for the theory of chromosomal crossing-over.

He first of all had to get data showing first that different genes assumed to be present on the same pair of chromosomes—the X-pair—undergo exchange. Second to show that they do this with characteristic frequencies, that is, that they manifest linkage.

As a consequence of the 'chiasmatype' theory of Janssens, it was seen by Morgan that if the genes are at various distances apart on the chromosomes, crossing over will be more frequent as they are farther apart.

The cautiousness of Morgan thus resulted in an epoch-making step forward. How much farther he would have gone by himself we do not know. But Morgan had a flair for leadership. He had got together a unique team of three young collaborators, Muller, Sturtevant and Bridges. One of these, Muller, was in the future also to be a recipient of the Nobel Prize.

In a generous tribute to his former chief, Muller may be quoted at some length: 'That the early findings of Morgan were so quickly followed up and generalised upon was due in no small measure to his having opened the doors of his laboratory and, indeed, of his mind to a group of co-workers, already trained in the chromosome theory by Wilson, who chose entirely their own leads and who would not have had the opportunity to carry on freely in most European or even American laboratories. Had Morgan been more of an authoritarian and less willing to be merely an equal member of the group in discussions, the young workers would not have had the opportunity they needed for the further development of the subject, and Morgan's own mind would not have become so opened to the full implications of the facts found in the Drosophila work as to have led him to agree that, after all, they lead inevitably to a theory of natural selection, now on a more rational basis, and provided with an elaborate mechanism for its operation. Morgan was won to this point of view only against his own very active opposition, yet it is to his enduring credit that he was finally willing to alter his whole viewpoint in accordance with the empirical facts.'

With the elucidation of sex-linked inheritance and the collaboration of Muller, Sturtevant and Bridges, the way was opened to the further work upon which that remarkable book *The Mechanism of Mendelian Heredity* was based, work on which Morgan later, in 1933, received the Nobel award. The book was published under their four joint names.

Morgan always insisted that the epoch-making series of researches on heredity using Drosophila as material were the work of a team, and he always gave full credit to his colleagues. Each of his co-workers was peculiarly gifted in his own way and the fact that each one found in Drosophila the medium of expression for his own intellectual diversity is a tribute to the great qualities of mind and heart of Morgan himself.

After Morgan in 1911 had put forward the novel idea that sex-linked genes are also linked to each other, and that close-ness of linkage implies proximity in a linear sense on the chromo-some, it was only a short step to the actual construction of chromosome maps for all the four Drosophila chromosomes in terms of units of crossing over, called after Morgan, 'centimorgans.'

Sturtevant has recently given us a picture of Morgan's laboratory at Columbia in those pioneer days. It became, he tells us, 'a very exciting place, as those of us who were there can testify; for there were new discoveries to be made by the dozen, and there was an air of excitement, enthusiasm and friendly and very vocal rivalry that can rarely have been equalled in a scientific laboratory.'

Julian Huxley has also given us an interesting reminiscence of Morgan. He says: 'When T. H. Morgan visited Oxford, I think about 1923, I took him up to the Hope Department of Entomology to see some of the wonderful series illustrating mimicry in butterflies which Poulton has amassed there. When I went back to fetch him for a luncheon, I could hardly prevail on him to move. "This is extraordinary!" he said, with his vivid enthusiasm; and then, "I just didn't know that things like this existed!" '

On the only occasion, in 1932, when the present writer met Morgan, he came away with two impressions. First his modesty and transparent honesty, and second his characteristic Kentucky sense of humour which inspired him to tell numerous earthy stories of the Abraham Lincoln type.

Something should perhaps be said about Morgan as an embryologist, a field in which he made contributions of great importance, and in which his ingenuity as an experimenter found great scope. A classical experiment in animal morpho-genesis was that of Roux. It consisted in the destruction of one of the blastomeres in the two-cell stage of a developing frog's egg. The result was the production of half-embryos. It was then found by Schulze that by turning frogs' eggs upside down at the two-cell stage they develop into double monsters. 'This,' says de Beer, 'is the background against which Morgan's investigation of frog development should be considered. He killed one blastomere at the two-cell stage of the frog and instead of leaving the preparation right way up, he turned it upside down. The living blastomere underwent a reorganisation and development into a perfect embryo. By this beautiful and simple experiment Morgan showed that the frog's egg was not, after all, the "mosaic" which it had been thought to be.'

This example will suffice to indicate the elegant simplicity of Morgan's method of experimentation. He also contributed largely to the study of regeneration, in which perhaps his most important contribution was the demonstration that regeneration did not take place solely as a response to injury. He found, for example, that the appendages of the hermit crab, not subject to injury, would also regenerate.

Morgan never deserted his special field of experimental embryology and towards the end of his working life he devoted increasing attention to it. Indeed, one of the papers published in the year in which he died dealt with the conditions that lead to normal or abnormal development of Ciona.

Morgan received many honours during his lifetime. In 1919 he became a foreign member of the Royal Society; he gave the Croonian Lecture in 1922; he received the Darwin Medal in 1924 and the Copley Medal in 1939. He was President of the International Congress of Genetics at Ithaca in 1932.

In 1904 he married Lilian Vaughan Sampson. She was a former research student at Bryn Mawr College and also worked on Drosophila. He left a son and three daughters.

The scientific output of Morgan was enormous. In all he published 376 papers and books. Seldom has a biologist written so extensively, so learnedly, and so prolifically. It is not too much to say that the monumental series of research on Drosophila inspired by Morgan constitute a landmark in human progress.

Hermann Joseph Muller

by S. C. HARLAND, D.Sc., F.R.S.

MANY great scientists have been individualists; they founded no schools; they left no disciples. But as already pointed out, Morgan was above all the leader of brilliant young associates whose minds were reciprocally attuned. And of the four workers whose combined efforts resulted in that classic *The Mechanism of Mendelian Heredity*, Hermann Muller has become perhaps the greatest biologist of his time, unique in the vast range of his imagination and in the wide sweep of his intellect.

Hermann Joseph Muller was born in New York City on December 21st, 1890. His grandparents on his father's side had emigrated to the United States from the Rhineland in the middle of the nineteenth century, attracted as many were by the atmosphere of greater freedom of the New World. They were of artisan and professional background and were at first Catholics. The grandfather established an art metal works, the first in the United States. His father was born in New York City and continued the works but was not a business man. He died in 1900, but although Muller was only ten years old at the time, he had already been led by his father to a lively interest in the nature of the universe, in the processes of evolution, as well as in the welfare and destiny of mankind. His mother was Frances Lyon Muller. She was also born in New York City. Her parents came from Britain but were descended from Spanish and Portuguese Jewish stock, the members of which had sought refuge from the Inquisition and had long been settled in England and Ireland. She also encouraged in the boy a love of Nature and of living things.

He was brought up in Harlem; he went to public school and then to Morris High School in the Bronx, where he, together with his classmates Lester Thompson and Edgar Altenburg, founded a high-school science club, perhaps one of the first in the United States. In spite of the limited income of his family (his mother, sister Ada and himself) they usually managed to spend the summer vacations in the country, which kept alive his love of Nature.

In 1907 he won the Cooper-Hewitt scholarship to Columbia University, but was obliged to supplement his resources by working during the summers at such jobs as bank runner and hotel clerk, for which work, for fourteen hours a day, he received twenty-five dollars a month and his board.

At Columbia, biology fascinated Muller from the beginning. During the summer of 1908 he had read R. H. Lock's (1906) well-known book on genetics, and this, together with the brilliant courses on cytology and cell biology given by E. B. Wilson, influenced him profoundly to specialise in the new science of heredity. He read widely in the domain of experimental biology and physiology, especially the works of Jacques Loeb. He founded, in 1909, a students' biology club of which Altenburg and his later to be research colleagues Bridges and Sturtevant were members.

After graduation he was not able to find a post in zoology, but after holding a scholarship (1910–11) and then a teaching fellowship in physiology at Cornell Medical College he finally obtained a teaching assistantship at Columbia (1912–15). The first summer (1911) of graduate work was spent at Wood's Hole, the rest in laboratory teaching at Columbia. From 1910 onwards he was drawn into the Morgan team of Drosophila workers, at first theoretically but from 1912 onwards also practically.

His doctoral thesis comprised the results of investigations of the simultaneous interrelationships of a number of linked genes—results which supported the theory of crossing-over.

At the same time he embarked on an analysis of variable, multiple-factor characters using the technique of 'marker genes.' This not only supported the chromosomal theory of inheritance of a gene stability but led later (1916) to Muller's first spectacular demonstration of balanced lethals.

After this intensely fruitful though relatively short period at Columbia, Muller came under another influence. In 1915 he was called to the Rice Institute of Houston, Texas, by Julian

Huxley. Here from 1915 to 1918 he not only gave various courses in biology, but began the monumental and unique studies on mutation which have continued to this day. Returning to Columbia (1918–20) as instructor, he worked out methods for the quantitative estimation of mutation rates. Partly in collaboration with Altenburg he obtained in 1918–19 the first series of definite results, including evidence of a probable effect of temperature on mutation rate.

Returning (1920) to Texas first as associate professor and from 1925 onwards as professor he was able to continue his work on mutation rates. As time went on he formulated the chief principles governing spontaneous gene mutation as now accepted. These included the ideas that most mutations were recessive and detrimental, 'being point effects of ultra-microscopic physico-chemical accidents arising in the course of random molecular motions (thermal agitation).'

During this period 'he put forward the conception of the gene as constituting the basis of life, as well as of evolution, by virtue of its possessing the property of reproducing its own changes, and he represented this phenomenon as the cardinal problem of living matter.'

Muller is, however, perhaps best known for the researches of himself and his pupils on the artificial induction of gene mutations and chromosome changes by X-rays. The first critical evidence was obtained in 1927. For the next twenty-five years he and his pupils explored this field in many institutions. A summary of the researches was given in the Nobel lecture, since it was on his vast studies of mutation that the Nobel award in physiology and medicine was given in 1946.

The work was carried out at a number of places. In 1932 he left Texas with a Guggenheim fellowship to work in Berlin with Timofeeff-Resovsky, himself a distinguished worker on mutation. He then, at the request of Vavilov, spent three and a half years as senior geneticist at the Institute of Genetics of the Academy of Sciences of the U.S.S.R., first in Leningrad and then in Moscow. With the rise of Lysenko to power and the defeat of Vavilov and all he stood for, Muller found that he could not continue his work in the U.S.S.R., surrounded though he was by an able group of workers. In succession he worked at the Institute of Animal Genetics in Edinburgh (1937–40) and at Amherst College (1942–5). Finally in 1945 he accepted a professorship in the Zoology Department at the University of Indiana, where up to the present day he has continued his work on radiation-induced mutations.

Of late, Muller has concerned himself greatly with the possible and probable effects of atomic radiation on man. In a series of trenchant articles, written with the full authority of a lifetime of study and with the wisdom of a world authority, he has issued grave warnings on the biological disasters which may result if we pursue our present policy of large-scale trials of atomic weapons.

Muller has been loaded with honours, both in his own country and in many others. He is a past president of the International Congress of Genetics (1948) and a foreign member of the Royal Society.

Ernest Rutherford

(Lord Rutherford)

by NORMAN FEATHER, F.R.S.

Norman Feather is Professor of Natural Philosophy in the University of Edinburgh. Born at Crimsworth in the West Riding of Yorkshire, he was educated at Bridlington School, winning a scholarship from there to Trinity College, Cambridge. He was for thirteen years a Fellow of Trinity and has also been an Associate in Physics of Johns Hopkins University, Baltimore. He became a Fellow of the Royal Society in 1945.

He has written a full-length biography of Lord Rutherford among other works, and is joint editor of the Cambridge Monographs on Physics.

IT is just about a hundred years since Lord Kelvin converted an old wine-cellar in a professor's house in Glasgow into a physical laboratory in which volunteer members of his natural philosophy class assisted him in his researches, and in so doing acquired a training in experimental methods in physics. University laboratories for the teaching of practical physics to undergraduate students are a later development, and the tradition whereby any university worth the name must provide such a laboratory, and furnish adequate facilities for organised research, is not more than some seventy years old. The realisation of these facts may well come as a surprise, but it is more surprising surely to reflect that, for at least half the period in question, one of these laboratories, the Cavendish Laboratory in Cambridge, should have been held in universal esteem to be pre-eminent amongst all the rest. Now, in the middle of the twentieth century, the whole scale of effort has changed; countries much more populous than Britain have taken the lead in technological advance, and physical research is prosecuted by ever-growing numbers of young men in new and well-equipped laboratories in universities and outside. A situation of undisputed pre-eminence for any one of them is unlikely ever to recur, but that it did occur over the years 1895 to 1935, or thereabouts, with the Cavendish the premier physical laboratory in the world, there can be no doubt. And there can be little doubt of the underlying reason: it is to be found in the genius of the men who were called to the Cavendish chair: Maxwell, Rayleigh, Thomson, Rutherford.

James Clark Maxwell was dead, at the early age of forty-eight, more than twenty years before the first Nobel prize for physics was awarded to Röntgen in 1901, but Rayleigh was still active in the seclusion of his private laboratory at Terling Place, Chelmsford, and as professor at the Royal Institution in London. In Cambridge, Thomson had just completed the experiments on the electron upon which his popular fame as scientist securely rests. Rutherford, then thirty, had already spent three years in the Cavendish, as personal collaborator with his professor for part of the time, in a research on the electrical conductivity of gases which has since become classical. By 1901, however, he too had been installed as professor in Montreal for three years, and his work on radioactivity stood at a critical phase.

Those who administered the new prize might have well been excused a backward glance, when the early awards were in question—there were great men still alive whose triumphs had been in the past—but the statutes of the Nobel Foundation strictly adjured them to pay attention on each occasion specifically to work which had 'appeared during the preceding year,' work 'of older standing to be taken into consideration only in case [its] importance [had] not previously been demonstrated.' Rayleigh, as we have said, was still at work; the physics prize came to him in 1904. It came to his Cambridge successor, J. J. Thomson, in 1906, and in 1908 Rutherford was awarded the prize for chemistry. Maxwell had been removed by early death, but the three men who next occupied his chair in Cambridge were all honoured in Stockholm during a period of five years, before the Nobel Foundation was ten years old. We shall have more to say of Rutherford's award later, here we need only remark his early fame: he was internationally renowned, and justifiably so, at the age of thirty-seven, and it was only eleven years before he was called to succeed Thomson in the Cavendish chair. But we should note, too, for here lies the chief reason for this recital of fact, how the fame of the Cavendish Laboratory at Cambridge, Rutherford's spiritual home, was reflected in these three awards in rapid succession to the men who with outstanding genius directed its activities over a period of nearly sixty years.

Ernest Rutherford was born at Brightwater, South Island, New Zealand, on August 30th, 1871. His father and mother had emigrated from the old country as children, his father from Dundee, when he was only three years old, his mother from Sussex when she was thirteen. His Scots grandfather had come to New Zealand to set up water-mills for the flax farmers who were colonising that fertile country, and James Rutherford, his son, Ernest's father, learned the trade of wheelwright from him, and when he married cultivated his own flax farm and built his own mills. Following this adventurous and sometimes precarious calling, he moved from Brightwater, successively to Foxhill and Havelock on South Island and finally to Pungarehu, North Island, before Ernest was sixteen years old. Ernest was the fourth child in a family which eventually numbered twelve—seven boys and five girls—though one boy died in infancy and two were drowned in a sailing accident aged eight and nine. The family circumstances, so recited, and the condition of the country—not more than a quarter of a million white people slowly bringing under cultivation a land larger in area than Britain, parliamentary government established for less than a generation—all this does not predicate the traditional background for the nurture of genius, least of all genius in the realm of science. But the natural hardiness of emigrants must not be forgotten, nor the Scot's century-old respect for education, nor that Martha Thompson, Ernest Rutherford's mother, herself shared that respect, having been a teacher at the time of her marriage. In the upshot the natural aptitude of her fourth child did not pass unrecognised by his parents; they sacrificed much in the cause of his schooling at Foxhill and Havelock, and from the latter school he passed to Nelson College at the age of fifteen.

It is not without significance that when Sir Ernest Rutherford was raised to the peerage in the New Year's honours list in 1931 he chose the title Baron Rutherford of Nelson, New

Zealand. It is to be supposed that he recognised, himself, as his biographers have done, that his entry into Nelson College was his first step towards eminence in science. True, at the age of ten he had been the proud possessor of a small volume on general science by the Scots physicist Balfour Stewart, but he did not come under the influence of a regular teacher of science until he entered the college. There W. S. Littlejohn, an Aberdonian, taught him mathematics—and such science as he knew. Of the science much was imparted informally, out of school, but the tuition which he obtained in this way enabled Rutherford to offer the two papers in mechanics and light and sound in the university junior scholarship examination, though these papers accounted for less than 20 per cent of the total marks available to the candidate. Offering mathematics, Latin, English and French, along with his science, Rutherford was placed fourth in the list of junior scholars of his year and entered Canterbury College, Christchurch, in the spring of 1890. It was his firm intention to follow a course in mathematics and science—and of that year's intake he stood highest amongst those with a similar aim—but the curriculum at Canterbury College was designed according to the Scottish model, three years for a pass degree followed by a fourth year for honours, so it was mathematics rather than physics which kept his interest alive during the first two years of his university course. Again he was lucky in his teacher; G. H. H. Cook, sometime fellow of St. John's College, Cambridge, a strictly scholastic and able man, was professor of mathematics and natural philosophy.

At the end of his pass degree course Rutherford was a candidate for the university senior scholarship in mathematics (not physics!)—and again he was successful. A year later he took his honours degree with first classes in mathematics and in physics. No one else in the whole university obtained a first class in either subject. Possibly his genius as physicist was denied outlet in the earlier years through the requirements of the curriculum; certainly in this honours year he took the opportunity for which he had striven with both hands. He sat his honours examination in November 1893, after not much more than a year's advanced work in experimental physics under a stimulating but highly heterodox teacher, A. W. Bickerton, professor of chemistry and physics in the college. Within five years he himself occupied a chair of experimental physics, in Montreal, and within ten had startled the world by the most revolutionary hypothesis ever to stem directly from experiment, the hypothesis of the spontaneous disintegration of atoms. Rutherford took his honours examination in November, and on December 5th, 1893, he started on his embryonic researches. Under that date he entered in his notebook a description of certain 'Experiments on secondary circuits,' quoting Faraday, Kelvin and Rayleigh in the first page of his account. Kelvin, with the authority of a professorship in an ancient university giving weight to his demands, had been able to convert an old wine-cellar to the sole purpose of physical research, Rutherford with nothing more than the enthusiasm of youth as his testimonial had found for himself a corner in another cellar, but he shared it with the students whose cloakroom, ill-appointed and draughty, it was reckoned to be. For more than eighteen months he worked there, and the two papers which he published in the *Transactions* of the New Zealand Institute report the weighty and original investigations which developed in natural sequence from his first trials with secondary circuits containing iron. The writings of Thomson are freely quoted in these papers, and when he had written them it must surely have appeared to him that he had indeed entered a profitable field of work and that the proper place to cultivate it was in Thomson's own laboratory at Cambridge. So to the Cavendish Laboratory Rutherford went, not without some luck in the manner in which he was nominated for the Exhibition of 1851 New Zealand Scholarship (replacing the first nominee J. S. MacLaurin, a chemist, who withdrew for family reasons), and started work there early in October 1895.

Rutherford had been fortunate in his teachers in New Zealand, he was lucky in the manner in which his entry into Cambridge became possible, on his arrival there he was to find himself doubly favoured by the circumstance of time. In the first place the university was then, for the first time, admitting to membership 'advanced students,' and providing a degree for them on the satisfactory completion of a course of research—he was in fact the first student to be enrolled in the Cavendish Laboratory under the new regulations—and secondly, and more importantly, the three years which lay ahead were to prove the most momentous in the history of physical science, at least since the time of the publication of Newton's *Principia*. Rutherford went to Cambridge with ideas for the improvement of a magnetic detector of Hertzian waves, a bundle of soft iron wires with primary and secondary circuits, which had already worked in New Zealand—and during his first two terms in the laboratory he made great progress with its development, studying fundamental problems on the way and catching the imagination even of some of the non-scientists in the university by his success in long-distance 'wireless' signalling. There was a future in such investigations for a young man of genius; such indeed was the future which Marconi realised in full, and those who followed him. There might be a fortune, too. But Rutherford was saved from that future, and denied the pecuniary gain which might have come to him as applied physicist or successful electrical engineer; he was saved by the accident of time—and the perspicacity of his professor. In April 1896 Thomson, keenly aware of his ability, took the young Rutherford to work with him on a problem which set the whole course of his future career. There is no doubting that at the age of twenty-four Rutherford was ambitious for his own advancement, but it is equally clear that the flattery of this invitation to collaborate put the possibility of financial reward out of mind for the time being, and as the investigation developed and time passed the temptation of wealth receded, and only the work in hand, the unravelling of the secrets of Nature, dominated his life. Two years later, on his appointment to the chair at Montreal, he wrote to his mother (August 4th, 1898) '. . . so I start up in life as a professor on £500 a year . . . and an unlimited prospect of work. . . . It is as good an opening for a start as I could wish.' These two years had settled his future.

In December 1895 Röntgen had communicated to the Physico-Medical Society of Würzburg his discovery of X-rays in a sober account, entirely convincing to all who read it (he sent reprints of this paper with accompanying photographs late in December to certain physicists and medical men throughout the world, being convinced of the novelty and importance of what he had found). The discovery, though made accidentally, had been well matured; the first unexpected effects of the new radiation had been noticed on November 8th, but nothing was published until the phenomenon had been thoroughly explored. Röntgen's first paper presented the world of science with something startlingly new—and entirely irrefutable. It created an immediate sensation, and, within a period of two or three weeks, its publication plunged all the physical laboratories in Europe and America into feverish activity. Rutherford observed this first impact in Cambridge. On January 25th, 1896, he wrote to his fiancée: 'The Professor has been very busy lately over the new method of photography discovered by Professor Röntgen . . . the great object is to find the theory of the matter before anyone else, for nearly every Professor in Europe is now on the warpath.' The immediate result in the weekly journals of science was chaos; a mass of observation reported in haste, much of it unchecked and a great deal trivial. Amateur and professional scientists alike rushed into print in the genuine excitement of the chase—or motivated, possibly, by some other less forgivable urge. Röntgen's had been a clear-cut discovery of great moment; in spite of the furore which followed, it was some months before much was added to what he had written of the essentials of the matter.

When the furore was at its height, the second outstanding discovery of this triad of years was made in Paris. Its immediate history was very different from the history of the discovery of X-rays. Becquerel's discovery of the spontaneous radioactivity of uranium resembled Röntgen's only in being in part accidental. Otherwise it started in a sequel to Röntgen's own work, and it was published originally in weekly instalments so that its impact was gradual. Moreover, the germ of the discovery—

that the radioactive property is intrinsic to uranium—was not arrived at until the third instalment. And later instalments reported conclusions which had afterwards to be withdrawn. It is perhaps understandable, then, that these communications of Becquerel to *Comptes rendus de l'Académie des Sciences* should not at once have been recognised at their true value amongst the welter of doubtful publications daily appearing in bewildering confusion. But Röntgen's discovery and Becquerel's were to provide equally the bases for Rutherford's work at the Cavendish Laboratory in the two years that followed—and Becquerel's, more than Röntgen's, was to provide him with his life's work.

In the midst of all this, a third 'discovery' was breaking upon the world, a discovery not made in a day or by accident: the 'discovery' of the electron. The final conclusive phase was working itself out in Cambridge in Thomson's laboratory during the early months of 1897. The problem at issue was the nature of the cathode rays. Its solution was obviously important also for an understanding of Röntgen's X-rays, since these are produced by the impact of cathode rays on matter, but it was a problem in its own right before the X-rays were discovered. Whether their discovery hastened the solution it would be rash to speculate, but it is certainly on record that Thomson wrote (Rede Lecture before the University of Cambridge, June 10th, 1896), 'One of the most remarkable phenomena connected with these rays [X-rays] is the way in which the absorption depends upon the density of the body . . . This appears to favour Prout's idea that the different elements are compounds of some primordial element, and that the density of a substance is proportional to the number of the primordial atoms; for if each of these primordial atoms did its share in stopping the Röntgen rays, we should have that intimate connection between density and opacity which is so marked a feature for these rays.' When, a year later, his experiments on the cathode rays finally reached their conclusion, it is equally certain that Thomson himself had discovered the first of the common constituents of atoms, the negative electron. It was not Prout's 'primordial element,' rather its counterpart—on the other hand it was just the constituent to which he had been led, in hypothesis, in his attempt to explain the early recorded observations on X-ray absorption.

These then were the favourable circumstances, with the ferment of new ideas, against the background of which Rutherford's Cambridge work was done. The statement of what he did can be made simply, almost prosaically, but it was none the less remarkable for that. That the X-rays possessed the property of discharging electrified bodies was an early observation made by many observers. Röntgen did not himself record this observation in his first paper, but in his second (dated March 9th, 1896) he wrote 'At the time of my first publication it was known to me that the X-rays are capable of discharging electrified bodies . . .', and he went on to describe the experiments which had convinced him that the essential action of the X-rays was on the circumambient air rather than on the charged body; moreover he also convinced himself that irradiated air 'retains this property for some time after being exposed to the X-rays.' He found that irradiated air lost its efficiency on passage through cotton wool, but 'whether it loses it in course of time spontaneously, that is without coming in contact with other bodies, is still undecided.' Röntgen had been cautious and exact as ever, but this time before his results could be published he had been anticipated. Late in January 1896, in collaboration with J. A. McClelland, Thomson began to investigate the discharging action of the rays, and he was able to present results and conclusions at a meeting of the Royal Society on February 13th which carried the matter at least as far as the quotations from Röntgen's second paper show that he had taken it three weeks later. Then, at Cambridge on March 9th, Thomson and McClelland described their investigations with a prototype parallel-plate ionisation chamber, and announced for the first time the discovery of the 'saturation' of discharge current. At Würzburg, on the same day, Röntgen was putting his signature to his belated report—but by that time the initiative had passed out of his hands. Within a few weeks Rutherford took McClelland's place as Thomson's collaborator in the experiments on gaseous conduction (McClelland turned to an investigation of the absorption of X-rays in solids); within five months the whole subject was in order. On September 18th, at the Liverpool meeting of the British Association, Thomson presented the work, essentially complete. It was published under joint authorship in the November number of the *Philosophical Magazine*.

Lord Rayleigh, Thomson's biographer, has written of this epoch-making paper, 'Rutherford gave me a copy of it one evening when I was in his rooms a few months later. . . . He allowed me to see that he was proud of his share in it.' He had every reason to be proud. The discharging action of the rays had been under investigation in many laboratories; only in Cambridge, in the investigation in which he had been involved, had quantitative results been obtained which were consonant with an acceptable theory. To our present way of thinking the theoretical ideas of Thomson and Rutherford appear natural, even inevitable, but that they were not seized on by others independently shows the extent of their novelty and the depth of the intuition which gave rise to them. The rays produce 'conducting particles' in the gas, these disappear spontaneously at a rate proportional to the square of the concentration (compare Röntgen's query quoted above), and move through the gas under an applied field with velocities proportional to the potential gradient. These were the assumptions: all the experimental evidence pointed to their validity. The steady-state concentration of 'conducting particles' was shown always to be extremely small, of the order of 1 in 10^{12} of the gas molecules with radiation of the intensity then available, and the drift velocities small compared with the thermal velocities of the molecules.

The terms *ion, recombination coefficient, mobility* were not used in the paper which we are discussing, but they have only to be introduced appropriately into the text to translate this classic original into modern language. As a first formal description of essential processes it was indeed a rounded statement. That Thomson regarded it as such is evident from the fact that the temporary collaboration of professor and student was immediately dissolved; that in addition he regarded it as a formal description only is equally evident from the next investigation which he assigned to his pupil. Rutherford was set to work on his own to investigate how the amount of ionisation produced in a gas is related to the rate of diminution of intensity (absorption) of the rays traversing it. The account of this investigation was published in April 1897. No simple numerical relation was obtained, but a wide variety of gases had been examined, and the general conclusion that 'good conductors under the rays are good absorbers of the radiation' was amply warranted. It was known that there was not much energy carried by the rays from an ordinary tube, but there was no need for mystery about the fate of this energy; when it was dissipated in absorption it was almost certainly used in the process of ionisation.

Having so far elucidated the first assumption of the formal description ('the rays produce "conducting particles" in the gas'), Rutherford proceeded to test the second and third assumptions regarding ionic recombination and mobility under controlled conditions. Within a few months this, too, had been accomplished and an account had been published in the *Philosophical Magazine* (November 1897). In a year's work on his own Rutherford had thus set the seal to his brief collaboration with his professor; from that time on no one has had need to re-think the question of how to describe the phenomenon of gaseous conduction at ordinary pressures and low field strengths; into the general kinetic theory description of gaseous behaviour it was necessary only to import the ideas of ionisation by the external agent and natural recombination of the oppositely charged ions to be able to proceed to a discussion of any situation. Rutherford was not, of course, the only worker in the Cavendish Laboratory who contributed to the solution of this problem in the last years of the last century, but it is fair to say that the essentials were settled by Thomson's strange genius, then at its zenith, and Rutherford's zest and natural flair as experimenter, then freshly released in full vigour of youth.

Yet our account of this one year's work has been over-simplified and has omitted much. As early as March 1897 Rutherford had begun to look into the question of the conductivity produced by the uranium radiation. Although his main investigation of this matter was reserved for a later occasion, he made preliminary experiments with uranium salts during 1897. His notebooks for that period show the manner of his working. Varying his experimental conditions from day to day, using now X-rays, now ultra-violet light, now the radiations from uranium, to produce the ionisation, he studied every aspect of the phenomenon as it began to make sense in response to his questioning. His investigations using ultra-violet light led to an elegant method of determining mobilities when ionisation can be confined to a very thin stratum of gas. This characteristic example of his opportunism as an experimenter was described in his next paper, published in *Proceedings of the Cambridge Philosophical Society* in February 1898.

Rutherford's study of the effects due to the uranium radiations produced results that were unexpected and new, and occupied him for the remainder of his time in Cambridge. A week before he sailed for Montreal he sent off for publication an account of these researches. This account occupied fifty-five pages of print in the *Philosophical Magazine* for January 1899. Here he gathered together his work on the recombination and mobilities of the ions produced in various gases by the uranium radiation—this part of the investigation proved beyond doubt that the ions produced by the uranium radiations were identical in properties with those produced by X-rays in a gas—and, of greater significance, his work on the absorption in various materials of the radiations emitted by layers of uranium and thorium salts of different thickness. For, early in 1898, thorium had been recognised, by Schmidt and Marie Curie independently, to have radioactive properties similar to those of uranium.

In these absorption experiments Rutherford came upon two striking and unexpected results; one he had time to examine in some detail, the other merely to note for future attention. The first result was that with a very thin layer of uranium salt (and consequently with a very small ionisation current to measure!) all but a per cent or so of the ionisation produced in a shallow ionisation vessel was cut out when a single sheet of paper (or its equivalent) was placed over the preparation (though afterwards the residual ionisation was cut out very much less rapidly when further similar absorbers were added). Not very different results were obtained with thin layers of thorium salts. It seemed as though Becquerel had discovered the radioactivity of uranium (which he detected by the photographic effect through sheets of black paper) under conditions in which all but a very small fraction of its full potency lay still unrevealed. This was startling enough, but to Rutherford, at the age of twenty-six, his unlooked-for result meant much more than this. It implied that uranium (and thorium) preparations emit radiations 'of at least two distinct types . . . which will be termed for convenience the α-radiation, and . . . the β-radiation.' Here was intuition and daring exposed, but Rutherford had noticed that the fraction of the ionising effect cut out by a single sheet of paper decreased as the thickness of the layer of salt was increased—which was sufficient evidence to convince him that two different radiations were in fact emitted independently (and uniformly) throughout the preparation. It was not long before Becquerel and others had shown that the β-radiation consists of electrons; the α-radiation became a preoccupying subject of study for Rutherford himself for the ten years which followed. Not perhaps until the end of that period was everyone convinced by the cumulative evidence of his experiments, as he shrewdly suspected at an early stage, that this easily absorbed radiation consists of streams of positively charged helium atoms projected with great velocity. In December 1908 his Nobel lecture was entitled 'The chemical nature of the α-particles from radioactive substances,' but we shall come to that lecture later; here we pay tribute to the experimental genius and the intuition of a young man of twenty-six who six years previously was just beginning for the first time to do some serious exercises in practical physics, under an undisciplined teacher whose fancy led him to many strange hypotheses—but never to a useful one.

The second unexpected result which Rutherford noticed in his work with the uranium and thorium radiations was 'that thorium nitrate when first exposed to the air on a platinum plate was not a steady source of radiation, and for a time . . . varied very capriciously.' Here was the germ of his discovery of the thorium emanation, but, as we have said, that discovery was not made in Cambridge: the 'capricious effect' with thorium nitrate was kept in mind for further study, as soon as opportunity should offer, in Montreal.

Rutherford's work as an advanced student in Cambridge in the years 1895–8 has been described in some detail, more systematically and in greater detail than much of his later scientific work can be treated in a notice such as this, but the emphasis has been intentional. In estimating his achievement we cannot forget that Rutherford was favoured by time and circumstance in growing to maturity as scientist during these particular years in Thomson's laboratory; equally, in assessing his stature we are bound to recognise the magnitude and importance of the work which he did in those three years, and that he was indeed scientifically mature, self-reliant and on the threshold of great success at their close. He could have stayed on in Cambridge, but he offered himself for the vacant research professorship at McGill University, Montreal, and it is not surprising that he was appointed to the chair. Nor was his future career surprising. If things went well he would surely come back, some time, to succeed Thomson in Cambridge. In fact, as we have noted, when Thomson resigned in 1919 Rutherford indeed was invited to succeed him. Professor John Cox, head of the department of physics at McGill, who had originally interviewed Rutherford for the Montreal chair, wrote to him then: 'So there you are at last! . . . It was 1898, wasn't it, when I fished you out of the Cavendish, and it has taken you just twenty years to come back to be its master. . . . You remember saying at McGill that you would not leave unless either Manchester or Cambridge came open. . . . And now you have had both.' Yes, Rutherford had left Montreal for Manchester in 1907, and by 1919 he was back in Cambridge, Sir Ernest Rutherford, Nobel laureate. But at one stage, in spite of his disclaimer, he had, in fact, seriously considered the possibility of leaving Montreal—for Edinburgh. That was in 1901, and again it must be conceded that the fates were kind; an older man with more teaching experience was elected to Tait's chair, and Rutherford was left in Canada to discover that his collaboration with a young Oxford chemist, Frederick Soddy, demonstrator in the chemistry department at McGill— a collaboration which was no more than a few weeks old at the time in question—was to mean more to him at that precise juncture than any chair in Europe.

In anticipation, we have already mentioned two aspects of Rutherford's work in Montreal during the nine years of his professorship there: the constantly preoccupying theme of the nature of the α-radiation, and now his collaboration with Soddy. There were many other themes, too, interwoven in the exciting tale of discovery which was told in the scientific journals of the day—and told, more particularly, in the pages of the *Philosophical Magazine*, for Rutherford never accustomed himself to publishing his original papers elsewhere until near the end of his life. But we cannot mention these other themes here, save to say that adventurous young men from all over the world flocked to Canada to help in their development towards the close of the period. The discoveries of Rutherford and Soddy in the years 1902–3 left no doubt in the minds of all but the most purblind that, for a season at least, Montreal was to be the centre of the universe for students of the new physics of the atom. Postponing consideration of the work on the α-radiation until, as already noted, we meet it in the Nobel lecture, let us look, then, at the results of this Rutherford–Soddy collaboration, the upshot of a chance conjunction, in the unlikely surroundings of a colonial university, of a young physicist of twenty-nine and a young chemist of twenty-three, each destined eventually to figure in the list of prizemen of the Nobel Foundation (the 1921 award for chemistry was made to Soddy in 1922). For this purpose we recall the 'capricious effect' with thorium nitrate, which Rutherford had observed in Cambridge in the summer of 1898. It provides the starting-point of the story.

In Montreal, in 1899, first in a short collaboration with R. B. Owens (then professor of electrical engineering at McGill), and later on his own, Rutherford examined this capricious effect further. He concluded that thorium compounds, sometimes more efficiently, sometimes less, depending on the precise physical state of the preparation, gave off a gas-like radioactive 'emanation' continuously. This substance could be transferred in a stream of air into a closed vessel, and, when so isolated, lost its activity 'in a geometrical progression with the time,' half-value activity being reached in about one minute. Then he found that inactive bodies left in the neighbourhood of thorium preparations acquired temporary radioactivity themselves 'as if [they] were covered with a layer of radioactive substance.' This acquired activity fell to half strength in a period of several hours. These results were described in detail in papers published in the *Philosophical Magazine* in January and February 1900. Thus the capricious effect has been reduced to order, but the investigation had raised more problems than it had solved. In the first place it had brought to light a number of short-lived radioactivities, strongly contrasted with the apparently permanent activities of uranium and thorium in their natural states, and in the second place it left open the question of the relation between the emanation and the acquired activity, which Rutherford suspected to be close. The particles responsible for the acquired activity appeared not to be the same as the particles of the emanation (for their activities decayed at different rates, and radioactivity seemed to be a property insensitive to physical or chemical state), but they appeared to be deposited on solids only when the latter were exposed to the short-lived emanation. The urgency of these problems was increased in Rutherford's estimation by the discovery, by Pierre and Marie Curie, and by Dorn, in Paris, of a similar acquired activity and a corresponding emanation from preparations of radium. He was spending the late (northern) summer of 1900 in New Zealand, but when he returned to Montreal he settled down at once to pursue the matter to its conclusion. At this stage he was joined by Soddy, who had arrived during his absence. Newly appointed to a position on the staff of the chemistry department, Soddy naturally expected to carry out research there, but it was not long before he was fully engaged in the thorium problem in collaboration with Rutherford.

In the two years of their collaboration Rutherford and Soddy published eight papers, and at the end of it they had acquired international renown. For the conclusion of the matter was the disintegration hypothesis, the realisation that the alchemist's dream was in essence continuously being enacted in Nature without the intervention of human agency in any form, the realisation that in the radioactive substances one kind of matter was changing into another with the gratuitous emission of energy associated with ionising radiations. At this distance in time it is difficult to appreciate either the rare insight and superb experimental skill required in the investigation to which Rutherford and Soddy set themselves, or the incredulity and hostility which their hypothesis aroused in some of their colleagues. We are not here concerned with the latter aspect of the matter, but in appraising the genius of our subject the former consideration is an essential one. Weighable amounts of emanation or active deposit were never available for experiment, yet Rutherford and Soddy correctly concluded 'the only known gases capable of passing in unchanged amount through all the reagents employed are the recently discovered gases of the argon family . . . the interpretation of the experiments must be that the emanation is a chemically inert gas analogous in nature to the members of the argon family.' They found that the emanation was evolved not from thorium itself but from a substance which they were able to separate from thorium compounds, again in unweighable amount (in all their experiments the 'amount' of a new substance was estimated by its radioactivity, not with the balance). They called this substance thorium X and wrote '. . . the manner in which it makes its appearance . . . dragged down by precipitates when no question of insolubility is involved . . . suggests the view that it is really present in minute quantity.' Both these quotations are from a paper published in April 1902 in the *Transactions of the Chemical Society*.

In the same journal in July 1902 they extended their observations 'Thorium can be freed ... from both ThX and the excited radioactivity ... and then possesses an activity about 25 per cent of its original value, below which it has not been reduced,' and they began cautiously to record the speculations which were forming in their minds: 'The idea of the chemical atom in certain cases spontaneously breaking up with the evolution of energy is not of itself contrary to anything that is known. ...' In the *Philosophical Magazine* in September 1902 they wrote '... the radioactive elements must be undergoing spontaneous transformation.' Early in the following year they were sufficiently confident of the worth of their ideas to devote a whole publication to setting them out in logical form. This classical paper, 'Radioactive change,' appeared in the *Philosophical Magazine* in the May issue. They faced the two aspects of the problem squarely: the emission of ionising radiations (radioactivity) and the appearance of new substances (chemical change). They wrote '... it is not possible to regard radioactivity as a consequence of changes that have already taken place. The rays emitted must be an accompaniment of the change ... the law of radioactive change ... may be expressed in the one statement—the proportional amount of radioactive matter that changes in unit time is a constant ... [which] possesses for each type of active matter a fixed and characteristic value. ... Apparent constancy [of radioactivity] is merely the expression of the slow rate of change of the radioelement ... the energy liberated in radioactive processes does not disobey the law of the conservation of energy. ... The law of radioactive change ... is also the law of mono-molecular chemical reaction. Radioactive change, therefore, must ... involve one system only ... the chemical atom ... in radioactive change the chemical atom must suffer disintegration.' The final statement, abbreviated as it has here of necessity been, may appear somewhat pontifical, but the earlier quotations surely indicate the intricacies of experiment which had to be devised, checked and re-checked, before this statement could be made. It stands today, accepted in its every positive assertion, a timeless monument to the surpassing genius of two young men.

Soddy returned to England in the summer of 1903 and was appointed to a lectureship in physical chemistry and radio-activity in the University of Glasgow almost immediately. Rutherford remained in Montreal until 1907. Thus the Rutherford–Soddy partnership was broken, but it had made a mark in the annals of science which will not be eradicated, and we may be excused, in a review such as this, from recount-ing the history of the four years that followed. As already described, they were years of great activity in the Macdonald physics laboratory at McGill, years of great personal triumph for Rutherford himself, but they produced no world-shaking hypothesis and we should follow him to Manchester.

In Manchester Rutherford found a large department and a numerous staff. He found a readership in mathematical physics newly endowed by his predecessor, Schuster, and he found Schuster's young assistant, Hans Geiger, already one year in the department. The work which Geiger did with Rutherford—by no means the collaboration of equals, as the Rutherford-Soddy episode had been, but a collaboration which was valuable, none the less—paved the way for the next great advances. In duty bound, in this place, we must give due regard to the award of the prize: in any review, however superficial, we could not exclude an account of the 'discovery' of the nucleus. The award of the Nobel Prize for Chemistry to Professor E. Rutherford 'for his investigations into the disintegration of the elements, and the chemistry of radioactive substances,' was announced in November 1908; the discovery of the nucleus was described in a paper in the *Philosophical Magazine* for May 1911.

Today, no doubt, it strikes the reader as strange that the greatest experimental physicist of the early years of this century should have been awarded the prize for chemistry. The reason for this designation was not regarded as crystal-clear even in Stockholm in 1908. At a formal dinner on the third day of the celebration, in speaking to the toast of the new laureates in physics and chemistry, the host of the evening referred to Rutherford as a 'young pioneer in that new science which is neither physics nor chemistry, yet which is, at the same time, both physics and chemistry,' and added 'we may hope to see him here a second time as laureate under the Nobel foundation.' That hope was never fulfilled (though Marie Curie, having shared a half-prize in physics with her husband in 1903, received the prize for chemistry in 1911). But the designation did not worry Rutherford unduly, nor did he regard himself as strictly bound by the terms of the citation in choosing the title for the formal lecture which he was to deliver before the Swedish Royal Academy. He did not find it very difficult to choose a title with a chemical flavour, but by his chosen title he implicitly disclaimed any personal contribution to new knowledge in the chemistry of radioactive *substances*; the investigations which he described (and illustrated by experiments) concerned the chemical identification of the heavy constituent of the radioactive *radiations*—the α-particles from radioactive substances. Radioactive substances, and radioactive radiations; the members of the Nobel committee might confuse the two, certainly Rutherford did not. Five years previously Soddy had anticipated this particular heresy, exposing it with his customary felicity: '[to make this confusion]' he wrote in the *McGill University Magazine*, 'would be to mistake a cannon for a cannon ball.'

In his Nobel lecture Rutherford gave the history of his thoughts and of his experimental investigations on the problem of the α-rays. Almost from the first he had imagined that these rays consisted in fact of projected particles—and that probably they were positively charged. He had persevered for two years, from 1900 to 1902, before obtaining any evidence of their deflection by a magnetic field, then he succeeded in observing the electric deflection also. The experiments were crude in the extreme (necessarily so because of the small activity of the sources available), but Rutherford had extracted, from measurements made with a gold-leaf electroscope as detector, numerical values for velocity of projection and specific charge (charge per unit mass) within about 20 per cent of the true values. Today it appears utterly incredible that he should have made such good use of such meagre experimental information. About this time too, as he told his audience, he had become greatly impressed by the fact that the then recently discovered light gas helium had not been found on the earth except occluded in minerals having uranium or thorium as an important constituent. He had become thoroughly convinced that this association implied a significant connection between the helium and the radioactivity; that this light gaseous element was one of the ultimate products of the disintegration of the heavy radioelements. The idea had taken root, and become at once simpler and more daring: the α-particles and the helium were merely the active and passive phases of the same ultimate product. The α-particles were, in fact, charged atoms of helium. It is probable that this notion was firmly fixed in Rutherford's mind by 1906 when, having refined his measurements on the electric and magnetic deflection of the particles, stronger sources of radiation having meanwhile become available, he showed that the α-radiation from all sources consisted of particles of a single kind.

At Manchester he had continued, with Geiger's help, to draw the net of proof closer. Using a new electrical detector, capable of recording the entry of a single α-particle (the distant prototype of the Geiger counter of today), he had counted the α-particles emitted from a given amount of radium, and in another experiment he had measured the total charge carried by these α-particles. If the α-particles were indeed charged helium atoms these experiments should have given a value for the charge carried by each equal to twice the fundamental unit of charge. He had been undismayed by the fact that his experiments gave a value much more nearly three times that charge, as then accepted (we know now that his intuition was unerring, the value of the fundamental unit of charge accepted as correct in 1908 was too small by a large margin). Finally, in collaboration with Royds, he had clinched the matter beyond question. He had fired the α-particles from a strong radioactive source into a piece of lead in an exhausted vessel. Afterwards he had found that helium was present in the lead: it could be released by melting the lead and detected spectroscopically. 'Dead' α-particles are atoms of helium gas; 'live' α-particles are fast-moving atoms of helium carrying two units of positive charge. It was an altogether convincing report which Ruther-ford gave in Stockholm on December 11th, 1908.

The identification of the α-particle as a particle of mass 4 and charge + 2 in atomic units gave new precision to the disintegration hypothesis. The whole sequence of disintegra-tions believed to occur as an atom of uranium changed suc-cessively into an atom of ionium, an atom of radium, and, so on, into an atom of lead, was the more easily accepted as the true sequence when it was pointed out that it was in general agreement with well-established facts of chemistry, namely the atomic weights of uranium, radium and lead. Thus Rutherford reinforced the strength of his own hypothesis. But he did more than that, because he was 'driven to the conclusion that the atoms of the primary radioactive elements . . . must be built up in part at least of atoms of helium . . . that other elements may be built up in part of helium, although the absence of radioactivity may prevent us from obtaining any definite proof.' Thomson had shown that all atoms contain negative electrons, Rutherford was here on a new line of thought. Soon after he returned to Manchester from the Nobel ceremony he was deeply involved in pursuing it. With it another line of thought with its roots in the past soon fused, and he was instantly on the threshold of the discovery of the nucleus. That was such a momentous discovery, it is small wonder that the flash of illumination did not come to him at once.

The older line of thought was given public utterance first in 1906. In that year Rutherford had noticed a very slight blurring of the 'shadow' image of a slit traversed by α-particles, when the particles passed through a sheet of mica less than a thousandth of an inch thick covering part of the slit (if he had covered the whole of his slit with mica he might never have noticed the difference, for he had not set out to look for this effect, but another!). He knew how difficult it was to deflect the particles in their paths by the electric or magnetic fields which he had at his disposal, and he wrote with utter directness '[the observed deflection] would require over that distance an average transverse electric field of about 100 million volts per cm. . . . clearly . . . the atoms of matter must be the seat of very intense electrical forces.' Here then were the two streams of thought: the first concerning the heavy constituents of atoms, the second concerning the strong electric forces. And note, that for the electric forces to be effective in changing the motion of the α-particles, except in minute degree at each encounter, they must have their origin in the heavy constituents; electric forces originating in the light electrons would not do. So the heavy constituents must be electrically charged. So, also, in 1908 Geiger was set to carry out some experiments on the scattering of α-particles in passing through thin foils. The new techniques of detecting the particles individually gave fresh scope to such experiments.

During the next year Marsden was added to the team, for the experiments were laborious, and the unexpected discovery was made. A few particles—a very few—were scattered back even from the thinnest foils on the side of incidence: they did not pass through at all. The idea that atomic projectiles might pass through solid matter, which appeared so incredible in 1894 when Lenard found the cathode rays emerging through the thin window of his discharge tube, but which with the passage of time had come to be accepted without demur, now seemed confounded again: just a few α-particles did not get through. The very great majority of the particles emerged on the far side of the foil, slightly deflected, as though they had been buffeted back and forth, ever so little by each atom which stood in their way; these few particles which were scattered back did not fit into the same picture at all. The problem as Rutherford saw it in its full magnitude was to provide a consistent description of the phenomenon as a whole. It took him nearly two years to provide that description. When he finally succeeded (in December 1910) the simplicity of his ideas was not the least of the marks of genius which his description bore.

The essential point on which Rutherford seized was that a single encounter with a heavy atom must be capable, in favourable circumstances, of turning an α-particle completely back on its path. Such favourable circumstances would occur very rarely indeed, but there would be a graded probability of deflection through all angles—falling off very rapidly as the angle increased. For the smaller angles the probability would be sufficiently high that for each α-particle passing through a thin foil almost every atom in its path would contribute such deflections; for the largest angles it would be so small that only one particle in many thousands would suffer such a deflection although several hundred atoms stood in its path through the foil.

To provide a model with these properties it has to be assumed that the atom is mostly empty space, space 'populated' by the negative electrons (which did not enter significantly into the phenomenon of α-particle scattering), with a minute heavy centre, or centres, carrying a considerable charge. As we have seen, Rutherford had earlier thought of a loose structure of helium atoms constituting the main heavy component in a heavier atom. Now, for mathematical simplicity—and for that simplification which so often in the past has appeared to be consonant with truth—he assumed that structure tightened, and postulated for each atom a single central 'nucleus,' carrying all the substance of the atom except that which the electrons carry, and carrying positive charge to balance the total negative charge of the electrons. He worked out for himself the mathematical consequences of his model on the basis of Newtonian dynamics and the classical law of electrostatic force, and, finding his predictions fully confirmed by Geiger's experiments early in 1911, he gave the nuclear atom to the world in the May number of the *Philosophical Magazine*, as has already been recorded. From the time of that publication we may date the opening of a new era in physics.

In this notice it is impossible to dwell on the early stages of the development of the nuclear atom model, which indeed proceeded so rapidly that its universal acceptance was all but immediate. Rutherford's laboratory at Manchester was the scene of most of them. Here, however, we have to follow his own wider-reaching notions to their triumphant vindication and his final success. For the job in hand he had hidden the complexity, which he knew to be of the essence of the matter,

E Rutherford

Charles S. Sheringh

in the simplicity of a single nucleus characterised by mass and electric charge only. But radioactivity was a property of the nucleus, the α-particles and the electrons were expelled from it—each α-particle to become later the nucleus of an atom of helium—and the whole problem of the varieties of the elementary substances of the world was fundamentally the problem of its structural laws. The synthesis of the elements was no doubt taking place in the stars (this was Lockyer's 'inorganic evolution,' now for the first time capable of discussion in terms of the current language of science), but 'it will prove a very difficult task to bring about the transmutation of matter under ordinary terrestrial conditions,' he wrote—difficult but not impossible—'the nucleus of an atom may be altered . . . by direct collision . . . with atoms of helium such as are ejected from radioactive matter. . . .' The quotations are from the William Ellery Hale lectures which Rutherford delivered in Washington in April 1914. So he returned to Manchester to his α-particles to make the attempt. Towards the end of the war of 1914-18 he succeeded.

But for the outbreak of war in August 1914, in all likelihood first proof of the artificial transmutation of nuclei would have been obtained by the end of the following year. The idea was there, it remained only to test it. Marsden had already begun work on the problem, before fundamental research was abandoned and the laboratory turned over to war work in the summer. In the upshot, however, it was left to Rutherford himself, with his laboratory steward, to make the crucial test in the months of September, October and November 1917, when at last he had a little respite from the urgent problems of the nation's defence. Several more months of observations followed, checking all possibilities of misinterpretation, then, as his last contribution from Manchester, Rutherford wrote an account of the work for the *Philosophical Magazine*. The four papers which resulted were published together in June 1919. In the last of them ('An anomalous effect in nitrogen') he wrote: 'It is difficult to avoid the conclusion . . . that the nitrogen atom is disintegrated under the intense forces developed in a close collision with a swift α-particle, and that the hydrogen atom which is liberated formed a constituent part of the nitrogen nucleus.'

For Rutherford, this was the last milestone; the long road had led from the scarcely differentiated atom-concept of the chemists to the nuclear atom, and now into the nucleus. At the beginning, for most scientists, there had been no problem; at the end there was no finality, only a host of new questions demanding an answer. For him, if for no one else, the road had been clear all the way: after Manchester, for the remainder of his life, no one else discovered such a broad high-road.

After Manchester, we know, Rutherford moved to Cambridge, to the Cavendish chair. To suggest that his work was done, or that his bright genius was thereafter eclipsed, is to deny the facts, which speak otherwise with unanswerable witness. But, for our estimate here, which is cast so as to reveal the essential quality of that genius, there is little more to be said. Rutherford led us to the confines of knowledge in respect of the ultimate structure and constitution of matter as it may be broadly comprehended in the language of everyday experience. He opened a new world, the world of the atomic nucleus, for the exploration of which new experimental techniques were required, and for the description of which a new language. At Cambridge he deployed a large force of attack, but the new techniques came slowly, and a new language must be used awhile before its grammar can be formulated. The campaign was planned with sure instinct and carried through with real power, but there was no large-scale break-through; there was no truce, equally no resounding victory as in Montreal or Manchester. Here and there was a major success, as when the last of the classical particles was discovered by Chadwick in 1932, the neutron of Rutherford's earlier prophecy, or, less fundamental, perhaps, when Cockcroft and Walton did with machines what Rutherford had done with a source of α-particles in 1919, but the advances were in general less spectacular than of old.

Not only was there a lull in the evolution of the subject, but conditions had changed in the world, and there were young men in large numbers to be trained in the methods of scientific research. Industry and the Government agencies were beginning to ask for such young men. Laboratories such as the Cavendish were no longer filled exclusively, or almost exclusively, with eager questing researchers, endowed possibly with some leisure for the adventure; instead they began to overflow with the less single-minded, the products of an age of keener economy, young men looking to be trained for a job. Rutherford was not slow to note the progressive change; he did not rebel against the inevitable. Indeed he saw that the life of the nation now demanded this sacrifice, that, in the research laboratories of the universities, training for its own sake should take equal place with the advancement of knowledge. Such policy is sowing for the future. Already it has borne a rich harvest. Ernest Rutherford was a great scientist, and a wise man in his generation.

Sir Charles Sherrington

by MACDONALD CRITCHLEY, M.D., F.R.C.P.

Macdonald Critchley qualified at the University of Bristol where he won the Markham Skerritt prize for original research. He is Senior Neurologist to King's College Hospital, London; Consulting Neurologist to the Royal Navy; and Physician to the National Hospital, Queen Square, the famous centre for teaching and research upon organic nervous disorders.

He is an honorary member of the French Academy of Medicine and of many foreign neurological societies. He has lectured in various parts of the world, including Australia, South America, the Middle East and California.

. His published works include the *Language of Gesture*, *Mirror Writing*, and *The Parietal Lobes*.

HIERARCHIES can be identified even within such a highly selected group as the band of Nobel prize-winners. Some recipients are conspicuous by reason of their exceptional intellectual stature and attainments; Sherrington certainly belongs among these few. The prestige of physiology has always been particularly high and the contributions made by Sherrington have perhaps exalted it in a way that no other exponent has ever done before or since. His work, from one decade to another, formed a coherent and logical construction, a house built upon a rock. By studying the workings of the nervous system in their elementary manifestations to begin with, Sherrington was able to build up from simple things to complexities, without being distracted by non-essentials.

Why is it that Sherrington stands out so loftily among other physiologists, and also among the whole congregation of Nobel prize-winners? Perhaps because he combined in an exceptional fashion three distinct accomplishments. In the first place he was a man of very high character. His personal attributes were quite unusual. He was esteemed as well as admired by physiologists throughout the world, and by his pupils and colleagues. Those who knew him well, and also those who met him on a more superficial level, have often referred to his modesty and his kindliness. He was generous with help and with advice, and a succession of young physiologists took advantage of his benevolent approachability. He was a quiet and essentially a good and unassuming man.

To these exceptional character-traits must be added his culture. He was a scholar versed in the humanities. A Latinist by dint of his schooling, he maintained his love of the classics throughout his life. He read widely. He collected books, particularly incunabula, and he endowed the British Museum with many valuable items. Medical history intrigued him, and he contributed much by his detailed study of Jean Fernel. His mode of thinking was reflective, and with advancing years he became more and more philosophical, even metaphysical. He sought to probe the fundamentals, for he could not tolerate obscurities or uncertainty when they touched upon problems of life. We witness these intellectual gropings in his volume entitled *Man on his Nature*. We must add to these capacities his love of poetry and his not inconsiderable creative writings.

Lastly, Sherrington was a scientist in the most strict sense of the word. His mode of thinking was speculative, it is true, but it was so rigidly disciplined that it never offended the rules of logic which ordain and govern the mental processes of deduction. He had the particular ability to seize upon the core of a problem, stripping away irrelevances like the leaves of an artichoke.

The unusual combination of these three qualities, namely character, culture and scientific probity, accounts largely for Sherrington's greatness. But he enjoyed other advantages too—advantages of a minor order. He was an uncannily dextrous technician, whose experimental methods were astonishing because of their precision, tidiness and success. He did not shrink from hard work, and hours spent in the laboratory, library or study were given ungrudgingly—even enthusiastically. Lastly he was blessed with that somewhat intangible gift of being lucky. He was fortunate in his early teachers—at school, in the university, and abroad. He was fortunate in his appointments. He was fortunate in his choice of career, and in the problems which he selected for investigation. Furthermore he was fortunate in his time, for he came to neuro-physiology at a most opportune moment, finding it something of a *terra incognita* and leaving it a well-charted though complex macrocosm. Furthermore, Sherrington was lucky in his possession of good health, which sustained him hour after hour of work, year after year, throughout an exceptionally long life.

Recital of these outstanding qualities may prompt one to inquire whether any weaknesses, foibles or eccentricity existed which a captious detractor could put in the debit column of the biographical ledger. There are a few indeed. Perhaps the severest criticism that can be adduced is to assert that Sherrington was an indifferent lecturer, being dull, unimpressive and uninformative. His true forum was not the auditorium, but the laboratory, where, in discussion with a small band of pupils—over tea perhaps—he proved inspiring and illuminating. Sherrington's writings—though far clearer than his set lectures—are not perhaps as simply expressed as might have been had Sherrington so contrived. His literary style can best be described as 'unusual,' for he indulged in unorthodox tricks of syntax. Indeed, in any of his prose works it would not be difficult for a linguist to identify Sherrington as the author, because of the individual choice of words and turns of phrase.

Again, it might be objected—though none has ventured to do so—that Sherrington did not possess that quality of personal physique or magnetism which would exercise an immediate impact upon a stranger. Thus he was not the domineering figure of a Claude Bernard; he was not endowed with the handsome physical presence of a Broca, a Jonathan Hutchinson, or a Michael Foster; nor the intriguing aloofness and austerity of Charcot. His was a modest charm, in which the softer shades of genial kindliness and sincerity became increasingly apparent with longer acquaintance. In this respect we are often reminded of his older colleague in clinical neurology—Hughlings Jackson.

Charles Scott Sherrington was born on November 27th, 1857, at Islington, London. His parents actually resided in Yarmouth, but his mother was visiting London at the time of her confinement. Sherrington's father died when Charles and his two younger brothers were quite small, and his mother subsequently married Dr. Caleb Rose, of Ipswich. This stepfather seems to have been a wise and able man whose medical and cultural interests exercised great influence upon the young Sherrington. We are told that Dr. Rose was an amateur archæologist and a collector of paintings—many of which now hang in the Norwich Art Gallery.

Sherrington attended Ipswich Grammar School, where he attracted the attention of two quite unorthodox masters, Thomas Ashe and H. A. Holden—both of them classicists of distinction. In his youth Sherrington also excelled in games, for he played soccer for the school (and later for Ipswich Town). When he went up to his university he rowed for his college and at his medical school he played rugger. Sherrington's slight frame was deceivingly powerful.

In 1871 he went to Cambridge, his college being Gonville and Caius. We are told that for a very short period he also studied at Edinburgh, but no details of this sojourn are available to us. At Cambridge he came under the authority of the great physiologist Michael Foster. J. N. Langley was also working in the Cambridge Physiological Laboratory at the time, and was five years older than Sherrington, being a Fellow of Trinity. Another great physiologist, namely W. H. Gaskell, was also in the same department. While still an undergraduate Sherrington wrote his first paper, published in collaboration with Langley, on 'Sections of the right half of the medulla oblongata and of the spinal cord of the dog which was exhibited by Professor Goltz at the International Medical Congress of 1881.' The article appeared in 1884 in the *Journal of Physiology*.

In 1883 Sherrington became a student-demonstrator in anatomy under Professor George Humphry, who wrote that he was '. . . much impressed by his ability and assiduity. He did his work well and the students were much attached to him. His genial friendly qualities made him a general favourite and a most agreeable colleague.' In 1884 Sherrington entered St. Thomas's Hospital, where for a time he was a demonstrator in histology. While still a medical student Sherrington paid a visit to Strasbourg in order to see Goltz, whose experimental work was exciting the keenest interest among physiologists, including Langley and himself.

After his qualification in 1885, Sherrington, who at that time aspired to a career in pathology, went to Spain, under the auspices of the Association for Research in Medicine, to assist C. S. Roy and Graham Brown in their investigation into cholera. Here Sherrington met Cajal, who was to exercise considerable sway over Sherrington's thought. The following year he proceeded to Italy and stayed awhile in Venetia and Puglia. A short period followed in Berlin at Virchow's laboratory, during which time he also saw something of the work of Waldeyer and of Zuntz. Later he studied some bacteriology with Koch.

In the summer of 1887 Sherrington returned to London as lecturer in physiology at St. Thomas's Hospital. At this time Sherrington was impressed by the work of his Cambridge colleague Gaskell. He it was who diverted Sherrington's attention away from the cortex to the spinal cord. As Sherrington himself afterwards said: 'My own work began by chance at the wrong end. It was certainly through Gaskell that I very soon felt that. One could not talk with him long without realising that the cord offered a better point of attack physiologically. Also, that the cord was originally and still must be a chain of "ganglia." . . .'

In 1891 Sherrington succeeded Victor Horsley as Professor (and Superintendent) of the Brown Institute for Advanced Physiological and Pathological Research. This foundation was an unusual but very valuable one located in the Wandsworth Road, in South London. It consisted in research laboratories attached to a veterinary hospital. Unfortunately it later fell into impoverishment and has since become merged with other institutions belonging to the University of London. At this period Sherrington had not altogether abandoned his interests in pathology and some of his work at the Brown Institute was immunological in scope. Sherrington was perhaps the first person in this country to prepare anti-diphtheritic serum and to utilise it in therapy. Gradually, however, his output became predominantly neurophysiological, and during the first ten years of his new career, Sherrington paid many further visits to Goltz.

It would be tedious to enumerate all of Sherrington's early researches. We may note that his interest in the nature and properties of the knee jerk began as early as 1891. Perhaps also we can mention his series of papers upon the segmental innervation of the motor and sensory nerve-roots in the monkey. These were the outcome of a deliberate and preliminary study which subsequently led to an investigation of the reflex functions of the spinal cord. These latter researches were described in his Croonian lecture of 1897 (at the Royal Society) on 'The mammalian spinal cord as an organ or reflex action.' In 1899 his Marshall Hall address 'On the spinal animal' appeared in print.

In 1895 Sherrington left London to succeed Gotch as the Holt Professor of Physiology at the University of Liverpool. He occupied this chair for the ensuing eighteen years. Much of his most brilliant pioneer work dates from that period. True, the notion of 'reciprocal innervation' had developed earlier, but it was in Liverpool that his views upon the phenomenon became consolidated.

The work of Goltz and of Pflüger was repeated, checked and corrected, and it appears in retrospect that much time had to be diverted from his other research in order to demonstrate the fallacies of Pflüger's 'laws' of reflex action.

Mindful of Cajal's histological studies Sherrington introduced the term 'synapse,' though it is possible that the actual creator might have been his old chief Foster, with whom he was now collaborating in a text-book. Sherrington also wrote three or four excellent chapters in Professor E. A. Schäfer's text-book of physiology which appeared in 1900. Of these the one entitled 'Cutaneous sensations' is of outstanding interest and it can profitably be read and studied even after a lapse of fifty years. In 1904 we find the first mention in physiological literature of a 'final common path.' Two years later came his study of the 'scratch reflex' with his eloquent demonstration of the discernible and predictable properties of reflex action in general.

During the first year of his professorial appointment in Liverpool, a steady continuity of fundamental research projects was accomplished at a rapid rate. The succession of papers is evidence not only of Sherrington's extreme industry and devotion to his laboratory, but of his unusual clear-sightedness. Each piece of work, each scientific communication, neatly and logically followed its predecessor, as in a masterly chess game.

It was at this period too that foreign scientists who were sufficiently curious began to make the unpromising expedition to Liverpool, or to interrupt their pilgrimage from America to the Metropolis. Most of these visitors were shrewd enough to realise and assess correctly the brilliance of the young physiologist. Not all, however. That assiduous notability-hunter Harvey Cushing—then thirty-two years of age—pausing at Liverpool to look up Sherrington was not impressed. Writing in his diary he said:

> Sherrington is a great surprise. He is young, almost boyish if 36 (?), near-sighted, wearing when he had not lost them a pair of gold spectacles. He operates well for a 'physiolog' but it seems to me too much. I do not see how he can carry with any accuracy the great amount of experimental material he has under way. He has as many strings to his bow as Spiller, and writes and publishes as much. As far as I can see, the reason why he is so much quoted is not that he has done especially big things, but that his predecessors have done them all so poorly before. It's a great surprise all through physiological work to find that practically all observations are open to dispute or various interpretations. . . . The whole thing referable to experimental neurology much to my surprise is still in a most crude condition. The problems offered are immense. S. goes at them too fast. Few notes are taken during the observations, which is bad. S. says himself he has a bad memory—potters around his laboratory till after seven in the evening trying to catch up on things and then is used up and doesn't begin till ten or eleven the next day.
>
> Grünbaum the 1st Assistant—chemical side, is rather sarcastic —just misses being a very nice fellow.

Soon, however, a friendship grew up between them and Cushing must surely have regretted his earlier assessment.

We come now to 1905—a year as memorable in neurophysiology as it was in Sherrington's career. A Mrs. Hepsa Ely Silliman Memorial had been founded at Yale in the form of a series of lectures. Sherrington was invited to deliver the second set of Silliman lectures, the first award having fallen to Professor J. J. Thomson. The following year Sherrington published his ten Silliman addresses in book form, entitled *The Integrative Action of the Nervous System*. Such were the circumstances which led to the appearance of that rare phenomenon, a medical classic. The *Integrative Action* received immediate recognition as a stupendous and fascinating exposé of the orderly synthesis of nervous function from the simplest reflex activity upwards to cortical levels. No reviewer failed to realise the magnificence of this monograph. Henry Head, the editor of *Brain*, took the unprecedented step of printing a formal acknowledgment of the reception of Sherrington's book, with a promise that it would receive detailed and serious attention in a later issue. In due course, Professor McDougall, the psychologist, contributed a thoughtful and laudatory review, seventeen pages in length. McDougall did not allow the opportunity to elude him for interpolating a few of his own private hobby-horses. Similar detailed and appreciative notices may be found in the contemporary issues of the world's medical and scientific Press. The *Integrative Action* contains so many treasures of information and insight that it never stales, and is not likely ever to do so. No aspirant in physiology can possibly neglect to study this monograph as part of his apprenticeship. Generations hence, Sherrington's book may well rank along with Thomas Willis's *De Anima Brutorum*, Pavlov's *Conditioned Reflexes*, Claude Bernard's *Étude de la Médecine Expérimentale* and Harvey's *De Motu Cordis*. Sherrington expressed in his Silliman lectures a favourable view of the future status of experimental psychology—indeed of its contemporary claims for recognition. The lectures included many ideas which were novel at the time, but which were subsequently to be incorporated within the terminology and structure of physiological acceptances. (Reprintings appeared in 1911, 1914, 1916, 1918 and 1920. Thereafter it became a most difficult volume to acquire.

Accordingly in 1947 the Physiological Society decided to prepare a new edition, the original text being retained unaltered, but with the figures redrawn. Sherrington supplied a new foreword and Samson Wright, who was responsible for this endeavour, wrote an editorial note and added a portrait frontispiece of the author. To mark the occasion of the XVII International Congress of Physiology which met at Oxford in July 1947, every member was presented with a copy of this interesting reissue.)

Throughout the first decade of the century Sherrington was concerned with problems of muscular tonus and he continued his analysis of what he had already, as far back as 1897, described as 'decerebrate rigidity.' But over and above his pursuit of a rigid design of research, a considerable versatility was also displayed, and we find him collaborating with A. S. Grünbaum in electrical stimulation of the primate brain. This was a project of much topical interest, and Sherrington and Grünbaum's immediate concern was chiefly directed upon the post-central gyrus and its function.

Sherrington had identified himself with the official activities of the Physiological Society, having served as its secretary from 1889 till 1905. Six International Physiological Congresses had taken place with Sherrington representing the British and American contingents as their secretary.

In 1913 Sherrington was invited to occupy the Waynflete Chair of Physiology at Oxford—an appointment for which, oddly enough, he had unsuccessfully applied in 1895. Although the practical facilities were disappointing compared with the well-equipped Thompson-Yates Laboratories of Liverpool, these were offset by the more leisurely pace, the prestige and the cloistered delights of an academic environment. But only too soon came the first world war, and he was saddled with a load of administrative and advisory work which distracted him from pure physiological research. He became Chairman of the Industrial Fatigue Board and there were many other Governmental committees which occupied his time. As if that were not enough he put in some hours every day at the bench of a Birmingham munitions factory. Sherrington's anxiety over his only son who was serving in the Army added to his burden of trouble.

The end of hostilities brought its compensations. In 1919 he published his practical laboratory notes which had served generations of Liverpool students under the title *Mammalian Physiology: a course of practical exercises.* In 1920 he was elected President of the Royal Society, of which he had been a Fellow since 1893.

A volume of poetry, much of which he had written during the war years, was issued in 1925, under the title *The assaying of Brabantius and other verse.* He was accorded in 1931 the most important compliment within the gift of British neurology, namely the Hughlings Jackson lectureship, and he took as his subject 'Quantitative management of contraction in lowest level co-ordination.' Sherrington's Rede Lecture (1933) was of a somewhat different genre from his other writings. *The Brain and its Mechanism*—as Professor Liddell has written— showed how the biologist, philosopher and poet combined in Sherrington. The Nobel Prize was not accorded to Sherrington until as late as 1932, a delay in recognition which has never ceased to astonish. Even then the Prize was shared with his much junior colleague E. D. Adrian. Why the Swedish Academy of Science did not award these two great physiologists independently and outright remains unexplained. Other honours had naturally enough been accorded him in profusion. The G.B.E. came to him in 1922, and the O.M. in 1924. At the Royal Society he had received the Royal Medal in 1907 and the Copley Medal in 1927. He held honorary doctorates of twenty-two universities.

In 1936 Sherrington retired from the chair at Oxford, having attained the age of seventy-nine years. But his work was not yet over. The following year he delivered the Gifford Lectures in Edinburgh, which were published in 1940 as a volume of thoughtful essays entitled *Man on his Nature.*

Ten years after his retirement another volume was published —full of scholarship and wisdom—the product of many years' historical reading. *The Endeavour of Jean Fernel* affords us considerable information as to the thinking of this medieval physician and scientist. Many resemblances can indeed be traced between Fernel and his biographer, both of whom deserve Professor Asher's appellation of 'philosopher of the nervous system.'

During his last years, Sherrington lived in a nursing home at Eastbourne tended by Catholic nursing sisters. Though he was very frail, his mind was clear and he welcomed visitors, and he corresponded with friends, colleagues and former pupils all over the world. His last writings were concerned with Goethe, whom he admired as an artist rather than scientist. Death struck him with merciful abruptness on March 4th, 1952, when he was in his ninety-fifth year of life.

.   .   .   .   .

It is a common and engaging conceit to look to the insect world for analogies with the province of scientific thinkers. In this respect, the symbol of Sherrington's life and work may be identified in the bee, whereof Francis Bacon wrote:

> The men of experiment are like the ant; they only collect and use: the reasoners resemble the spiders, who make cobwebs out of their own substance. But the bee takes a middle course, it gathers its material from the flowers of the garden and of the field, but transforms and digests it by a power of its own. Not unlike this is the true business of philosophy. . . .